THE PROFESSIONAL PRACTICE SERIES

The Professional Practice Series is sponsored by the Society for Industrial and Organizational Psychology (SIOP). The series was launched in 1988 to provide industrial/organizational psychologists, organizational scientists and practitioners, human resource professionals, managers, executives, and those interested in organizational behavior and performance with volumes that are insightful, current, informative, and relevant to organizational practice. The volumes in the Professional Practice Series are guided by five tenets designed to enhance future organizational practice:

1. Focus on practice, but grounded in science
2. Translate organizational science into practice by generating guidelines, principles, and lessons learned that can shape and guide practice
3. Showcase the application of industrial/organizational psychology to solve problems
4. Document and demonstrate best industrial and organizational-based practices
5. Stimulate research needed to guide future organizational practice

The volumes seek to inform those interested in practice with guidance, insights, and advice on how to apply the concepts, findings, methods, and tools derived from industrial/organizational psychology to solve human-related organizational problems.

Previous Professional Practice Series volumes include:

Published by Jossey-Bass

Resizing the Organization
Kenneth P. De Meuse, Mitchell Lee Marks, Editors

Implementing Organizational Interventions
Jerry W. Hedge, Elaine D. Pulakos, Editors

Organization Development
Janine Waclawski, Allan H. Church, Editors

Creating, Implementing, and Managing Effective Training and Development
Kurt Kraiger, Editor

The 21st Century Executive
Rob Silzer, Editor

Managing Selection in Changing Organizations
Jerard F. Kehoe, Editor

Evolving Practices in Human Resource Management
Allen I. Kraut, Abraham K. Korman, Editors

Individual Psychological Assessment
Richard Jeanneret, Rob Silzer, Editors

Performance Appraisal
James W. Smither, Editor

Organizational Surveys
Allen I. Kraut, Editor

Employees, Careers, and Job Creation
Manuel London, Editor

Published by Guilford Press

Diagnosis for Organizational Change
Ann Howard and Associates

Human Dilemmas in Work Organizations
Abraham K. Korman and Associates

Diversity in the Workplace
Susan E. Jackson and Associates

Working with Organizations and Their People
Douglas W. Bray and Associates

Improving Learning Transfer in Organizations

Elwood F. Holton III

Timothy T. Baldwin

Editors

Foreword by Eduardo Salas

 JOSSEY-BASS
A Wiley Imprint
www.josseybass.com

Published by Jossey-Bass
A Wiley Imprint
989 Market Street, San Francisco, CA 94103-1741 www.josseybass.com

Page 328 constitutes a continuation of this copyright page.

Jossey-Bass books and products are available through most bookstores. To contact
Jossey-Bass directly call our Customer Care Department within the U.S. at 800-956-7739,
outside the U.S. at 317-572-3986 or fax 317-572-4002.

Jossey-Bass also publishes its books in a variety of electronic formats. Some content that
appears in print may not be available in electronic books.

Library of Congress Cataloging-in-Publication Data
Improving learning transfer in organizations / edited by Elwood F.
Holton, III and Timothy T. Baldwin.—1st ed.
        p. cm.
Includes bibliographical references and index.
    ISBN 0-7879-6540-5 (alk. paper)
  1. Organizational learning. 2. Knowledge management. 3.
Employees—Training of. I. Holton, Ed, 1957- II. Baldwin, Timothy T.
    HD58.82.I47 2003
    658.4'038—dc21
                                                    2003007927

FIRST EDITION
HB Printing   10 9 8 7 6 5 4 3 2 1

The Professional Practice Series

Contents

Foreword

In an era of lifelong learning and of increasing competition for skilled employees, organizations can not waste the limited resources they have to develop their workforce. Organizations should ensure that the newly acquired knowledge, skills, and attitudes of their workforce are applied and used to fulfill their goals and objectives. It is (or should be) a business imperative. Thus, organizations need to create, promote, and support a climate where employees can positively transfer the newly acquired skills to the job. Simple? Not so; this is easier said than done. There are many reasons for this. For example, organizations often have a poor understanding or a misconception of what and how training systems can help them. Another problem is that those who design, deliver, evaluate, or manage training have little guidance from the literature to help them create and foster such a transfer climate—at least until this book.

The now classic transfer-of-training piece published in 1988 by Tim Baldwin and Kevin Ford set the stage for this book. In that piece, they provide a framework outlining the key issues involved in the transfer of training. Since then we have seen a plethora of research in the topic, which has generated a body of knowledge that organizations can now use. This is what is compiled in this book. And it's quite remarkable.

Ed Holton and Tim Baldwin have assembled a rich and innovative set of chapters on what should be done to facilitate the transfer of training to the job. They have brought together a number of authors who are well versed in applying learning systems to organizations. These authors in their chapters provide tips, guidelines, and practical recommendations on what to do to promote transfer of training and how to do it. This is, in my opinion, a true contribution not only to the field but more important to the organizations that use it. Holton and Baldwin (and the rest of the authors) have done a great job in ensuring the chapters present practical information to them and also are concerned with the design, delivery, and management of training. Well done!

The Editorial Board of the Professional Practice Series continues to seek volumes that help practitioners manage their human resources. This book is another example of what we hope is useful guidance to them. On behalf of the Editorial Board, Ed and Tim, thank you and congratulations for a wonderful volume. Our thanks also go to all the authors who contributed to the volume. We will continue our relentless effort to translate our science to practice.

University of Central Florida   Eduardo Salas
May 2003   *Editor*

Preface

Businesses, government agencies, and nonprofit organizations have devoted increased resources to the training and development of their own workforce in an effort to increase competitiveness and to improve service. While increased resources have been devoted to training and learning activities, concerns remain about the impact of the training and developmental activities on organizational effectiveness. Clearly, the main objective of training is to enhance employee performance in the transfer or work setting. Demonstrating transfer requires clear linkages between the expected changes during training and observable changes in behaviors in the work setting. Enhancing the likelihood of transfer requires active attention to transfer-enhancing strategies.

In 1988 Tim Baldwin and I published a review in *Personnel Psychology* that called for greater research attention to transfer-of-learning issues. Over the past fifteen years, industrial and organizational psychologists and human resource professionals have made great progress in several areas, especially the development of theoretical perspectives and models of what is meant by learning and transfer; the derivation of testable models and the conduct of empirical research on the factors that impact learning during training and the transfer of training to the job; the identification, design, delivery, evaluation, and improvement of training programs; and study of key issues beyond individual training to broader issues of team training and organizational change and development.

In this volume, Baldwin has joined with Ed Holton to compile a set of thought-provoking chapters that now translate these types of research findings into action-oriented steps professionals can take to enhance training transfer. The chapters provide a multidimensional view of transfer and the identification of conditions for successful transfer to job situations. The authors also anticipate the variety of challenges training professionals typically face when designing training activities and promoting transfer. Throughout the chapters of this book, these challenges are examined in order to lead to a number of innovative strategies to improve the efficiency and effectiveness of training for transfer.

This book on improving learning transfer in organizations clearly fits the goals of the Society of Industrial and Organizational Psychology Professional Practice Series. The book provides industrial-organizational psychologists, human resource professionals, and all those interested in promoting learning in organizations with a number of clearly defined opportunities for effectively dealing with the threats to learning and development in the work environments of today. Now the cycle of training improvement can continue as ideas and strategies from this book are tested and further refined through new research and experience.

Michigan State University   J. Kevin Ford
May 2003

The Authors

Elwood F. Holton III is Jones S. Davis Professor of Human Resource, Leadership, and Organization Development in the School of Human Resource Education at Louisiana State University, where he coordinates the B.S., M.S., and Ph.D. degree programs in HRD. He holds an M.B.A. and an Ed.D. in Human Resource Development from Virginia Tech. He is past president of the Academy of Human Resource Development and is the founding editor of *Human Resource Development Review,* a new quarterly refereed journal devoted to theory and theory building in human resource development. He has also served on the editorial boards of *HRD Quarterly, Human Resource Development International,* and *Advances in Developing Human Resources.* In 2002, he was honored with the Outstanding HRD Scholar Award, the highest award given by the Academy of Human Resource Development. His research focuses on analysis and evaluation of organizational learning and performance systems, improving learning transfer systems, new employee development and retention, adult learning, management and leadership development, and HRD policy and strategy. His research has won numerous awards, including the Richard A. Swanson Research Excellence Award from the Academy of Human Resource Development and six Citations of Excellence from ANBAR Management Intelligence. He is the author, coauthor, or editor of eighteen books, the most recent being *Approaches to Training and Development* (coauthor; forthcoming from Perseus) and *Human Resource Development: Foundations of Theory and Practice* (coauthor; Berrett-Koehler, 2001). He is the author of more than two hundred publications, including academic and professional articles in journals such as *Advances in Developing Human Resources; Human Resource Development Quarterly; Human Resource Development International; Performance Improvement Quarterly; Human Resource Management Review;*

Human Resource Planning; Human Performance; International Journal of Training and Development; Public Personnel Management; Journal of Organizational and Occupational Psychology; Training and Development; and the *Journal of Business and Psychology.* He has more than seventeen years' experience consulting with a wide variety of private, public, and nonprofit organizations on human resource development and performance improvement issues. The organizations he has consulted with include Formosa Plastics Corp., Baton Rouge City Police, J. P. Morgan, Cigna Corp., Entergy Corp., Enterprise Rent-a-Car, Ciba-Geigy Corp., Ford Motor Company, Honeywell, U.S. Department of Energy, U.S. General Services Administration, eleven Louisiana state government departments, the Multiple Sclerosis Society, and Louisiana Workers' Compensation Corp.

Timothy T. Baldwin is professor of management and Subhedar Faculty Fellow at the Indiana University Kelley School of Business. Baldwin holds M.B.A. and Ph.D. degrees in human resource management from Michigan State University and has published his research work in leading academic and professional journals such as *Academy of Management Journal, Personnel Psychology, Journal of Applied Psychology, Human Resource Management,* and *Academy of Management Executive.* He has won several national awards for his work, including six from the Management Education and Development Division of the Academy of Management. He has also twice been the recipient of the Richard A. Swanson Excellence in Research Award presented by the American Society for Training & Development (ASTD). Baldwin is actively involved in executive education in the United States and abroad and has recently worked with firms including Eli Lilly & Co., FedEx, Cummins Engine, Whirlpool, EDS, Dow Chemical, and several others. His current research focuses on chief learning officers and their use of organizational systems to promote talent pool management and leadership development.

Reid A. Bates is an assistant professor in the Human Resource and Leadership Development Program in the School of Human Resource Education at Louisiana State University, where he teaches undergraduate and graduate courses in HRD. He received his Ph.D. from Louisiana State University. He is an active researcher and author and has published in journals such as *Adult Education Quarterly, Human Resource Development Quarterly, Human Resource Development International, International Journal of Training and Development, Human Resource Management Review,* and *Performance Improvement Quarterly.* His research interests include employee development; learning transfer; the role of values, ethics, and culture in human resource development; and global and international human resource development. He has nearly twenty years of experience working with a variety of private- and public-sector organizations in the United States, Africa, and the Pacific region pursuing a range of goals and objectives related to HRD.

Mary L. Broad, with *Performance Excellence,* consults with public- and private-sector organizations to improve the payoff from investments in training and other performance improvement initiatives. She works with clients to enhance workforce learning and performance as well as organizational results, and to gain the support of key stakeholders throughout the complex systems that are increasingly common in the global marketplace. She has a master's degree in adult education and a Doctorate of Education in human resource development, both from the George Washington University, where she has served as adjunct associate professor of HRD. Recent clients have included Pfizer Pharmaceuticals Group, the Georgia State Department of Human Resources, the Centers for Disease Control and Prevention in the National Institutes of Health, the Long Term Care Institute of Southwest Ontario, the U.S. Marshals Service, and H.G. Electronics (South Korea). Broad managed the training departments at several federal agencies (1976–1981), and headed the Human Resource Development Division at the Defense Information Systems Agency (1982–1993). She served on the ASTD Board of Directors from 1993 to 1995, and received ASTD's Torch Award in 1998. She is coauthor of *Transfer of Training: Action-Packed Strategies to Ensure High Payoff from Training Investments* (1992, Addison-Wesley, now in its ninth printing) and edited *In Action: Transferring Learning to the Workplace* (1997, ASTD). She also has written chapters in six recently published books and journals on training and performance improvement (1998–2003). She has consulted and presented in Canada,

El Salvador, Indonesia, Ireland, Kuwait, Panama, Mexico, South Korea, Singapore, and throughout the United States, and is a regular presenter at international conferences of ASTD and the International Society for Performance Improvement (ISPI).

Lisa A. Burke is an associate professor of management at Louisiana State University in Shreveport. Her doctorate is in organizational behavior and human resources from Indiana University Kelley School of Business and she teaches organization theory, staffing, training, strategic human resources management, and general management to undergraduate and M.B.A. students. Burke's research interests include management training, development, and education and she is on the editorial board for the *Academy of Management Journal.* Her book *High-Impact Training Solutions* (2001) addresses strategic training, needs assessment, training technologies, training transfer, performance consulting, and contemporary roles of corporate trainers. Burke is certified as a Senior Professional in Human Resources (SPHR) from the Society for Human Resource Management and has published her research work in leading academic and professional journals such as *Academy of Management Learning and Education Journal, Journal of Applied Psychology, Human Resource Management Review,* and *Academy of Management Executive.*

Janis A. Cannon-Bowers is a senior research psychologist in the Science and Technology Division of the Naval Air Warfare Center Training Systems Division. In 1988, she received her Ph.D. in industrial and organizational psychology from the University of South Florida. Her research interests include team training and performance, crew coordination training, training effectiveness, and tactical decision making.

Camden C. Danielson is executive director of Kelley Executive Partners, the executive education arm of the Kelley School of Business, Indiana University. Over the last seventeen years he has designed or conducted executive development programs for major corporations around the world. His research focuses on the formulation of corporate learning strategies and the role of chief learning officers and has appeared in the *Academy of Management Executive,*

Human Resource Development Quarterly, and *Business Horizons.* Previously Camden was a speech writer for the president of Indiana University and a member of the faculty at the U.S. Air Force Academy.

Erik R. Eddy is a member of the Group for Organizational Effectiveness. He has worked for the group since 1996, first as a consultant then as a project director, to support organizations in their organizational development, change management, management and employee development, and knowledge management efforts. A few of the recent projects he has worked on include facilitating strategic planning and conducting sessions to build managerial talent at Core Staffing Services, helping guide internal experts at Tiffany & Co. to develop a certification program for their sales and operations professionals, facilitating working sessions with U.S. Air Force fighter pilots to identify the "Mission Essential Competencies" required to be successful, and researching the requisite characteristics of successful mentoring programs and consulting with the U.S. Navy in developing a mentoring program. He has also worked with such firms as Whirlpool, BP Amoco, and The St. Paul Companies. He continues to be an active researcher and author. He has presented at national conferences and published in several journals and book chapters on such topics as job design, training, quality management, mentoring, and continuous learning. He holds a master's degree in business administration and a master's degree in organization development from Bowling Green State University, and a Ph.D. in organizational studies from State University of New York at Albany.

J. Kevin Ford is professor of psychology at Michigan State University. His major research interests include improving training effectiveness through efforts to advance understanding of training needs assessment, design, evaluation, and transfer. Ford also concentrates on building continuous learning and improvement orientations in organizations. He has published more than fifty articles, chapters, and technical reports and serves on the editorial board of *Human Performance.* He was the lead editor of the book *Improving Training Effectiveness in Work Organizations* and is coauthor with Irwin Goldstein of the fourth edition of *Training in Organizations.* He is an active consultant with private industry and the public sector on training, leadership, and organization development issues. He is a fellow of the American Psychological Association and the Society of Industrial and Organizational Psychology. He received his B.S. from the University of Maryland and M.A. and Ph.D. in psychology from Ohio State University.

Jerry W. Gilley is a professor of organizational performance and change at Colorado State University and was previously a principal at William M. Mercer Inc., responsible for human resource and organizational development. He received his doctorate from Oklahoma State University in HRD. He has coauthored thirteen books and more than seventy-five articles, book chapters, and monographs. His books include *Organizational Learning, Performance, and Change: An Introduction to Strategic HRD* (Perseus), which was selected the HRD Book of the Year (2000) by the Academy of HRD, as well as *Principles of HRD,* 2nd ed., *Beyond the Learning Organization, The Performance Challenge, Strategically Integrated HRD* (Perseus), and *Stop Managing, Start Coaching* (McGraw-Hill).

Erik Hoekstra is vice president for people and organizational development at The Harbor Group, the parent company for a variety of firms in the construction, engineering, and factory automation industries. He holds an M.B.A. degree from the Rotterdam School of Management in the Netherlands and is a Ph.D. candidate in organizational learning and human resource development at Iowa State University. Prior to his current position, Erik led several companies in retail and wholesale distribution and was a member of the business faculty at Dordt College.

Robert D. Marx is an associate professor of management, Isenberg School of Management, University of Massachusetts, Amherst, and a visiting professor, with formal affiliation, at the Athens Laboratory for Business Administration (ALBA), in Athens, Greece. He received his doctorate from the University of Illinois, Champaign-Urbana. He is coauthor of *The Wisdom of Solomon at Work: Ancient Virtues for Living and Leading Today* and coauthor of *Management Live: The Video Book.* Marx's research interests include relapse prevention in management training, the optimal use of video in management education, and spirituality in organizations. His research efforts on the problem of skill retention following management development programs have resulted in numerous published articles on this topic in journals such as the *Academy of Management Review,* the *Journal of Management Development,* and the *Training and Development Journal.* He has presented his research at the Academy of Management, the Eastern Academy of Management, the Organizational Behavior Teaching Society, and other national, regional, and international meetings. He serves on the editorial board of the *Journal of Management Education.* He has taught internationally at the Management Training Center in St. Petersburg, Russia, and at the Graduate School of Business Leadership (UNISA), the University of South Africa in Pretoria, and as a faculty member at the Athens Laboratory for Business Administration in Athens, Greece. He has chaired the board of the Organizational Behavior Teaching Society. Marx consults on issues of leadership, teamwork, communication, improving skill retention in management training, and spirituality in organizations. His clients have included Danaher Tools, Lego Systems Inc., Glaxo SmithKline Pharmaceuticals Inc., Springfield Mo. Healthsystems, and—in Greece—Thenamaris Shipping Co., NetMed Cable Television, Macedonia Thrace Bank, and Adel Saatchi and Saatchi Advertising. He is a regular presenter at The Physician Executive Institute at Case Western Reserve University and has presented at the Cape Cod Institute in Wellfleet, Massachusetts.

Patricia McLagan consults, speaks, and writes on organization and people development. Her focus is on successfully guiding organizational changes that optimize the interests of all stakeholder groups: customers, employees, and shareholders. She is the author of two major studies of competencies required by people in the HRD field, and is the author or coauthor of many books and articles on management, change, learning, and communication, including *Change Is Everybody's Business, The Age of Participation: New Governance for the Workplace and the World, On the Level: Performance Communication That Works,* and *Helping Others Learn.* She is the second woman and the fifteenth person inducted into the Human Resource Development Hall of Fame, and holds the American Society for Training and Development's highest award, the Gordon Bliss Award. She is professor of HRM at Rand Afrikaans University,

Johannesburg, a member of many HRD-related editorial boards, and the former cohost of the Internet radio show *The Changing World of Work*. She lives in both the United States and South Africa and works and speaks around the world. See http://www.mclaganint.com.

Laura Martin Milham received her Ph.D. from the University of Central Florida. She has served as a research assistant at the Team Performance Laboratory of the Naval Air Warfare Center Training Systems Division, where she has worked on projects relating to team training and team performance measurement.

Sharon S. Naquin has her doctorate in HRD and undergraduate degrees in finance and human resource management. She is a faculty member in the School of Human Resource and Workforce Development at Louisiana State University and is also the executive director of the Public Management Program. She is also an active consultant specializing in public- and private-sector HRD-related issues. Her published works include journal articles and four books. She has also coedited three issues of *Advances in Human Resource Development*.

Eduardo Salas is professor of psychology at the University of Central Florida, where he is also project director of the Department of Human Systems Integration Research at the Institute of Simulation and Training. Previously, he was a senior research psychologist and head of the training technology development branch of the Naval Air Warfare Center Training Systems division for fifteen years. During that time, he was principal investigator for numerous R&D programs on teamwork, team training, and performance assessment. He has coauthored more than 150 journal articles and book chapters, has coedited eight books, and is on the editorial review boards of several top-tier journals. A fellow of the American Psychological Association and the Human Factors and Ergonomics Society, and a recipient of the Meritorious Civil Service Award from the Department of the Navy, he received his Ph.D. in 1984 in industrial and organizational psychology from Old Dominion University.

Richard A. Swanson is professor of human resource development at the University of Minnesota. He is an internationally recognized authority on organizational change, performance improvement at the organizational, work process, and individual and group levels, and the strategic roles of human resource development. Swanson has authored more than 250 publications on human resource development and performance improvement. He served as president of the Academy of Human Resource Development and was the founding editor of two scholarly journals, *Human Resource Development Quarterly* and *Advances in Developing Human Resources*. Swanson's recent books include *Analysis for Improving Performance* (1996), *Results* (1999), *Foundations of Human Resource Development* (2001), and *Assessing the Financial Benefits of Human Resource Development* (2001). In 2000 he received the Outstanding HRD Scholar Award and was inducted into the International Adult and Continuing Education Hall of Fame, and in 2003 he received the Distinguished Alumni Award from the University of Illinois.

Scott I. Tannenbaum is a founder and president of the Group for Organizational Effectiveness. Throughout his career, he has served as a consultant and adviser to many Fortune 1000 organizations. The well-known organizations he has supported include Johnson & Johnson, Tiffany & Co., BP Amoco, Whirlpool, The St. Paul Companies, UBS Warburg, Bank One, USAA, PSEG, GE Capital, CNA, American Express, Binney & Smith, First USA, the U.S. Navy and Air Force, Citicorp, Progressive Insurance, and NASA. He is an active author and presenter on human resource, training, and technology issues. His research has received awards from the National Academy of Management and the American Society for Training and Development. He has also served as a business school professor, where he helped build the world's first M.B.A. specialization in human resource information technology, and coauthored the first university-level text on the topic. He recently coauthored a book on the emerging topic of knowledge management. He holds a Ph.D. in industrial and organizational psychology from Old Dominion University.

William Wiggenhorn is chief learning officer at CIGNA Corporation. He has also been CLO at Xerox and Motorola, and executive vice president of human resources at Providian Financial Services. His numerous awards include the McKinsey Award for best article in the *Harvard Business Review* (1990), the Rose-Huhlman Institute Award of Excellence in Corporate Education, the China Society/Xilin

Association Educator of the Year Award 2000, the University of Dayton Alumni Award for work in the field of education, and the State of Penang Malaysia's Governor's Award and honorary title of the monarchy for contribution to development of citizens of the state.

Lyle Yorks is an associate professor in the Department of Organization and Leadership at Teachers College, Columbia University, where he is also director of the AEGIS doctoral program. He regularly consults with companies worldwide on issues related to organizational change, executive development, and performance management. He is the author of several books and chapters and has authored and coauthored articles in the *Academy of Management Review, California Management Review, Human Resource Development Quarterly, Sloan Management Review,* and other scholarly and professional journals. His current research interests center around the use of action learning, collaborative inquiry, and related participative strategies for executive development and organizational change. He holds master's degrees from Vanderbilt University and Columbia University and earned his doctorate at Columbia University.

Transfer of Learning in Today's Organizational Reality

CHAPTER 1

Making Transfer Happen

An Action Perspective on Learning Transfer Systems

Elwood F. Holton III, Timothy T. Baldwin

This chapter presents the fundamental premise that guides this book: Researchers studying the transfer of learning have not focused sufficiently on interventions to improve this transfer, so the time has come for more action-oriented strategies. Our core assumptions about transfer are explicated, especially the notion that transfer can be improved significantly, particularly if the focus is on the learning transfer system. We also introduce a transfer distance framework as an approach to understanding the gap between learning and application and to analyzing exactly which parts of the transfer gap are addressed by various interventions.

Most corporations die prematurely from learning disabilities.
They are unable to adapt and evolve as the world around them
changes.
    —ARIE DE GEUS, ROYAL DUTCH SHELL

Recent years have seen an explosion of organizational interest in becoming "learning organizations," creating "corporate universities," and generally being more proactive in approaching education and learning. Many organizational leaders are increasingly sensitive to the reality articulated by de Geus and recognize that their firms' future success will depend on the speed with which people can learn and transfer new ideas and information.

There is no question that transfer of learning is a formidable challenge for organizations. The most commonly cited estimate is that only 10 percent of learning transfers into job performance (although there is little empirical basis for this claim) and reports from the field suggest that a substantial part of organizations' investment in HRD is wasted due to poor learning transfer.

Of course, transfer of learning has long been an important HRD research issue. Since Baldwin and Ford's (1988) review of the literature over a decade ago, considerable progress has been made in understanding factors affecting transfer. Much of the research has focused on training design factors that influence transfer (see Kraiger, Salas, & Cannon-Bowers, 1995; Paas, 1992; Warr & Bunce, 1995). Another stream of research has focused on factors in the organizational environment that influence individuals' ability and opportunity to transfer (Rouillier & Goldstein, 1993; Tracey, Tannenbaum, & Kavanaugh, 1995). Other researchers have focused on individual differences that affect the nature and level of transfer (Gist, Bavetta, & Stevens, 1990; Gist, Stevens, & Bavetta, 1991). Finally, recent work has focused on developing instruments to measure transfer and its antecedent factors in the workplace (Holton, Bates, & Ruona, 2001; Holton, Bates, Seyler, & Carvalho, 1997).

Unfortunately, the existing research is, for the most part, not action-oriented. That is, most existing authors have stopped at the point of identifying, describing, or measuring factors that may influence transfer without investigating how those factors might be effectively changed or managed. For example, of the fifty-eight studies described in the two most comprehensive reviews of the transfer literature (Baldwin & Ford, 1988; Ford & Weissbein, 1997), only those concerning training design dealt much with change or intervention. One notable exception involves studies examining the effectiveness of two post-training interventions (goal setting and relapse prevention training), with all of them finding enhanced transfer (Burke & Baldwin, 1999; Gist, Bavetta, & Stevens, 1990; Gist, Stevens, & Bavetta, 1991; Tziner, Haccoun, & Kadish,

1991; Werner, O'Leary-Kelly, Baldwin, & Wexley, 1994; Wexley & Baldwin, 1986).

Of course, the lack of a prescriptive, action-oriented focus characterizes much of the academic literature and often reflects an appropriate conservatism and reluctance to go beyond one's data. At the same time, it creates a disconnect between HRD researchers and research consumers who rightfully ask, "With your comprehensive knowledge of the research literature, what would you recommend we do in our organizational context?" With respect to transfer of learning, we find that question very difficult to answer. Consumers have had only one source to which to turn for action-oriented strategies (Broad & Newstrom, 1992). It was our recognition of that disconnect that provided the stimulus for this book.

Purpose of This Book

The purpose of this book, then, was to invite leading authors in transfer of learning to contribute their most recent thinking on how to intervene in organizational contexts to influence transfer of learning. Our plan is to expand beyond questions of how transfer occurs or is inhibited, to questions of *how organizational systems can be changed* to enhance transfer. It is perhaps important to note that we are not critical of the existing research. Indeed, many of the studies designed to understand the transfer system will guide explorations into changing that system. Moreover, we see the mission of the SIOP Professional Practice series to provide guidance to practitioners based on sound theory and research, so we are not interested in prescriptions that do not stem from such a foundation. That said, it must be recognized that there are many unanswered research questions about learning transfer; authors have had to go out on a limb at times.

Our Core Assumptions About Transfer

Much has been learned over the past twenty years that has affected our understanding of transfer and its antecedents and inhibitors. At the same time, some persistent misconceptions linger, and we suspect they have served to constrain progress on the transfer problem. Our choice of authors and topics reflects several core assumptions we share about transfer:

• *Transfer is a function of a system of influences—not just learning design.* Questions of transfer are hardly new. In fact, they were among the first issues addressed by early psychologists such as Thorndike and Woodworth (1901). However, until fairly recently, the majority of transfer attention has been focused solely on the design and delivery of the learning event. We have adopted Holton, Bates, and Ruona's (2001) concept of the *transfer system,* which they defined as all factors in the person, training, and organization that influence transfer of learning to job performance. *Transfer climate,* the more common term, is actually but one subset of the factors that influence transfer, though the term is sometimes incorrectly used to refer to the full set of influences. Other influences on transfer include training design, personal characteristics, opportunity to use training, and motivation. Thus, the transfer system is a broader construct than transfer climate but includes all factors traditionally referred to as transfer climate. Transfer can only be completely understood and influenced by examining the entire system of influences.

• *Transfer is not necessarily resistant to intervention.* Clearly, achieving transfer of learning is a complex and difficult challenge, and the amount of transfer from the learning initiatives in our organizations has been disappointing. Left to chance, the likelihood that significant transfer will occur from most learning initiatives is truly very small. However, to conclude that transfer is resistant to intervention is based on the assumption that interventions have regularly been designed and implemented and yet failed to yield transfer. That is not the case. Although a number of exceptions exist (some chronicled in this volume), the reality is that transfer has generally not been actively pursued or managed with planned interventions.

Ironically, we find the lack of active transfer intervention to be a source of optimism and a large part of the impetus for this volume. That is, we believe that transfer can be greatly affected by intervention. But you have to intervene! Moreover, the most successful transfer-inducing interventions will be those based on the accumulating evidence of what affects transfer in organizational contexts. In short, transfer is difficult but has not been shown to be resistant to intervention. Indeed, most reported interventions have produced at least modestly positive results. We contend that the dismal reports of transfer yield are far more a function of "leaving transfer to chance" than any statement of the failure of thoughtful and research-based interventions. The chapters in this volume were chosen to help bring such interventions to life.

• *Achieving transfer does not require substantial new processes and systems.* One of the justifiable fears of practicing professionals is that prescriptions for improvement (particularly those stemming from academic authors) will involve new systems and more infrastructure and additional resources—at a level often not realistically available. To be clear, transfer of learning in organizations will not dramatically improve with a business-as-usual mindset. At the same time, we do not believe that the solution to the transfer problem lies in a radical increase in systems, people, or organizational infrastructure. Rather, we contend that the most significant gains in transfer will come when learning is more tightly integrated into the process and reward systems that already matter in the firm. The challenge is not how to build a bigger and more influential transfer support system, it is how to make transfer a more integral part of the existing organizational climate.

• *Transfer interventions will be most successful where the explicit goal is performance improvement.* It is a rare organizational learning context where transfer would not be included as a desirable outcome. But the reality is that learning activities have often been created more as a reward (top salespeople seminar), an evaluation and assessment tool, or a designation of status than as a way to truly improve work performance. It is hardly surprising to see little performance improvement when such improvement is not the ultimate objective of the initiative. Our experience is that the importance of performance improvement varies widely across learning contexts and some low-transfer outcomes may well be because improved performance was never the primary goal to begin with. If we are to truly understand and build interventions that will improve transfer, then it is important that we do so when and where performance really matters to the learning sponsors.

• *Transfer is multidimensional.* Most authors in the discipline of industrial and organizational psychology have adopted the definition of transfer as the application of learned skills to the workplace. However, at the risk of stating the obvious, transfer is not just one thing. Distinctions among types of transfer are not new, but they are often obscured. We find it particularly useful to think in terms of transfer *distance*. To illustrate, learning to drive a car and then finding yourself in a small truck would be a situation that would demand transfer, but of a short distance. On the other hand, learning principles of organizational change in a management development seminar and then attempting to practice behaviors stemming from those principles over time as head of a merger and acquisition team would define much greater distance. It is important to have some degree of clarity about the nature of the transfer of interest before designing and evaluating particular interventions.

Conceptual Framework for Transfer System Intervention

Previous conceptual frameworks have been largely descriptive, so we adapted existing frameworks to fit a more intervention-oriented approach. Our framework (see Figure 1.1), consistent with other existing models (for example, Baldwin & Ford, 1988),

Figure 1.1. Conceptual Framework for Managing Learning Transfer Systems.

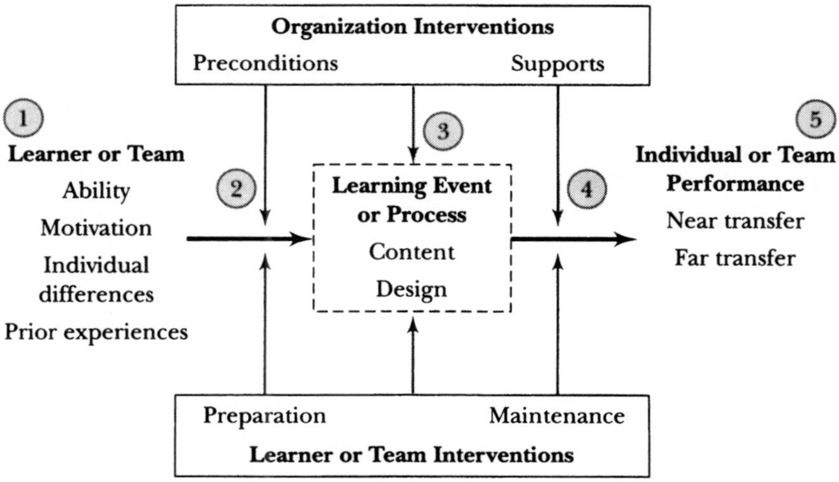

begins with three general foci for transfer interventions: the learners, the learning event, and the organizational context, which we call system design. These are the essential elements of any learning transfer system. However, we also expand the notion of learner to include individual learners and teams. Like Broad and Newstrom (1992), we incorporate a temporal dimension into the framework. Whereas they suggested three simple stages (before, during, and after), we expand it to five time dimensions as described in subsequent paragraphs.

Then we adopt Holton, Bates, and Ruona's (2001) and Naquin and Holton's (2002) emphasis on individual differences by recognizing that the learner or team is both an input to the process (time point 1 in the figure) and a unit in the model that may be shaped by interventions. At time point 1, the learner or team is viewed as bringing to the learning transfer process four key elements: ability, motivation, individual differences, and prior experiences with the transfer system (Holton, Bates, & Ruona, 2001).

Time point 2 is similar to Broad and Newstrom's (1992) "before" stage. Similarly, time point 3 is analogous to their "during" stage, and time point 4 is analogous to their "after" stage. It is at points 2 and 4 that the two major intervention sets, *learner and team interventions* and *organization interventions,* influence the process. Organization interventions include both preconditions and supports, while learner or team interventions include preparation and maintenance. Both intervention sets have before and after components, and on some occasions might also influence the learning event itself. It should also be noted that both the before and after stages may be quite lengthy and consist of multiple interventions.

Time point 3, the learning event itself, is composed of two dimensions: content and design. That is, the learning event must be built around content that is viewed as valid and complete to attain job performance outcomes. Furthermore, as noted by Baldwin and Ford (1988) and emphasized by Holton, Bates, and Ruona (2001), the content must be taught in a manner that enables learners to use it in real work situations, which is called transfer design.

The fifth time point in the model represents the performance outcomes from learning. Two dimensions of performance outcomes are noted: near transfer and far transfer. The transfer literature has inadvertently focused mostly on near transfer. In reality, performance outcomes from learning must provide an appropriate balance between short-term results (near) and longer-term transfer and generalization of learning to new situations (far).

Collectively, these elements comprise what we call the *learning transfer system*. The model shown here is just a conceptual framework of the system, as many individual variables would fit within each element. This transfer process model points out the multiple opportunities available to organizations wishing to manage or change the learning transfer system. Subsequent chapters will develop each element more fully and discuss ways to manage or change them.

The Transfer Distance Concept

Much has been made of the potential for new, nonclassroom learning designs to do away with the learning transfer problem. We disagree. Newer learning designs are tremendous advances and do improve the transfer problem, but they do not fix it. To understand their impact, it is useful to think of a concept we call *transfer distance*. Metaphorically, transfer distance refers to the gap between the learning environment and application in the job environment. Various labels have been applied to this gap, including lateral versus vertical transfer, specific versus nonspecific transfer, literal and figural transfer, and—best known to HRD learning professionals— near versus far transfer (Royer, 1979). Actually, all of these terms were originally used by educational and cognitive psychologists to talk about various levels or types of cognitive learning.

Transfer distance integrates the cognitive notions of transfer as well as the learning to performance concepts into a single continuum. As Figure 1.2 shows, the transfer distance continuum progresses through two phases with six key events representing points along the journey from cognitive learning to broad performance application. The first phase, moving from knowledge to performance capability, is the learning process and the traditional domain of training. Node 1 represents the starting point for most training: acquiring cognitive knowledge or "know that." However, real transfer requires that learning be expanded to node 2, acquiring knowledge for how to use the learning, or "know how." Nodes 1 and 2 represent the minimum learning required to make trans-

Figure 1.2. Transfer Distance Conceptual Model.

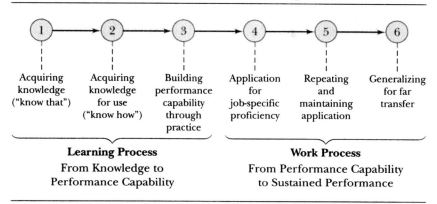

fer possible. We suggest that node 3, building performance capability through practice, is likely to significantly enhance transfer by providing learners opportunities to practice what is learned.

The second phase moves the learner from performance capability to sustained performance and represents the work process using the learning. Node 4 represents the traditional notion of near transfer, and that is the application of learned material to the learner's immediate job and for the tasks at which the learning was targeted. Note that node 4 also represents proficiency, not just attempts at application. Learning transfer does not stop here, even though common uses of the term imply that it does. Node 5 represents the next step, repeating and maintaining learned performance. That is, the desired outcome is not just limited use of what is learned but continuing use of the learning on the job. Node 6 then represents the pinnacle of transfer, the generalization of learning for application to tasks or jobs not originally anticipated by the training, but related in a way that allows the learning effects to multiply.

The traditional view of learning transfer in training has been from node 1 to node 4. Usually this represented classroom instruction to immediate job application. Nodes 5 and 6 have not been discussed as heavily because, frankly, the challenge of closing the gap from nodes 1 to 4 has been so significant. Newer learning designs that integrate learning with work significantly improve the transfer problem because they shorten the distances between nodes 1, 2, 3, and 4 until they are so small that they seem to disappear. Indeed a strong argument can be made that work-based learning initiatives move learning at least to node 3. However, it should also be apparent that they do not make the transfer problem disappear completely. At best they leave nodes 5 and 6 (repetition, maintenance, and generalization) still unresolved—and node 4 (job application) is usually not fully addressed because the work systems (social and process) that support learning on the job are not incorporated into many learning initiatives.

Consider management development training in coaching skills as an example. In this case, each node could mean the following:

- Node 1: learning the characteristics of effective coaching
- Node 2: learning the steps effective coaches use to conduct coaching sessions
- Node 3: role-plays during training to practice coaching skills
- Node 4: trying out the new skills in a coaching session with an employee a few weeks after training
- Node 5: continuing to coach employees on a regular basis, so the new coaching skills become more natural for the learner as success is experienced
- Node 6: building on the principles of coaching to create more empowered employees who are more self-directed

Transfer distance provides a useful means of thinking about learning transfer systems. First, it helps by locating the type of learning event on the continuum. Second, it is useful to locate the type of transfer that is being targeted. That is, is the goal limited to job-specific transfer (node 4), long-term performance (node 5), or generalized learning application (node 6)? Together these provide a conceptual map of the distance to be closed by transfer improvement interventions.

About This Volume

We sought authors whose expertise reflected each of these intervention targets. The result is that different chapters are likely to be more relevant to some practitioners than others but the volume as a whole will speak to most of the major elements of a total transfer system. A recurrent theme throughout this volume is that there are many things we don't know about managing and changing transfer systems. All the authors have had to extend their thinking in order to move to the action orientation asked of them. While all operated from a base of sound research, in most cases they have had to stretch beyond their comfort zone of what is known from empirical research. In that sense, this volume also challenges researchers to extend their research agendas to test the propositions advanced here.

Part One frames this volume by putting it in the context of today's organizational realities. Chapters Two and Three present the chief learning officers' views of learning transfer in organizations, followed by a discussion of how new forces have shaped learning in today's organizations in such a way that transfer demands some different strategies.

Part Two tackles three critical questions:

- How do you diagnose learning transfer systems?
- What is a transfer-ready profile and how do you assess and place employees to maximize transfer?
- What process should be followed to design a learning transfer system improvement intervention?

Part Three focuses on the learning process, that is, moving from knowledge to performance capability (nodes 1–3). Key topics include

- Using front-end analysis to avoid transfer problems
- Transfer issues in increasingly popular work-based learning initiatives such as action learning and communities of practice
- Transfer in e-learning contexts
- Transfer of team training

Part Four addresses the work process, the second phase of the transfer distance model. This includes

- Relapse prevention as a tool to maintain learned skills over time

- Competencies required by managers as key agents in the transfer system
- How managers create a workgroup climate that encourages not only initial transfer but maintenance and generalization of learning over time

In short, our goal is to be representative of what we see as the key areas for interventions that may improve transfer in organizations. We hope that the volume will substantively contribute to the literature in the area of transfer and will ultimately lead to fewer organizations perishing as the result of learning transfer disabilities.

References

Baldwin, T. T., & Ford, K. J. (1988). Transfer of training: A review and directions for future research. *Personnel Psychology, 41*, 63–105.

Broad, M. L., & Newstrom, J. W. (1992). *Transfer of training: Action-packed strategies to ensure high payoff from training investments.* Reading, MA: Addison-Wesley.

Burke, L., & Baldwin, T. T. (1999). Effects of relapse prevention training and transfer climate on the use of trained skills. *Human Resource Management, 38*(3), 227–241.

Ford, J. K., & Weissbein, D. A. (1997). Transfer of training: An update review and analysis. *Performance Improvement Quarterly, 10*, 22–41.

Gist, M. E., Bavetta, A. G., & Stevens, C. K. (1990). Transfer training method: Its influence on skill generalization, skill repetition, and performance level. *Personnel Psychology, 43*, 501–523.

Gist, M. E., Stevens, C. K., & Bavetta, A. G. (1991). Effects of self-efficacy and post-training intervention on the acquisition and maintenance of complex interpersonal skills. *Personnel Psychology, 44*, 837–861.

Holton, E. F., III, Bates, R. A., & Ruona, W.E.A. (2001). Development of a generalized learning transfer system inventory. *Human Resource Development Quarterly, 11*(4), 333–360.

Holton, E. F., III, Bates, R., Seyler, D., & Carvalho, M. (1997). Toward construct validation of a transfer climate instrument. *Human Resource Development Quarterly, 8*, 95–113.

Kraiger, K., Salas, E., & Cannon-Bowers, J. A. (1995). Measuring knowledge organization as a method for assessing learning during training. *Human Factors, 37*, 804–816.

Naquin, S. S., & Holton, E. F., III. (2002). The effects of personality, affectivity, and work commitment on motivation to improve work through learning. *Human Resource Development Quarterly, 13*, 357–376.

Paas, F.G.W.C. (1992). Training strategies for attaining transfer of problem-solving skill in statistics: A cognitive load approach. *Journal of Educational Psychology, 84,* 429–434.

Rouillier, J. Z., & Goldstein, I. L. (1993). The relationship between organizational transfer climate and positive transfer of training. *Human Resource Development Quarterly, 4,* 377–390.

Royer, J. M. (1979). Theories of the transfer of learning. *Educational Psychologist, 14,* 53–69.

Thorndike, E. L., & Woodworth, R. S. (1901). The influence of improvement in one mental function upon the efficiency of other functions. *Psychological Review, 8,* 247–261.

Tracey, J. B., Tannenbaum, S. I., & Kavanaugh, M. J. (1995). Applying trained skills on the job: The importance of the work environment. *Journal of Applied Psychology, 80,* 239–252.

Tziner, A., Haccoun, R. R., & Kadish, A. (1991). Personal and situational characteristics of transfer of training improvement strategies. *Journal of Occupational Psychology, 64,* 167–177.

Warr, P., & Bunce, D. (1995). Trainee characteristics and the outcomes of open learning. *Personnel Psychology, 48,* 347–375.

Werner, J. M., O'Leary-Kelly, A. M., Baldwin, T. T., & Wexley, K. N. (1994). Augmenting behavior-modeling training: Testing the effects of pre- and post-training interventions. *Human Resource Development Quarterly, 5,* 169–183.

Wexley, K. N., & Baldwin, T. T. (1986). Posttraining strategies for facilitating positive transfer: An empirical exploration. *Academy of Management Journal, 29,* 503–520.

CHAPTER 2

The Strategic Challenge for Transfer

Chief Learning Officers Speak Out

Camden C. Danielson
William Wiggenhorn

Escalating corporate investment in learning, and the accompanying expectations of that investment's impact on firm performance, have combined to create greater urgency in the search for models and strategies for evaluating and improving the transfer of learning. Unfortunately, many existing transfer prescriptions suffer from one or more latent assumptions that are inconsistent with the reality of learning in today's organizations. Drawing on conversations with leading learning professionals and our own experience, we contend that the reality facing today's learning professional involves three fundamental challenges: aligning learning with the business, organizing for impact, and affecting *real* learning. Making liberal use of the voices of those at the front, we describe and illustrate each of those three challenges and present some examples of how firms are attempting to enhance transfer as a path to better business performance.

Much of the research and writing in the area of transfer of learning has emerged from authors not directly responsible for learning outcomes in organizations. Our charge, therefore, was to provide a perspective from the front—that is, to explore the challenge of transfer through the lens of learning professionals' experience. In doing so, we relied on our own work leading the learning function in organizations (for example, Motorola, CIGNA) and on conversations with leading learning executives. (See Table 2.1 for a complete list of learning executives interviewed by the first author.)

Today's progressive corporations have moved from treating learning as an obligatory cost factor to regarding it as a weapon in the battle for competitive advantage. Expenditures on both traditional and technology-driven learning activities have risen substantially and the level of resources devoted to all aspects of the learning enterprise (salaries, technology, facilities) has grown rapidly. The escalating level of investment corporations have made in learning, and the accompanying expectations of that investment's enhancing firm performance, have combined to create greater urgency in the search for models or tools for both evaluating and improving the transfer of learning.

While transfer of learning is clearly top of mind for today's learning executives, achieving it remains problematic. A large part of the challenge is that the learning contexts in organizations have become increasingly complex and demanding. For example, any firmwide sales learning initiatives at Cisco need to reach tens of thousands of people (internal and external to the firm), located in different regions of the world. At Sun Microsystems, the majority of revenue comes from products and services less than eighteen months old, so the demand for "big learning fast" is acute. At NCR, new electronic learning applications change the educational dynamic in ways that make some conventional measures of learning effectiveness inapplicable. For example, how does one assess the level of transfer from a series of quick Internet hits—all fruitless except for one that contained a transferable gem? Perhaps most important, for all firms, the level of uncertainty in markets and strategy (what industry *are* we in, what competencies do we need?) has risen significantly. The implications of these contextual realities for the management of transfer are self-evident and imposing.

We contend that the existing literature on transfer of learning suffers from at least three latent assumptions inconsistent with the reality facing today's learning professional. First, there is a preoccupation with training outcomes vis-à-vis business performance. Second, evaluation of transfer effectiveness (or often lack thereof) is frequently reported uncoupled from organizational culture and

Table 2.1. Participants in CLO Study.

Company	Participant Name	Participant Title
AT&T	Albert Siu	Chief Learning Officer
Andersen UK	Nick Holley	Partner, UK Learning and Performance
Boeing	Steve Mercer	Vice President, Learning and Leadership
Cisco Systems	Tom Kelly	Vice President, Internet Solutions
Dana Corporation	Larry Lottier	Dean, School of Business
Dow Chemical Company	Frank Morgan	Director, Executive Development & Leadership Programs
Eli Lilly & Co.	Sharon Sullivan	Vice President, Human Resources and Chief Learning Officer
FedEx Express	Steve Nielsen	Managing Director, Leadership Institute
General Motors	Donnee Ramelli	President, GM University
Hewlett-Packard	Susan Burnett	Director, Enterprise Workforce Development
Home Depot	Gary Jusela	Vice President and Chief Learning Officer
Johnson & Johnson	Allen Andersen	Vice President, Education and Development
3M	Margaret Alldredge	Staff Vice President, Selection and Learning
NASA	Bonnie Acoveno	Director, Training and Development
NCR Corporation	Brad Luckhaupt	Vice President, Global Learning
Rolls-Royce plc	Jim Butler	Director, Training and Development
St. Paul Companies	David Owens	Chief Knowledge Officer
Sun Microsystems	Jim Moore	Director, Workforce Planning and Development

context. Third, there is a perpetuation of a bias toward activities and programs in defining the scope of learning. As a result, training and development groups have been admonished for their disconnect between learning and strategic objectives, a preoccupation with activity rather than outcomes (an overemphasis on formal classes or events to address organizational performance issues), fragmented delivery, and the lack of linkage with other influential systems and processes (such as performance management, succession planning, and compensation).

Fortunately, the current reality is that progressive (certainly not all) learning executives are consumed with making the business performance case for learning; they struggle to link learning into the critical business processes and reward systems of the firm, and they now view learning as far broader than narrowly defined programs or events. In fact, we believe that those are the three most fundamental challenges facing learning executives today. More specifically:

- *Aligning the learning enterprise with the business:* Identifying and translating key strategic objectives into learning initiatives and identifying metrics that capture learning's impact on business-related outcomes
- *Organizing for impact:* Building a learning infrastructure that connects with the people and processes that matter in the firm
- *Affecting real learning:* Understanding and managing the forms of learning (traditional classroom experiences being only one element) that can improve the work performance of individuals and nourishing a culture where learning takes place as a natural consequence of work and progression in the firm

Of course, it is overly simplistic to talk in terms of "solving" or "overcoming" such broad challenges. Rather, our objective in this chapter was to simply explicate the nature and dimensions of those challenges and the kinds of initiatives that are being led in response. Our hope was that a fuller and more explicit understanding of these contexts would help direct future transfer research away from simplified and outdated notions and toward the issues of most salience to practicing professionals. The ultimate goal is to help bridge the chasm between science and practice.

Aligning with the Business

My role is not to deliver programs but to be a catalyst for business performance.
—NICK HOLLEY, CLO, ANDERSEN UK

We consider ourselves staunch advocates of the value of learning and have found that most senior business executives are passionate about the value of education and insatiable learners in their own right. But the reality today is that organizations do not consider learning an imperative—performance and survival are the imperatives. Learning is essential only to the degree that it contributes more to performance than other allocations of scarce resources. This is in direct contrast to much of the academic writing on transfer, which has often tended to divorce learning objectives from business performance objectives. So the charge is not to focus on learning for learning's sake but to contribute to helping the business win in the marketplace. Put another way, before asking, "Are we doing all we can to maximize the transfer of our learning experiences?" we should first be asking, "Are our learning experiences instrumental to the performance requirements of the firm?"

Clarifying Business Objectives and Stakeholders

If you do not have a customer, you have a problem.
—FRANK MORGAN, CLO, DOW CHEMICAL

Aligning with the business requires a systemic view of organizational performance that is highly contextual in nature. To make a difference to the business requires clarity in (and perhaps even having input toward the creation of) the firm's key strategic objectives and the ability to make the business case for learning. In a world of resource scarcity, if any learning initiative is not viewed as being mission critical to key stakeholders then it is destined for a subordinate role and hopes of significant transfer are probably in vain. A primary challenge, therefore, is to clearly identify and understand the strategic objectives and to translate those into learning initiatives for such key stakeholders. That is no easy undertaking and varies considerably across organizations.

In some cases, learning executives have direct access to the most senior management of the firm and strategic objectives are relatively straightforward. For example, Sharon Sullivan, CLO at Eli Lilly & Co., is very mindful of the key strategic foci of the firm (for example, the end of patent protection for Prozac, improved manufacturing quality, and cost containment). Similarly, Margaret Alldredge at 3M is intimately aware of the strategic competitive platforms (narrow diversification focus on winners, speed to market and commercialization, cost-effective sourcing, e-productivity, and the like) advocated by her CEO. Both Sullivan and Alldredge point out that if their learning priorities do not reflect those strategic thrusts, then no matter how successful certain programs or initiatives may be in terms of transfer, they are nonetheless destined for low "mindshare" in the firm and risk funding and support.

At CIGNA, the strategic challenge is to build on a strong heritage of financial management while developing a marketing mindset and capability within all units of the firm. The difficulty is overcoming the organizational tension created by this new top management imperative. The CIGNA culture is risk averse as a result of its focus on asset management over the years (minimize risk and make a decent annual return on investments). Similarly, decision making became highly centralized, with little input from the market centers. To reposition the firm means both developing information-gathering systems linked to customers and consumers in every market and developing a new discipline in key decision-making forums that is based on market intelligence. This latter point is critical to innovation because of the conservative nature of the firm.

All and all, learning transfer involves a major cultural overhaul. The imperative is therefore building an environment of frank and open dialogue from top management down through the different lines of business. Here the learning strategy is less programmatic and more facilitative in terms of framing or modeling the dialogue within structured senior management meetings. However, the dialogue will not prove fruitful without rigorous systems of market intelligence and data analysis. As a result, another feature of the learning strategy is building a marketing community within the company that is based on a set of competencies for which more formal learning environments are well suited.

Of course, neither publicized strategic directives nor access to top decision makers ensures the alignment of the learning enterprise with the business. The ability to recognize cues regarding where and how learning can contribute to the achievement of business objectives (however vaguely stated) is a critical competency in these contexts. Toward that end, Sharon Sullivan organized two trips for the firm's executive council to visit other organizations highly regarded in terms of one or more of Lilly's current strategic thrusts. She notes that, in the course of those visits, a number of learning gaps have emerged, which are immediately salient to the most senior decision makers in the company. Her job is to prioritize and execute initiatives that are responsive to those recognized gaps.

Both Frank Morgan at Dow Chemical and Susan Burnett at HP initiated 360-degree evaluation processes with their most senior management teams—including CEOs. The idea was to understand the competency gaps that may constrain execution of strategic initiatives and then design learning to address those gaps—ultimately cascading the learning down from the very top of the firm. Again, the challenge is to get *aligned,* and one path to that end is to be central to the personal learning agendas of the most senior leaders of the firm.

Of course, many learning professionals do not have a direct pipeline to the CEO or other top decision makers and thus have to discern key strategic directives and "hear the voice of customers" in other ways. The process of learning stakeholder needs may be top-down or bottom-up. It may mean creating some infrastructure (advisory boards, learning councils), targeting key thought-leaders as champions, or building a database regarding learning expenditures that necessitates one's involvement in discussions regarding strategic resource allocation. Further, not every firm, even among some of those referenced here, could really be said to have a top management team that views learning as mission critical. In those cases, the challenge is more acute and the necessity for making the case for relevance even greater.

Along these same lines, we are struck by the ambiguity of the conventional training effectiveness axiom of "top management support." For example, such support is often referenced as if it is dichotomous (you either have it or you don't) when obviously it may occur in many forms and degrees, and all forms are not equal in their utility for accomplishing learning objectives. Further, we submit that lasting support comes less from general satisfaction ("I like what you guys are doing") and more from commitment ("Eliminating you would constrain my goal accomplishment and be too costly"). As Jim Butler of Rolls-Royce noted, real support is easy to confuse with cheerleading or politicking or just permission. Others noted that transfer is enhanced in those cases where it is a "pull" (if they come, we will build it) approach to educational programming rather than the more common "push" (if we build it, they will come) protocol, though there are trade-offs associated with each.

For example, among the more difficult pieces of clarifying objectives and stakeholders is making decisions around priorities and determining which customers will *not* be served. Focused and efficient use of resources requires clarity both about what you are trying to do and what you are leaving for others. Susan Burnett's work at Hewlett-Packard nicely captures this difficult trade-off.

Burnett describes the challenge of focus or scope in terms of her learning strategy: "We have to shift from an expense mentality of responding to every need that the business units identify to a capability building mentality." It is a challenge of managing the tension between decentralized decision-making authority at the business unit level and centralized corporate initiatives that affect the overall capability of the firm. In other words, Burnett is part of an effort to establish core capability standards that have measures linked to business performance. Within the learning function this means "educational initiatives must be linked to business performance and not offered just because people want them."

It is an interesting tension, because Burnett could run her office like a business that paid its way based on her success in responding to business unit requests. However, in her mind, to do so would be to diverge from the key strategic directions of the firm. Therefore, she has invested her time working with the top management team in defining a set of core competencies and measures that will enhance the integration strategy of common platforms and processes and shared profit-and-loss statements. At the same time, she recognizes that the largest need is workforce development to deliver on the strategy.

What Transfer Means in the Firm: Making the Business Case

We will not measure our learning systems in the same way that we do other business initiatives. To do so would only trivialize them.
—JACK WELCH, CEO, GENERAL ELECTRIC CO.

Isolated in the context of a single training program, the notion of transfer of learning is relatively easy to understand. To what degree was learning from the program applied in the workplace? However, in the context of business performance, the notion of what constitutes successful transfer is broader and more complicated. First, progressive firms today are beyond thinking solely about a focus on the individual learner. They know that the learning function cannot work exclusively at the level of the individual performer but must contribute to the development and performance management of teams, product lines, divisions, joint ventures, and wherever else performance is strategically important.

Second, the focus of evaluation is heavily dependent on the business case (or cases) for learning in the firm. Moreover, the business case may vary rather dramatically from firm to firm and even within a given firm. We have found that the answer to the question, "What is your business case for learning in this firm?" generally falls into one of the six categories summarized in Table 2.2. Evident from the chart is that the business case for learning need not be one-dimensional. Moreover, the dimensions of a compelling business case can range from the direct (effective learning yields higher sales revenue or new product innovation) to the indirect (effective learning will help us attract and keep good people, facilitate intraorganizational knowledge sharing, or create a deeper bench of leaders capable of running our growing businesses). Obviously, metrics based on business performance are more straightforward to obtain than, say, culture building or employer of choice, but some interesting ways of gauging success are emerging in each of those cases.

At Cisco Systems, Tom Kelly builds his learning case around "selling more boxes." That is, products change rapidly, and getting knowledge about those products into the hands of salespeople, both internal and external distributors, is critical to making sales. Steve Nielsen at FedEx Express says that his role could be likened

Table 2.2. CLOs Make the Business Case for Learning.

Employer of Choice	Culture Building	Leadership Development and Bench Strength	Source of Innovation	External Value	Functional Excellence
• Learning is key weapon in war for talent	• Exposure to shared values, organizational conscience, creating denser people networks and awareness of resources	• Growing, global firms depend on skilled leadership and current demand exceeds supply	• Learning can be window on the world, gestation source for new ideas, skunk works	• Learning products or services help customers make the purchase decision (training material becomes attractive product feature)	• Defining high levels of operational competence for functional units
• Means of protecting our investment in people	• Potent lever for change—vehicle for getting people's attention	• Provides safe environment for risk taking and noble failures	• Create living laboratories to experiment with new processes and systems	• Business partners and customers venture with us in part because of our learning enterprise	• Facilitating the transfer of knowledge to day-to-day performance of individuals (for example, a better-trained market analyst targets better opportunities for the firm)
• Good management is key to retention—good management is key to good development	• A megaphone for new corporate initiatives	• Can influence development at key career stages	• Knowledge generation, not just dissemination	• Analysts value the firm in part on the basis of our learning enterprise	• Enhancing the economic or business literacy of employees
• Inoculate against success derailers and the key reasons people leave	• Sharing best business practices, establishing boundaryless culture	• Tied to challenging jobs, can accelerate individual development and reduce talent gaps	• Knowledge management and an incubation center		
• Serve as the organizational chaplain—nurture whole person; preserve integrity and dignity in the firm	• Organizational glue—makes us better together than the sum of our parts				

to organizational "chaplain," a key source of conveying shared values and a common experience that is crucial to a cohesive culture—long a trademark of FedEx. He playfully points to the movie *Cast Away* as an idealized illustration of what he is trying to accomplish. In that film, Tom Hanks's character, a FedEx employee, holds to the customer service values of the firm even under the most extreme test.

Gary Jusela, CLO at Home Depot, believes that learning is a critical weapon in the war for talent, but not solely because people like to have lots of attractive learning opportunities available to them. Rather, he contends, and research supports, people leave firms largely because of their supervision. Put simply, people do not leave companies, they leave bosses. Thus the case for good managerial training can be tied to attraction and retention of key people. Similarly, Susan Burnett of HP reports that all managers at HP are evaluated on how well they mentor and develop people in the company and a piece of their annual bonus is tied to the retention of top talent.

Others use components of employee surveys or 360-degree feedback reports to gauge learning effectiveness. At Boeing, Steve Mercer, who runs the Leadership Development Center, helps makes his case by comparing the higher satisfaction level of employees in units that have a critical mass of graduates versus those units without this same depth of exposure to the curriculum of the Leadership Center. In a recent annual employee survey (calendar year 2000), units with more than 25 percent of their managers participating in Boeing Leadership Center programs (compared with those units with less than 10 percent) had an 8–10 percent higher rating from their employees on involvement in decisions that affect their work, support and recognition for the work they do, and challenging assignments that take advantage of their skills and abilities.

As a gauge of the value of Motorola University (MU) throughout the 1990s, business leaders at the time often noted, "Motorola enters no new markets without MU." The business case for MU was to influence the environment in which the company did business. A striking example of this was a telecommunication consortium organized by MU jointly with the U.S. State Department's Office of International Development. The consortium was made up of ministers of telecommunication from developing countries around the world. They participated in programs on wireless technology in forums that were instrumental in the formulation of public policy. These educational sessions helped inform individual perspectives on the role of wireless technology in the economic vitality of developing nations and, ultimately, country strategies on the regulation of telecommunication.

As a final point on aligning with the business, we want to make clear that we do not subscribe to the view that the ultimate metric of transfer should be firm financial performance. It is true that pressures for "hard" business performance outcomes have become acute in today's organizations. At the same time, it remains subject to debate whether the best case for the efficacy of learning really does reside in the demonstration of correlations with overall firm financial performance. Our experience is that good businesspeople understand well that reported financial performance is influenced by many factors over time (economic environment, accounting practices, new product and service releases, and the like). They also recognize that few learning interventions are ever *specifically* directed at affecting overall financial performance. Consequently, using a measure of overall firm financial performance as a dependent variable for assessing the success of learning strategies and interventions is not very proximate and can therefore be misleading, if not downright dangerous. Along those lines, work on the utility of HR interventions such as training and staffing has sometimes shown impressive dollar values of cost savings and gains and yet often garnered great skepticism from practicing managers who do not see the proximity between the interventions and the financial benefits claimed.

We should be cautious of falling prey to an obsession with financial performance data as the direct consequence of learning initiatives. To be sure, in some cases and for some learning initiatives (as in the External Value column of Table 2.2), learning professionals do seek to make their business case through direct impact on financial performance indices. Far more often, however, they make the case through the positive effects of learning on attraction and retention of good people, intraorganizational knowledge sharing, or the creation of a deeper bench of leaders capable of running growing businesses.

Organizing for Impact

What gets measured and rewarded, gets done.
   —ANONYMOUS

One disappointing aspect of much existing research work on HR in general, and transfer of learning in particular, is that so little attention has been devoted to distinctions related to the environment, industry, markets, or culture of business firms. Despite a great deal of rhetoric related to "becoming strategic partners" and "enabling business success," much of the literature still neglects to have any measurement, consideration, or even mention of the type of environment, strategic initiatives, history, culture, or values of the firm or firms under study.

A number of authors (Baldwin & Ford, 1988; Broad & Newstrom, 1992) have highlighted the importance of the transfer context or culture and our experience is that such culture, particularly those processes and reward systems that really matter in a given firm, can make or break the transfer of learning.

For learning to be respected and gain mindshare in any firm, it simply cannot be an isolated activity. As noted earlier, it must emanate from firm strategy and have identifiable customers. Further, given the political reality of all major organizations, addressing two questions is central to the ultimate effectiveness of the learning function: Who has the means and the will to support our initiatives? and What systems, processes, and data garner attention in the firm both at senior levels and through the ranks? Thoughtful consideration of those two questions can help chart a direction for the organization and positioning of learning that will facilitate transfer.

"Learning is too important for HR" is a provocative epigram, and one that we frankly debated about whether to include. HR units have earned sterling reputations in many firms (including those referenced here) and have been strategic partners and responsive staff functions. We do not think that the issue is one of organizational structure—the location of learning on the organization chart is far less important than its place between the lines, in the informal organization that actually functions on a day-to-day basis within the firm. The lesson to be taken from that seemingly caustic comment, in our view, is not that learning should be taken out of the hands of HR. Rather, to be effective, it cannot be limited to or seen as just an HR program. Any learning professional would be well served to find and nurture champions of learning in the line functions of the business. Like it or not, HR does not always enjoy the most business-oriented reputation, and the effectiveness of a learning program will be diminished to the extent that it is viewed solely as one of the HR roles and functions.

With respect to the linkage with people, Nick Holley of Andersen UK has learned that he need not pursue support from a critical mass of his senior management constituents. Rather, he seeks visible support of a few recognized thought leaders in the firm. He also notes that those with a history of skepticism toward learning, or budget frugality, can make excellent champions. Of course, to get such support requires some small wins and demonstration that learning can add value to their business. Key people are not limited to the senior management ranks. Up-and-coming managers (HIPOs) can be excellent champions as well. Steve Nielsen at FedEx Express talks about how some of what he calls the "young tigers," recently promoted into general management roles and on a rapid career incline in the firm, are among his most visible and effective champions of learning.

Connections with processes, not just people, are part of this equation as well, and every firm has core capabilities that are distinctive. For example, at HP and 3M it is research and development. At Lilly it is scientific innovation and sales and marketing. At FedEx it is customer service and continuous improvement. At Dana and GM it is manufacturing and quality. What makes these distinctive in each firm are the major systems or business processes linked to them. The learning function needs to leverage these systems as part of its value contribution role, both for taking advantage of what is core to the firm and for extending best practices in the learning function itself. HR systems are often of particular importance in the coupling of learning with performance management. Compensation, career and succession planning, and knowledge management are all means of making learning relevant to things that matter most to organization members. Two good illustrations of efforts to make those connections are Donnee Ramelli at GM and Jim Moore, former CLO at Sun Microsystems.

Since Ramelli arrived at GM in late 1999 after a stint as CLO at AlliedSignal, working for Larry Bossidy, his focus has been to evaluate and address the performance gaps in the organization. While on first blush this seems standard practice, the difference in this case is the linkage he has forged between learning and other classic levers of organizational change: performance management, talent development, and succession planning with a focus on improving business performance and results. In Ramelli's words, "As the CLO I have to be involved in the systems and processes that help you succeed as a company. Learning systems may be 40 percent of this, but it is only one part."

What is becoming apparent in this description of Ramelli's role as CLO is the degree of emphasis he places on the interrelation between improving organizational performance and business results and the systems that have to interact to accomplish this goal. For example, Ramelli has helped develop a performance evaluation instrument for top management. The function of the instrument has been to look at leaders' business results and individual behavior in terms of how well they are addressing four key values: acting as one company, embracing stretch targets, acting with a sense of urgency, and focusing on product quality and customer loyalty. The process will eventually cascade throughout the management ranks of the organization and create a tight linkage to various change initiatives such as quality improvement, speed to market, innovation, and growth of profitable services.

The role of learning systems in Ramelli's strategy is to act as a pull mechanism based on individual performance measures. As individuals realize how their careers will be derailed if they don't have the proper skills, knowledge, and tools, they will turn to the education cupboard for the things they need. In this model, the emphasis is to make knowledge as readily accessible as possible. Consumers know what they want because they have an immediate need to be addressed, and they are operating in a world of time and cost constraints. Yet here is where GM University comes to play, and with sixteen deans reporting to senior managers in functional leadership roles there is a clear link to the processes that employees need to know and the means to transfer that knowledge.

Key to Ramelli's strategy is to build a market for education within GM stemming from individual business performance requirements tightly linked to business goals. With more than eighty thousand technical and professional people in the firm, Ramelli's approach underscores his efforts to extend the reach of his unit and touch more people—thus addressing organizational performance and business results from a very wide base.

Jim Moore, former CLO at Sun Microsystems, cites compelling evidence that the performance of people managers is critical to the attraction and retention of top talent, correlates significantly with financial performance, and even has an impact on institutional investors' perception of stock value. While CLO, he set out to make the learning function central to the improvement of people manager skills.

Toward that end, Moore spearheaded a program now in place at Sun that defines manager expectations and synthesizes those into a straightforward scorecard they call the "people management dashboard" that includes the four competencies and their specific behavioral indicators measured via 360-degree feedback. One of Moore's particular objectives was to link meaningful outcomes to the attainment and demonstration (or lack thereof) of people management competence—and he has done so. Among the outcomes are skip-level promotion, visibility for the top fifty people managers, a targeted stock plan, and the phased termination of the bottom 5 percent of managers. The result is that learning and honing people management skills has become highly critical, not just in the rarefied air of senior management circles but to the rank-and-file managers that are the lifeblood of the firm.

Affecting Real Learning

I never let my schooling get in the way of my education.
—MARK TWAIN

Everyone is incredibly busy. But you cannot be so busy that you allow yourself to get stupid.
—TOM KELLY, CISCO

We no longer even use the terminology of someone "going to a class." Rather we say they "join a learning community."
—DAVID OWENS, ST. PAUL COMPANIES

While the whole education profession wants to believe that their efforts are instrumental in the growth and development of their constituents, there is no consensus as to what constitutes impact or what may be referred to as "real learning." As research by the Center for Creative Leadership and others has documented (McCall, Lombardo, & Morrison, 1988), much of what gets referenced as critical to the success of a manager's career occurs outside of a classroom. Such things as challenging assignments, job performance, good mentors, and an organizational climate of success are factors that rank higher than training and education. While this may be true, generally speaking, what it fails to do is differentiate the nature of learning that occurs across all these factors.

Every situation that contributes to the growth and development of an individual has a learning dimension to it. As such, to stress one kind of learning experience at the cost of others misses the point that different learning experiences put together in an integral way can undergird the success of an individual career. The challenge is to understand this balance and intervene in ways that support integral learning for a critical mass of individuals.

Though much maligned these days, the reality is that well-designed classroom programs can create learning environments where managers step out of their day-to-day decision-making roles in order to think more broadly and creatively about the business environment. Big-picture thinking, which is the hallmark of the liberal education model, can stimulate new perspectives on oneself as a leader and the needs of the business.

Outside the classroom, one increasingly popular learning strategy is to place high-potential managers in stretch assignments (sometimes referred to as taking over popcorn stands) where they make decisions affecting the overall performance of that unit or business. Hardly a controlled environment, a stretch assignment is a potentially powerful (although also potentially inefficient) learning tool because decisions have implications. In a similar way, good mentoring or coaching can provide a learning experience that helps managers translate generic business practices into unique solutions for unique situations.

Finally, learner-centered education becomes a viable element of a learning strategy with the advent of electronic learning media that enable managers to seek information and knowledge on a just-in-time basis. Knowledge systems that organize data into easily referenced content for rapid dissemination and application helps make learning integral to the way a company works.

In our view, the best learning professionals develop a portfolio of initiatives to address different individual learning requirements in ways that can influence the performance of the company as a whole. With respect to transfer of learning, the challenge is how to assess and facilitate transfer across the full spectrum of real learning that occurs in a firm and not to limit our explorations to those formal and identifiable events that may lend themselves to transfer measurement. To illustrate this challenge, we present three examples we believe nicely illustrate the widely varying types of learning activity taking place in today's firms and underscore the complexity of managing and researching transfer.

Steve Mercer at Boeing is a believer in simulated business environments where people have the freedom to fail. Mercer has created a "school" of leadership, an intervention strategy to increase the degree of success for managers on the job where someone is keeping score. At the heart of his learning strategy is the notion that individuals have to get out of the scorecard environment to really have a shift of perspective. In other words, they have to be given the opportunity to take risks without fear of failure. Without this change of venue, much that happens under the label of training and education leads to merely incremental changes in individual growth trajectories. In Mercer's view, big bucks can be spent in training and education for the benefit of a lot of people with relatively little return to the company unless there is a clear focus in the education that "it's all about business results."

Mercer played a similar role at GE before coming to Boeing to take charge of the Boeing Leadership Center. His emphasis on residential educational experiences goes beyond the traditional defense of classroom education. While big-picture thinking tends to be linked to conceptually based instruction, such instruction has relevance only to the degree that individuals are given the means to "internalize" the learning through application. At the Leadership Center, converting concepts into experience is heavily emphasized in various action learning contexts. In one case, it may be a customized global business simulation where individuals assume roles they have never been in before and get a chance to "fly the plane without fear of crashing." In another case, it may be as coaches and mentors to other program participants of more senior standing in the firm. In this example, selected managers who have gone through a series of coaching workshops get a chance to work one-on-one with senior managers in providing feedback to those managers on their leadership behaviors. Within this experiential learning context, both the manager as coach and the senior manager as student are testing their comprehension of leadership principles.

An ambitious example of the type of nonclassroom action learning increasingly popular in organizations is that initiated at Motorola. In 1995, senior leaders at Motorola discussed the problems it faced in Latin America at a meeting of the board of trustees of Motorola University. The general consensus was that the company needed a much better understanding of economic, cultural, and political realities in the major markets of Latin America. The question was how to develop this knowledge in a way that leaders in the company could formulate and deploy a successful business strategy.

In a bold move, Motorola University developed a market assessment process disguised as an educational program. Teams of managers spent several weeks collecting information within different market centers—São Paulo, Brazil; Santiago, Chile; Buenos Aires, Argentina; Mexico City, Mexico. They met not only with Motorola customers, vendors, and employees within those cities but with bankers, government officials, and business leaders across other industries. Their goal was to immerse themselves as much as possible within the local cultures in order to discover what made these markets unique.

The output (that is, transfer) was a new business strategy for Latin America that incorporated, among other things, the key insights of "very successful business people who had overcome hyperinflation, unstable political regimes, black markets, and corruption" (Baldwin, Danielson, & Wiggenhorn, 1997). As a result of these lessons and others, a much greater emphasis was placed in Latin America on the cross-functional development of all managers to help them more effectively identify, interpret, and respond to market opportunities; define and develop organizational processes to manage unique solutions within unique markets; and stimulate greater collaboration across functional disciplines to leverage different perspectives and capabilities. The strategy produced solid financial results: revenues tripled over a five-year period.

While the pedagogical model illustrated here is based on a fairly open-ended inquiry process, which is not always appropriate for every educational need, the point is that the boundaries on the learning event begin with the question of business requirements (the Motorola University trustees meeting) and conclude with organization and individual performance that have consequences (weighted outcomes in Latin America that had positive or negative effects on corporate and individual goals).

With respect to learner-centered approaches and e-learning, one prominent example is Tom Kelly at Cisco. Over the past four years, Kelly has led the charge to reinvent the way that the company delivers ideas, information, and best practices to what may be the most important part of the Cisco empire—the tens of thousands of people who have the closest day-to-day contact with customers. The first challenge, says Kelly, was to overcome a mindset that the learning function was not a real part of the business. Despite a lot of rhetoric, says Kelly, very few high-tech companies truly understand and act on how much learning has to happen to allow them and their people to stay current.

The learning model that Kelly is building at Cisco distinguishes between structured learning and emergency learning and tries to customize each form of learning to the needs of the individual. The ultimate goal (now in the works) is to give each person at Cisco a customized Web page. That Web page will serve as a learning portal where people can chart a long-term structured learning plan, get all relevant short-term updates, and automatically receive some content based on their job title, area of expertise, field of interest, and learning preferences—time-critical information for emergency learning situations.

Kelly has also championed the aggregation of information by audience. For example, his team launched the Field E-Learning connection—a Web site where content is aggregated in curriculum maps based on job titles, work theaters, specific technologies, and products. Another interesting innovation from Cisco is the means to let people outside the training operation create training content.

Today Cisco has no content developers. Rather, if you are involved in developing a product (say, as a chip designer or a software engineer), then developing educational content is also a part of your job.

Finally, Kelly has pushed Cisco to come up with a framework for its educational offerings—a kind of digital shorthand that creates a tag for every piece of content generated for training purposes, so that it can be stored in and retrieved from a central database. Ultimately, Kelly wants a system where the field people can rank both the quality and relevance of the content, creating a level of accountability uncommon in educational arenas. His ultimate goal is to match content with the people who need it—dynamically and quickly.

Clearly, all these forms of learning are real—and yet none make the assessment and evaluation of transfer straightforward. The goals of classroom education today often extend beyond mastery of facts to changing mindsets and overcoming fear of failure. Action learning opportunities often yield insights and discoveries that could never reasonably have been included in some a priori list of learning objectives. And learner-centered, e-learning approaches require a rethinking of conventional terms and metrics whereby notions of reusable learning objects, time to mastery, resource accessibility, and the like supersede traditional classroom-oriented notions.

Summary

Managing the transfer of learning in today's business organizations is a role fraught with complexity. The three fundamental challenges we describe are neither simple nor straightforward. Here are a few summary comments regarding each challenge.

Alignment and Business Impact

It's essential to focus on alignment and business impact vis-à-vis courses and curriculums. The traditional tenets of training success in organizations—great coursework, stimulating learning environments, and senior management support for quality education—are no longer sufficient. Learning must be viewed as helping the firm compete and win in the marketplace. The charge for today's top learning professionals has less to do with the design of specific educational programs and more to do with articulating the business objectives for the company and defining the business case for the learning function in support of those objectives. As a consequence, an effective business case will address the scope of the learning enterprise to both enhance the firm's existing capabilities and develop new ones, while deciding which factors to influence most strongly because of their contribution to the growth and development of individuals.

Organize for Impact

All organizations are different, and it is folly to think that any particular learning initiative will succeed in isolation of the people and processes that matter in a given firm. The challenge is to understand the explicit and implicit reward system of the firm and to manage learning in a way that is cognizant of that system. Salient linkages to performance management and succession in the firm seem essential to maximize transfer.

Affecting Real Learning

Anyone who has been around educational environments in organizations these days knows that not much learning takes place in a class with people assigned to attend and not sure why they are there. Real learning comes from a need to know. A need to know might spring from intrinsic or extrinsic sources, but unless it is something that people care about, learning will be minimal. In addition, for real learning to take place people have to struggle with feeling incompetent. They have to recognize they will make many errors before attaining a fundamental level of competence, so the fear of failure cannot be overwhelming.

The ongoing challenge for today's learning professionals is how to harness and manage the contexts that lead to real learning and transfer. Finding ways to embed knowledge in organization processes, to spark innovation and future-oriented thinking, to distribute information and know-how in readily accessible forms, and to accelerate the acquisition of requisite competencies are key objectives. Making learning a part of how people do their jobs is perhaps the ultimate test of integrating learning into the culture of the firm.

References

Baldwin, T. T., & Danielson, C. (2002, August). Formulating learning strategy in organizations: Challenges facing the chief learning officer. Paper presented at the annual meeting of the National Academy of Management, Denver, CO.

Baldwin, T. T., & Danielson, C. (2000). Making learning strategy at the top: Lessons from 10 of America's chief learning officers. *Business Horizons, 43*(6), 5–14.

Baldwin, T. T., Danielson, C., & Wiggenhorn, W. (1997). The evolution of learning strategies in organizations: From employee development to business redefinition. *Academy of Management Executive, 11*(4), 47–58.

Baldwin, T. T., & Ford, J. K. (1988). Transfer of training: A review and directions for future research. *Personnel Psychology, 41,* 63–105.

Broad, M., & Newstrom, J. (1992). *Transfer of training: Action-packed strategies to ensure high payoff from training investments.* Reading, MA: Addison-Wesley.

McCall, M., Lombardo, M. M., & Morrison, A. (1988). *Lessons of experience.* Lexington, MA: Lexington Books.

CHAPTER 3

New Organizational Forces Affecting Learning Transfer

Designing for Impact

Patricia McLagan

In this chapter, McLagan suggests that we change how we think about "transfer of learning." Rather than asking "How can we ensure learning transfer?" she proposes that we ask, "How can we stimulate and harness learning for optimal impact in today's organizations?" She describes the new forces that are changing how we view the relationship between work and learning. Here she focuses on insights from the new science, new understandings of learning, and the shift of organization attention to work processes. Against this backdrop of the past and shaping forces for the future, McLagan then proposes six important implications for learning designers: help structure the organization for optimal learning, create the cultural conditions for learning, embed learning practices into management and work processes, create practices and processes that accelerate the spread and sharing of both explicit and tacit learning, provide opportunities for everyone to develop the skills and mindsets for self-directed learning, and integrate once-off interventions with work. She concludes by reiterating that learning is not an add-on to organizational activities (a view implicit in the transfer question), but is a central and inseparable dynamic of performance.

Our concern about learning transfer reflects the larger questions we have about the relationship between learning and life. The Industrial Age model that separated learning and work (go to school, then go to work), as well as thinking and doing, doesn't meet today's needs. Continuous learning, lifelong learning, action learning, knowledge management, and learning organization are all terms that tell us something different is happening. Learning and work are merging, and this has implications for what we must do if we want to intensify or accelerate the effectiveness of both. The old transfer question assumes a separation of work and learning. A more relevant question related to learning and work, though, is "How can we stimulate and harness learning for optimal impact in today's organizations?" This is a design question we'll answer after we review the transfer approaches of the past and after we look at some shaping forces for the future.

The Last Half of the Twentieth Century

There are four main ways that designers addressed the transfer problem in the last half of the twentieth century. I'll call them the *add-on* approach, the *performance engineering* approach, the *cognitive intervention* approach, and the *technical training* approach.

The Add-On Approach

Workplace training and development was born in the 1950s and began to get organized in the 1960s. In the 1960s, 1970s, and 1980s, most organizations' designed learning happened in a traditional classroom, with a focus on theory and concepts. Links with the real world of work usually occurred through in-class case studies and post-class application assignments. In the late 1980s and through the 1990s, this more pedagogical model started to bend. Program participants often worked on their own work problems while in the classroom, or applied their learnings to real operational or strategic projects where they were responsible for showing results. Learning designs sometimes included structured project reviews and even presentations of results to senior management and other real-life evaluators. Blending classroom learning with business projects became a very common learning transfer tactic in major U.S. corporations by the end of the century.

The Performance Engineering Approach

A second way the transfer problem was addressed in the late 1980s and 1990s relates to the increase in system-wide change initiatives like SAP, Total Quality Management, and organization redesign. These changes used training as a key vehicle for communication and skill development—but in the context of larger interventions designed to get better productivity. The "trainer" of old became a more results-focused "performance consultant" responsible for redesigning all the pieces of the performance system: processes, tools, rewards, roles, information flows, as well as programs to develop personal knowledge and skills. Task, performance, and competency analysis ensured that the training focus was relevant, while providing the focus for reinforcement and reward strategies back on the job.

The Cognitive Intervention Approach

Simultaneously, systems thinking, self-directed learning and learning to learn, action learning, and other cognitive approaches like those of Argyris (1999), Knowles, Holton, and Swanson (2000), Watkins and Marsick (1993), and Senge (1990) became a big part of some formal work-related learning agendas and events. The goal was to develop people's meta-cognitive skills for recognizing and redirecting their own learning, behavior, and routines. The underlying assumption was that if people could identify and modify beliefs and patterns related to the status quo, and if they could develop thinking, learning, and self-management skills, they could and would become more active forces for change. The goal was to democratize and diffuse the responsibility for learning, learning application, and transfer.

The Technical Training Approach

A fourth stream is the technical training stream. Here, the transfer problem was less "how to transfer concepts and theory" and more "how to generalize specific technical skills learned in a formal learning setting to a broader range of problems faced on the job." Technical training often used real or simulated machines and technical problems, but the challenge was to generalize learning to different but related technical challenges and problems.

So we left the 1990s armed with several dominant strains of formal and designed learning—each struggling in a different way to ensure greater relevance and bottom-line impact: the traditional theory and concept-oriented education model—augmented by various ways of linking theory to on-the-job applications; the behavioral systems–oriented performance consulting model; a smattering of approaches focused on developing mental models, self-awareness, self-directed learning, and systems thinking; and the technical training models that usually used real equipment and processes but grappled with how to generalize specific skills to the messy real world. All of these approaches floated in a new, highly networked and technology-facilitated economy demanding speed, relevance, competitiveness, and results.

Shaping Forces for the Twenty-First Century

To speculate about design options for the future, we need to recognize that technology, new science, and other forces are dramatically changing the world, the nature of work, and learning itself. Our quest for greater impact through learning can and must take these into account—and harness their energies.

Here are some of the forces that seem to be shaping the relationship between learning and work, people and organizations. As we'll see, they have major implications for how to ask and answer the "how to design for transfer" question. I'll describe three categories of forces. Specifically, there are changes in the way we view the world and ourselves in it, in technology, and in the sociopolitical scene. These don't cover everything—but, taken together, they present a pretty good picture of the future we are creating and the design opportunities and challenges we face.

Worldview

Our view of the world and organizations is profoundly changing. This creates a new conceptual and emotional backdrop for dealing with transfer issues. Here are a few of the paradigm changers:

• *Insights from new science.* Physicists and life scientists tell us that living systems (and organizations are living systems) are built up from simple basic units and operating codes (like the genes in the human body) but they rely on very complex and decentralized interactions with the environment. Living organisms thrive because their various parts continuously process and act on information from the environment—not because they rigidly follow predetermined rules. For example, each organ in the human body operates according to a set of principles, but continually adapts to current conditions. *(Implication for learning design: we can't predetermine, dictate, or control learning. We can provide a unifying framework but then allow and support lots of exploration and local decisions and actions)* (Capra, 1997).

• *Understanding of the learning process.* Here are some of the things we "know" about learning: Learning is a natural process that occurs within a social context and is driven by the need to solve problems. This is true for all living things. For some life forms, including humans, learning also appears to be an end in itself. It is self-rewarding. It keeps us interacting with something new and satisfies and stimulates curiosity.

We also know that people have different styles and orientations in learning. Different topics and methods naturally turn individuals on, and we process information in different ways. We use varied routines as we learn, and we vary in our conscious use of these routines. Over time, we can and do learn more effective ways of learning—and may apply those in familiar situations or (with intent and consciousness) bring our learning routines into unfamiliar settings. *(Implications: Facilitating learning requires unleashing a natural process in a way that engages individuals' learning styles, helps people refine or develop learning routines that they can use consciously, and makes it more likely that they will recognize situations where these routines may be useful.)*

• *Process-awareness and expertise.* Thanks to the total quality and reengineering movements of the 1980s and 1990s and the systems thinking work of people like Argyris (1999) and Senge (1990), we can understand the bigger picture of behavior in organizations. We have tools to analyze organization processes and systems and technologies for dramatically redesigning them. These tools and insights are even more important as we move into the world of more virtual organizations. Virtual organizations are primarily connected by processes and systems rather than organization charts, cultures, hierarchies, and bureaucracies. *(Implication: Processes are becoming the main linking mechanisms for people at work. Process excellence has to be a major focus of any organization improvement and learning intervention.)*

- *The power (and responsibility) of one.* Individuals work inside processes and systems, but they are also important performance units. If you don't believe it, think about the impact of one computer virus, of one accusation of abuse, of one shareholder raising an embarrassing corporate issue. On a more mundane level for all of us, we find ourselves constantly shifting roles. One minute we lead and innovate, the next we follow and support. One minute we are involved in one process, the next in another. Bill Bridges calls these the days of "You, Inc." Tom Peters calls it "Brand You." Accountants call it the era of the contractor. New-style organizations acknowledge it by calling people *associates* rather than employees, *coaches and stewards* rather than managers. It all points to the individual as a key player and decision maker in an increasingly complex web of value-stream activity. *(Implication: With individuals in such powerful and self-managing roles, it's imperative that the learning transfer responsibility be theirs. Individuals are the only people who are constantly present at their own performance!! A democratization of transfer needs to occur.)*

- *Evolution of consciousness.* Our global economy and information and communication systems are profoundly changing our views of the world, our interconnectedness, and society (Persaud, Kumar, & Kumar, 2001; Porter et al., 2000). These changes present us with some new learning problems. We need more systemic and global views and values that can accommodate massive diversities and innovations at the interorganizational, intersocial, international, and interregional levels. Humanity seems to be responding. New kinds of international agreements, the increased interest in spirituality, the big focus on dealing with change, concerns for the environment and longer-term consequences of actions—these are all signs that a new kind of global thinking and responsibility are emerging. *(Implication: We are developing the psychic and intellectual mandate and capacity to be responsible organization members—free from the authoritarian controls and assumptions of the past. That is, people can and must be more active in and responsible for continually improving their contributions at work.)*

- *Experiential base from the last century.* Of course, we've been doing a lot to accelerate individual and team learning for the benefit of organizations. All the methods described in this book are a reservoir of practices we can use in designing learning interventions that will work. Our challenge is to unleash more of their potential—possibly by helping learners be more consciously involved in making them work. *(Implication: We must draw on what we've learned about impact-focused learning. There is an experience base.)*

Technology Breakthroughs

Technology advances make many dreams possible. And technology dramatically changes how we view our design options. Here are some of the main issues of the moment:

- *The Web.* With the Web, *all* individuals (including those who use Internet cafés in underdeveloped countries) can instantly reach others globally, have quick access to the world's information and resources, can collaborate on problems and interests, and become part of a transparent world that can't hide information. With so many nodes in the Web, the permutations and combinations of information exchange and learning are endless! These will increase as technologies for voice and image communication via the Web develop. *(Implication: The action and resource possibilities are too vast to try to control through traditional methods of learning design. We must unleash the individual to assemble the best resources and organize the best conversations for applied learning. And, of course, the Web opens up lots of new design options.)*

- *Workplace technology.* Whether a person is filing claims, working clients through a sale, designing or manufacturing a product, consulting with a remote partner, or managing a global project, technology can do the routine and dangerous parts of the work. This obviously frees individuals up to do more of the thinking and design work—to take on a fuller knowledge role. *(Implication: As technology pushes up the skill and knowledge requirements and opportunities of work, more and more people are going to have strategy and design as well as implementation responsibilities. The stage is set for people to be more involved in all the activities associated with learning transfer, including the design and structuring of activities that HRD specialists and other third parties have done in the past.)*

• *Information technology.* Computers and information storage and processing technologies make it possible to have information available everywhere, 24/7. This raises the promise that we can get the information we need whenever we need it—the ultimate learning support system! The promise remains, but technology has not yet been able to deliver on this promise, for several reasons: The information may be there, but it's not always stored for easy access; individuals are not yet skilled at the kinds of problem analysis and questioning needed to focus their enquiries; people at work often favor action rather than the reflective and analytical processes associated with research and search; computers are still too literal in finding information (if you don't ask the question or do a search in a particular way, you won't find what you need); a great deal of learning is a social process that requires conversation; and much of the important knowledge is tacit and can't be easily recorded in computers.

As technology develops, and as we become more attuned to the requirements of the Information Age, many of these limiting factors are being addressed, however. Our designs for learning impact can accelerate this adjustment.

The Sociopolitical Context

The world around us is changing. These changes spill over into all our social institutions, including the workplace. We have to explore the future of design against the emerging sociopolitical context:

• *Democracy as the major sociopolitical format.* Since the early 1990s democracy has emerged as the world's only viable political structure able to handle the complexities of the new global economy (McLagan & Nel, 1996). This continues to be true even as we face global threats like terrorism or corporate malfeasance. *(Implication: The design processes we use will be affected by the norms and expectations we are developing in our social institutions. This applies to anything we do to design and facilitate impact-focused learning.)*

- *Research validation of the effectiveness of open systems management.* Virtually all studies of effective organizations and institutions validate the superior performance of organizations that inform, involve, empower, support, and expect high performance from their people. This same research shows that authoritarian controls have the opposite effect. *(Implication: The design methods we use to ensure learning and transfer must use open system principles: involvement, transparency, correction, and opportunity-identifying feedback loops.)*
- *Diversity.* The world continues to struggle with the conflicts that come from acknowledging and unleashing diversity. But changes are occurring as gender, racial, religious, socioeconomic, and cultural differences receive more protection under national and international law—and within organizations. As we begin to embrace more diversity, we open up to the fact that people's mindsets and ways of operating are different. We also realize that these differences are a great source of creativity. *(Implication: Our learning and transfer interventions should unleash and encourage this diversity energy.)*
- *Population demographics.* A new wave of people is moving into and up in organizations. There is no doubt that the next generations are more skeptical of authority and globally aware than previous generations. *(Implication: We have to design for the mix of people—but more and more, for people who are more questioning, technologically savvy, and open-systems oriented).*

Impact-Focused Learning in the Future

All the shifts discussed thus far contribute to a big shift in how we must think about learning and work. Rather than being an add-on and an exception in the operations and success of an organization, learning is integral to its success. The learning designer's role today thus must operate on strategic and process levels, as well as on tactical levels. The question shifts from, "How can we ensure learning transfer?" to "How can we stimulate and harness learning for optimal impact in today's organizations?" This is a dramatic change of emphasis, with at least six major implications for learning designers:

- Help structure the organization for optimal learning.
- Create the cultural conditions for learning.

- Embed learning practices into management and work processes.
- Create practices and processes that accelerate the spread and sharing of both explicit and tacit learning.
- Provide opportunities for everyone to develop the skills and mindsets for self-directed learning in both formal and informal learning situations.
- Integrate once-off interventions with work.

Designing for impact involves all of these tasks.

Design Task 1: Help Structure the Organization for Optimal Learning

The designer's first job is to make sure the organization is structured for learning. Traditional organizational designs localize thinking and learning at the top of the pyramid. They emphasize rule-based action everywhere else. They keep people with similar expertise together in functional groups. Strategic scanning and planning happens at the top, and the top is the only place where all the multifunctional knowledge about the organization and its context, goals, and performance come together. This kind of structure may be fine for a stable and relatively closed organizational context. It may be fine in situations where the people at the top have all the answers. But it's disastrous if the environment is changing quickly or is very uncertain. In the latter situation, everybody who interacts with the world outside the organization is a potential source of competitive intelligence and creative ideas—of learning.

Today's learning designers must make the business case for more open organization designs. Project-focused structures, multifunctional and regional teams, skunk works, customer- and market-focused structures, and alliances all help keep everyone aware of the larger picture. These structures enable the organization's own processes to match the complexity of the environment—the only condition under which any organization facing change and complexity can continue to thrive and grow. Why is this true? It's because they ensure that the conflict and complex problems that stimulate learning occur.

If the structure of the organization restricts the exposure necessary for success and renewal, then any other attempts to design for optimal learning will be inadequate. They will fail.

Design Task 2: Create the Cultural Conditions for Learning

Peter Senge (1990) defines a learning organization as one where people continually expand their capacity to create the results they truly desire, where new and expansive patterns of thinking are nurtured, where collective aspiration is set free, and where people are continually learning how to learn together.

Watkins and Marsick (1993) focus on seven "action imperatives" of a learning culture: create continuous learning opportunities, promote inquiry and dialogue, encourage collaboration and team learning, establish systems to capture and share learning, empower people to have a collective vision, connect the organization to the environment, and ensure that leaders model and support learning at the individual, team, and organizational levels.

Ellinger, Watkins, and Bostrom (1999) note that in learning organizations, formal leaders put a lot of emphasis on their coaching roles. Specifically, they help individuals learn and take empowered action, they help individuals and teams connect with larger visions and goals, they provide reflective feedback on employee behavior and its effects, they open up learning and growth opportunities, and they make sure that people get feedback from internal and external stakeholders.

Today's designers must focus on creating conditions like these. We can draw the same conclusions as for structure. If learning isn't a value embedded in the culture, it's unlikely that a fancy course or intervention design will have much impact.

Design Task 3: Embed Learning Practices into Management and Work Processes

It's time to bring learning into the ongoing practices and processes of the business. These processes range from strategy planning, budgeting, and performance management to project management and processes for manufacturing or engineering or customer service. Whatever the process, it consists of explicit or tacit steps and questions to guide action.

Until recently, process steps tended to emphasize action rather than reflection, fixing and correcting rather than experimenting. Yet we know that reflection and experimentation are critical success factors when change and uncertainty dominate. Action, fixing, and correcting are important, too. But they have dominated management and work processes. This retards and constrains learning and the innovation and adaptation that depend on it.

Designers now need to rectify this situation. They need to modify strategic planning so that it involves more people, stretches people's thinking about what-ifs, draws on experiences and insights of people everywhere, sets the stage for learning and surprise, and allows for major shifts of direction. Designers can add formal review and learning events like project reviews and the After Action Reviews (AARs) developed by the Army (an AAR is a regularly occurring, open, multilevel conversation about what worked and didn't work in a battle or other situation).

There are also many opportunities for action learning when people try out new things, assess the consequences, and feed their learning into new actions for the future (Mohrman & Cummings, 1989). Action learning differs from AAR. People intentionally try something new and then examine what worked and didn't. It is deductive rather than inductive. Both need to be part of the organization's ongoing management process in order to be effective.

There are other possible enhancements to management processes. Designers can help mandate data gathering, reflection time, and review and analysis time. They can build in requirements to collaborate with other internal and external groups—including customers, suppliers, other functions. They can provide incentives and time for innovation, as 3M has always done. When these are built into the organization's formal processes, they help complete and enhance the learning cycle. Work is more reflective. Experimentation is more legitimate. Plans are more grounded in exploration and possibility thinking. In short, learning and work integrate. Transfer becomes a moot point.

Design Task 4: Create Practices and Processes for Diffusing Learning

Organizations must formalize and accelerate the spread and sharing of both explicit and tacit learning. Simonin (1997) investigated the barriers to knowledge transfer in companies that required high levels of innovation and creativity. The major impediment related to the nature of the knowledge itself was its tacitness. Tacit knowledge is unspoken. It's "how things work around here." It relates to the subtleties of connecting explicit knowledge and skill to the requirements and nuances of specific situations.

It's difficult to spread tacit knowledge by using books, articles, instructions, videos, tapes, or even courses. Tacit knowledge, rather, spreads through interpersonal interactions and shared experiences—like project teams, networks, stories, and examples (O'Reilly & Pfeffer, 2000).

Communities of practice (Wenger, McDermott, & Snyder, 2002) are one emerging design option for accelerating the spread of tacit knowledge. These are self-forming, open, and sometimes organization-supported groups of people who have common interests or face common problems and learning goals. They use every means possible, including technology, to stay connected, share problems and insights, experiment, and advance their field of knowledge or interest.

Of course, whenever it's possible to make knowledge explicit—to reduce successful action to replicable steps—then designers must attend to that, too. But that's where we've excelled in the past. The bigger challenge today is design for the spread of tacit knowledge.

Design Task 5: Provide Opportunities for Self-Directed Learning

Everyone in an organization needs a chance to develop the skills and mindset for self-directed learning in both formal and informal learning situations. The pressure is on to decentralize organizations, diffuse accountability and power, and ensure that everyone becomes a sensor and contributes to both the productivity and the continual development of the organization. Information and workplace technology and cost-reduction pressures deliver the same message: organizations today can't afford layers of management. And they need people at all levels to be vigilant, responsible, and creative.

But workplace precedent and personal experience are still steeped in a more authoritarian and dependent model of organization and relationship. People at work sometimes lack the mindset, skills, self-image, or will to participate in the learning and change that organizations need today. This is partly a problem of structure, culture, processes, and other conditions I've described in this chapter. But the mindset, skill, self-image, and will problem is still valid. Most of us grew up in families, churches, communities, organizations, and countries where few governed and many followed. We learned how to learn in schools where teachers lectured, where the focus was on theory, and where knowledge application was often irrelevant. The problem wasn't the focus on theory. It was that we never learned how to consciously and deliberately complete the learning cycle—bring learning to action, or bring insights from action to learning.

Today's designers have a chance to help everyone learn how to participate fully in the learning cycle. It's a cycle that integrates rather than separates learning and application. David Kolb many years ago presented a powerful integration model (1983). He told us that learning required "concrete experience," "reflection," "conceptualization," and "experimentation"—all four experiences. He presented these as a cycle requiring a variety of processes: *inducing*—making sense out of our experience by reflecting on it; *assimilating*—bringing the lessons of our reflection together into coherent theories that can guide us; *deducing*—using our theories about the world to help us set up experiments and try things out; and *accommodating*—bringing our lessons from experimentation into our day-to-day habits and practices.

Each of these points on the model (experience, reflection, conceptualization, and experimentation) and the processes they trigger (inducing, assimilating, deducing, and accommodating) are areas of expertise for everybody at work. We all need to be skilled and capable of self-direction in every aspect of the learning process: only then can we realize the full learning potential of any organization. Developing these capabilities and ensuring that all learning completes its cycle is another challenge to today's designers.

Design Task 6: Integrate Once-Off Interventions and Work

I've focused so far on the less traditional aspects of the relationship between learning and work. Even if we do these things well, we still need off-the-job interventions where people learn new mindsets, knowledge, skills, and behaviors. Interventions may include conferences, workshops, courses, books—educational communications of all kinds and using all sorts of media. These interventions can never be fully integrated into work because their intent is to be a formal and planned driving force for change. These interventions usually focus on one of two types of broad objectives:

- Expose people to knowledge, information, beliefs, and values that are *beyond the current culture and practices of their own organization.* By this "expanded range" learning, individuals and teams *may become equipped and inspired* to introduce and implement new ideas and practices. Once-off learning (learning that is not embedded in structure, process, culture, practice, and so on) can help crack the organization open and set forces in motion to change structures, culture, and processes. A few people who are committed to change can help redirect any organization.

- Help expand people's range of skills and knowledge for *success within* the current organization structure, processes, and culture.

These interventions are obviously designed either to shake people and the organization up or to optimize performance in the current system. Both *can* be successful if what people learn *is related to success in the organization or to the organization's success in its environment.* Success (that is, individuals or teams consistently use and produce valued organizational results with what they learn) *can* occur without extra attention to transfer, but research suggests that success is more likely if the design includes transfer-support actions.

Here's where the research on learning transfer is useful. Some key facilitating conditions include management support for the new behaviors, workplace design that makes new behaviors easy, ready access to the technology and equipment for success, and supportive coworkers (Kupritz & Reddy, 2002).

Holton, Bates, and Ruona (2001), in an attempt to create a valid basis for investigating learning transfer, identified sixteen factors related to once-off learning transfer. These factors relate to the organization's climate relative to implementing the learning, the value of the learning for the job and the organization, the relationship between learning and rewards, and the behavior of supervisors.

Moving into the New Era of Design for Impact

All six design tasks, one way or another, reflect the implications of these twenty-first-century shaping forces described earlier:

- We cannot predetermine, dictate, or control learning, but we can provide a unifying framework and support.
- Learning is a natural process that needs unleashing, refining, and focusing rather than control.
- Process excellence has to be a major focus of any organization improvement interventions—including the design of learning for work.
- A democratization of transfer needs to occur: learning is ultimately an individual as well as a social process.
- People are developing more conscious abilities to transfer their own learning.
- We must draw on what we've learned about impact-focused learning. There is an experience base.
- We can't control transfer through traditional methods of learning design. The world is too complex and changing too rapidly.
- As technology pushes up the skill and knowledge requirements and opportunities of work, more and more people are going to have strategy and design as well as implementation responsibilities.
- The structures we design to do anything in and around organizations will be affected by the norms and expectations we are developing in our social institutions. This applies to anything we do to design and facilitate impact-focused learning.

- The design methods we use to ensure learning and transfer must use open system principles including involvement, transparency, correction, and opportunity-identifying feedback loops.
- Our learning and transfer interventions should unleash and encourage the energy of diversity.
- We have to design for a mix of people—but more and more, for people who are more questioning, technologically savvy, and open-systems oriented.

Today's designers of learning have to be more than creative course and curriculum planners. They have to go beyond performance consulting. Design for learning relates to the core design of any business. People who do this design work require extensive knowledge of how organizations work and of how learning and change happen at the social, group, team, and individual levels. They need systems-thinking capacity and an ability to guide changes in the culture, strategies, processes, roles, and mindsets and skills of people. They need to understand the full range of learning experience options—both formal (courses, simulations, media-based interventions) and informal (mentoring, job experience, interactions with others).

We are moving way beyond the old days of add-ons, performance engineering, learning-to-learn, and technical training approaches to transfer. What we learned from these transfer approaches is still valuable. But the new challenge is to virtually eliminate, or at least minimize, the importance of the transfer question. Our challenge is to replace "How can we ensure learning transfer?" with "How can we stimulate and harness learning for optimal impact in today's organizations?" The questions lead us in two different directions. Designers today must travel the path of the second question, for learning is now the central dynamic in the organizations we serve.

Bibliography
Argyris, C. (1999). *On organizational learning.* London: Blackwell.
Capra, F. (1997). *The web of life: A new synthesis of mind and matter.* London: Flamingo.
Christensen, C. (1997). *The innovator's dilemma: When new technologies cause great firms to fail.* Boston: Harvard Business School Press.

Ellinger, A., Watkins, K., & Bostrom, R. (1999). "Managers as facilitators of learning in learning organizations." *Human Resource Development Quarterly, 10*(2), 105–125.

Holton, E. F., Bates, R. A., & Ruona, W.E.A. (2001). Development of a generalized learning transfer system inventory. *Human Resource Development Quarterly, 11*(4), 333–360.

Knowles, M., Holton, E., & Swanson, R. (2000). *The adult learner: The definitive classic in adult education and human resource development.* Burlington, MA: Gulf Professional.

Kolb, D. (1983). *Experiential learning: Experience as the source of learning and development.* Upper Saddle River, NJ: Prentice Hall.

Kupritz, V. W., & Reddy, T. Y. (2002, March). "The impact of workplace design on training transfer." Proceedings of AHRD Conference, Honolulu.

McLagan, P., & Nel, C. (1996). *The age of participation: New governance for the workplace and the world.* San Francisco: Berrett-Koehler.

Mohrman, S. A., & Cummings, T. J. (1989). *Self-designing organizations: Learning how to create high performance.* Reading, MA: Addison-Wesley.

O'Reilly, C., & Pfeffer, J. (2000). *Hidden value: How great companies achieve extraordinary results with ordinary people.* Boston: Harvard Business School Press.

Persaud, A., Kumar, U., & Kumar, V. (2001, March). "Harnessing scientific and technological knowledge for the rapid deployment of global innovations." *Engineering Management Journal, 13*(1), 12–18.

Pettigrew, A. M., Woodman, R. W., & Cameron, K. S. (2001, August). "Studying organizational change and development: Challenges for future research." *Academy of Management Journal, 44*(4), 697–713.

Porter, M., Sachs, J., Warner, A., Cornelius, P., Levinson, M., & Schwab, K. (2000). *The global competitiveness report 2000.* New York: Oxford University Press.

Senge, P. (1990). *The fifth discipline: The art and practice of the learning organization.* New York: Doubleday.

Simonin, B. (1997). "The importance of collaborative know how: An empirical test of the learning organization." *Academy of Management Journal, 40*(5), 1150–1174.

Watkins, K., & Marsick, V. (1993). *Sculpting the learning organization: Lessons in the art and science of systemic change.* San Francisco: Jossey-Bass.

Wenger, E., McDermott, R., & Snyder, W. (2002). *Cultivating communities of practice.* Boston: Harvard Business School Press.

PART TWO

Transfer Diagnosis and Intervention

CHAPTER 4

What's *Really* Wrong

Diagnosis for Learning Transfer System Change

Elwood F. Holton III

Transfer problems are just like any other organizational problems—a good diagnostic analysis is a prerequisite for targeted interventions with high impact. This chapter presents a framework for diagnosing learning transfer systems that consists of three components: a set of sixteen factors that influence transfer, a diagnostic instrument, and a change process model. The diagnostic instrument presented here, the Learning Transfer System Inventory (LTSI), offers a simple and quick approach to pinpoint learning transfer system problems. Developed through extensive research, it is the only validated instrument available to diagnose learning transfer factors in organizations. Also included is an audit checklist derived from the LTSI that offers learning professionals an approach for a quick preliminary analysis of transfer problems.

Note: The complete LTSI instrument is available by contacting the author at Louisiana State University, HRD Program, Baton Rouge, LA 70803. You can phone 225-578-2456, fax to 225-578-5755, or e-mail eholton2@lsu.edu. The instrument is available free of charge to researchers or practitioners wishing to engage in collaborative research projects. Readers interested in using the full version of the instrument may find more information at http://www.edholton.com, including how to contact the authors and how to obtain permission to use the instrument.

Most HRD professionals realize learning transfer improvement is needed in their organizations, but few have an accurate sense of what the problem is (Baldwin & Ford, 1988; Ford & Weissbein, 1997). As a result, even those aware of strategies to improve transfer (such as Broad & Newstrom, 1992) are left with only intuition and guesswork to guide them to those most likely to yield high returns. Yet most would agree that improving learning transfer systems requires an ability to accurately diagnose factors inhibiting transfer.

The primary reason for this paradox is that, until recently, no diagnostic tool had emerged. In recent transfer research, a wide variety of instruments and measures have been used, most with either questionable or unknown psychometric properties. As a result, neither practitioners nor researchers have had a well-validated, effective diagnostic instrument. This presents a key barrier because it is hard to change a transfer system without accurate diagnosis of system problems.

This chapter presents a framework for diagnosing learning transfer systems that consists of three components: a set of factors that influence transfer; a diagnostic instrument; and a change process model. The diagnostic instrument presented here, the Learning Transfer System Inventory (LTSI), emerged from an ongoing research program (Holton, Bates, & Ruona, 2001; Holton, Bates, Seyler, & Carvalho, 1997) committed to building an assessment tool validated for research, but equally useful for practice and intervention. The instrument offers a simple and quick approach to pinpoint learning transfer system problems.

Diagnosis with the LTSI

Having valid and reliable measures enhances transfer because practitioners can use the LTSI to

- Assess potential transfer factor problems prior to conducting major learning interventions.
- Follow up on evaluations of existing training programs.
- Investigate known transfer problems.

- Target interventions designed to enhance transfer.
- Incorporate evaluation of transfer as part of regular employee assessments.
- Conduct needs assessment for training programs to provide transfer skills to supervisors and trainers.

My colleagues and I have argued that what is needed, and should be an important goal for HRD research, is development of a valid and generalizable set of transfer system scales (Holton et al., 2001; Holton et al., 1997). Scales with validated constructs and known psychometric qualities would facilitate cross-study comparisons and add significantly to understanding the transfer process. A general transfer system instrument would not preclude adding situation-specific scales. Rather, it provides a foundation of validated constructs with established applicability across populations and settings. Research in organizational behavior, which produced a series of generally accepted job attitude scales, provides a strong example of such a goal's value.

Thus the development of a research-quality diagnostic instrument to assess critical transfer factors is important to both researchers and practitioners. There is no reason that a single tool can't be useful in both arenas. Indeed, far too many diagnostic instruments are sold for HRD practice without prior testing, which have no known validity.

LTSI Structure

The LTSI is based on the theoretical framework of the HRD Research and Evaluation Model (Holton, 1996). The macro structure of that model hypothesizes that HRD outcomes are a function of ability, motivation, and environmental influences (Noe & Schmitt, 1986) at three outcome levels: learning, individual performance, and organizational performance. Secondary influences such as attitudes and personality are also included, particularly ones that impact motivation.

Figure 4.1 shows the LTSI conceptual model, which is a subset of the full theoretical framework. The sixteen factors measured by

Figure 4.1. Conceptual Model of the LTSI.

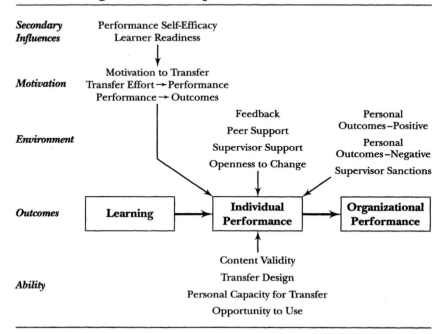

Note: For more information on the constructs in this instrument, see Holton (1996) and Holton, Bates, & Seyler (1996).

the LTSI are grouped by the macro structure of the HRD Research and Evaluation Model:

- Ability can be a barrier on the job or in the learning event. Two factors focus on ability to use learning on the job: the lack of opportunity to use learning (Ford, Quinones, Sego, & Sorra, 1992), and a lack of personal capacity to try out learning. Two other factors deal with elements of the learning event that enable learners to transfer the learning. The learning content may have little perceived content validity, making it difficult for learners to understand how it relates to their jobs. Finally, it may be taught with low transfer design so that learners have little chance of turning knowledge into workplace expertise.
- Motivation factors form the second group. Workers need both the ability to apply knowledge and the motivation to do so.

Motivation has two components: workers have to believe both that the expended effort will change performance and that changed performance will lead to valued outcomes (Facteau, Dobbins, Russell, Ladd, & Kudisch, 1995).

• Work environment factors form the third group. Research consistently shows that the work environment can be a tremendous barrier to workers' use of knowledge and expertise (Huczynski & Lewis, 1980; Mathieu, Tannenbaum, & Salas, 1992; Smith-Jentsch, Jentsch, Payne, & Salas, 1996; Xiao, 1996). Three factors deal with the worker-supervisor relationship: feedback and performance coaching about learning use, amount of support for learning use, and the extent to which supervisors actively oppose using new knowledge and expertise (Tziner, Haccoun, & Kadish, 1991). Two factors deal with the work group: peer support for using new approaches and the extent to which the group norm is openness to change (Tracey, Tannenbaum, & Kavanaugh, 1995). And two factors deal with the reward systems: the extent to which the outcomes for the person are either positive or negative.

• Secondary influences include two factors influencing motivation. Learner readiness addresses the need to prepare learners to participate meaningfully in training (Warr & Bunce, 1995). Workers also need to have high performance self-efficacy (Gist, 1987), or the general belief that they *can* use learning to change their performance.

Development of the LTSI

A nine-factor version of the instrument was first developed (Holton et al., 1997) from research using the Rouiller and Goldstein (1993) instrument. It was expanded to the current sixteen-factor version (Holton et al., 2001). The sixteen factors emerged through factor analysis of responses from 1,616 people in a wide variety of organizations and training programs. A convergent and divergent validity study showed that most of the constructs had only low correlations with other related variables (Bookter, 1999), further reinforcing the uniqueness of the transfer system constructs. Some scales have also shown initial evidence of criterion validity in predicting motivation to transfer, learner perceptions of the training utility, and operating procedure use on the job (Bates, Holton, & Seyler, 2000; Ruona, Leimbach, Holton, & Bates, in press; Seyler et al., 1998).

Items were designed to measure individual perceptions of constructs, including individual perceptions of climate variables. While *climate* often refers to group-level shared interpretation of organizations, it can also be an individual-level construct, called psychological climate (James & McIntyre, 1996). Studying climate from the individual perspective is important because people perceive particular climates differently and respond in terms of their perceptions (James & MacIntyre, 1996). Because transfer of learning refers to individual behaviors, it is most appropriate to assess individual perceptions of transfer factors because those perceptions will shape the individual's behavior.

LTSI Description

Defining these sixteen factors was an important step in learning transfer system research. They represent factors most commonly identified in transfer research and have been validated by construct validation studies. They also define the targets for learning transfer system diagnosis and change interventions.

The items on the LTSI instrument are divided into sections representing two construct domains. The first contains seventy-six items measuring eleven constructs representing factors affecting the training program attended. Respondents are directed to "think about *this specific training program.*" This section is program specific because transfer system factors vary depending on the training program. For example, it is possible for a technical training program but not an interpersonal skills program to have strong transfer. Thus it is best to assess some constructs on a program-by-program basis.

Table 4.1 shows the constructs, their definitions, a sample item, and coefficient alphas for each of these scales. Another thirty-six items measure five constructs that are not program-specific, but represent general factors that may influence any training program. Here, trainees were instructed to "think about *training in general* in your organization." Table 4.1 also describes these scales.

Administering the LTSI

The LTSI has been administered to approximately five thousand people, so our experience with it is extensive. Most HRD professionals are initially concerned about its length, but our experience is that it is quick and easy to complete, usually taking only fifteen to twenty minutes. Few have objected to its length, and most understand it easily.

The LTSI can be administered in a variety of ways. Primarily, it has been administered at the end of a program, when it can provide diagnostic information about the transfer environment in time to enhance it. This has also proven to be the most practical approach to obtaining data because the participants are a captive audience. Data obtained at this point reflect participants' beliefs about what they will encounter when they return to the job. While some might argue this is only a forecast, it is also likely that participants' initial transfer attempts will be shaped by these beliefs. As Naquin and Baldwin argue in Chapter Five, a single training program is actually an episode in a series of training events so trainees' behavior will be shaped by their beliefs based on past experiences.

The LTSI might also be administered thirty to sixty days after training to diagnose what actually occurred. Pragmatically, it is much harder to administer in that fashion because follow-up surveys have to be mailed and participants encouraged to respond. Often, participants are too busy. In instances where we have been successful with post-training administration, the data is particularly rich because it reflects actual experiences.

The Learning Transfer System Change Process

Assessing and improving learning transfer systems is best viewed as an organizational change process. Organizational change interventions are typically structured using the action research model except in transformational change (Cummings & Worley, 1998). Figure 4.2 shows the learning transfer system change process model used to implement diagnosis with the LTSI. Each step is briefly described, with specific substeps, following the figure.

Table 4.1. LTSI Scale Definitions and Sample Items.

Factor	Definition	Sample Item	Number of Items	α
Training-Specific Scales				
Learner Readiness	Extent to which individuals are prepared to enter and participate in training	Before the training I had a good understanding of how it would fit my job-related development.	4	.73
Motivation to Transfer	Direction, intensity, and persistence of effort toward utilizing in a work setting skills and knowledge learned.	I get excited when I think about trying to use my new learning on my job.	4	.83
Positive Personal Outcomes	Degree to which applying training on the job leads to outcomes that are positive for the individual.	Employees in this organization receive various perks when they utilize newly learned skills on the job.	3	.69
Negative Personal Outcomes	Extent to which individuals believe that *not* applying skills and knowledge learned in training will lead to negative personal outcomes.	If I do not utilize my training I will be cautioned about it.	4	.76
Personal Capacity for Transfer	Extent to which individuals have the time, energy, and mental space in their work lives to make changes required to transfer learning to the job.	My workload allows me time to try the new things I have learned.	4	.68
Peer Support	Extent to which peers reinforce and support use of learning on the job.	My colleagues encourage me to use the skills I have learned in training.	4	.83
Supervisor Support	Extent to which supervisors and managers support and reinforce use of training on the job.	My supervisor sets goals for me that encourage me to apply my training on the job.	6	.91
Supervisor Sanctions	Extent to which individuals perceive negative responses from supervisors and managers	My supervisor opposes the use of the techniques I learned in training.	3	.63

Scale	Definition	Sample Item	Items	α
Perceived Content Validity	Extent to which trainees judge training content to accurately reflect job requirements.	What is taught in training closely matches my job requirements.	5	.84
Transfer Design	Degree to which training has been designed and delivered to give trainees the ability to transfer learning to the job, and training instructions match job requirements.	The activities and exercises the trainers used helped me know how to apply my learning on the job.	4	.85
Opportunity to Use	Extent to which trainees are provided with or obtain resources and tasks on the job enabling them to use training on the job.	The resources I need to use what I learned will be available to me after training.	4	.70

General Scales

Scale	Definition	Sample Item	Items	α
Transfer Effort–Performance Expectations	Expectation that effort devoted to transferring learning will lead to changes in job performance.	My job performance improves when I use new things that I have learned.	4	.81
Performance-Outcomes Expectations	Expectation that changes in job performance will lead to valued outcomes.	When I do things to improve my performance, good things happen to me.	5	.83
Resistance or Openness to Change	Extent to which prevailing group norms are perceived by individuals to resist or discourage the use of skills and knowledge acquired in training.	People in my group are open to changing the way they do things.	6	.85
Performance Self-Efficacy	An individual's general belief in the ability to change performance at will.	I am confident in my ability to use newly learned skills on the job.	4	.76
Performance Coaching	Formal and informal indicators from an organization about an individual's job performance.	After training, I get feedback from people about how well I am applying what I learned.	4	.70

Figure 4.2. Learning Transfer System Change Process.

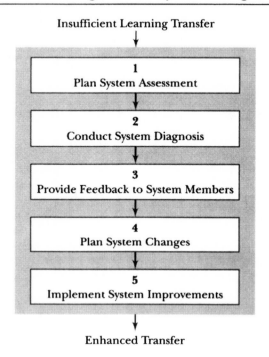

1. *Plan system assessment.* Any effective diagnosis begins with good planning. Part of the planning is focused on logistical issues and part on political issues with managers. It is particularly important to build political support because the LTSI assesses elements of managerial behavior. Substeps:

- Determine employee groups to be assessed.
- Build partnerships with managers.
- Address confidentiality issues.
- Obtain management support.
- Decide logistical issues.

2. *Diagnose system.* The LTSI is administered to collect diagnostic data as a pulse-check to identify areas for further inquiry. Focus groups are employed to investigate areas the LTSI identifies as potential problem areas and to provide more specific information about how the problems should be addressed. Substeps:

- Collect initial diagnostic data.
- Conduct focus groups to understand meaning behind data.
- Identify key transfer system gaps.

3. Provide feedback to system members. If diagnosis is to become action and solution oriented, system members should be involved. Consistent with the action research model, it is recommended that the diagnostic findings be reported to system members. Substeps:

- Arrange feedback meeting (or meetings, if needed).
- Report diagnostic data.
- Avoid blame and criticism.
- Overcome objections to identified gaps.

4. Plan system changes. Continuing with the action research approach, attempts should be made to involve system members in joint change planning. System members frequently are best equipped to recommend specific improvements. Substeps:

- Build support from management and transfer agents for change.
- Engage transfer agents in collaborative decision making.
- Make realistic decisions.

5. Implement system improvements. System improvements are most likely to endure if ownership is shared with system members. Part of the plan should include monitoring changes and periodic reassessment. Substeps:

- Share ownership of system improvements.
- Overcome resistance of system members.
- Monitor change progress.
- Plan for reassessment.

Finding Leverage Points for Change

Research has not established whether there is an optimal norm level for the sixteen LTSI factors. Theory suggests that the most potent learning transfer systems are those with high levels on all factors. However, cultural variations across organizations suggest that not all organizations will or should build the same types of transfer systems. Case evidence supports this. For example, one organization in which the author has worked had a very strong team culture that made peer support a more powerful predictor of learning transfer than supervisor support. In a state government agency the exact opposite was true.

Such case evidence suggests that a different conception is needed. First, it is possible that a total *overall* level of transfer system factors is needed—not an absolute level on any one of them. That is, transfer system factors operate together as a constellation to influence transfer. Some elements might be interchangeable or compensate for missing elements. For example, strong reward systems might compensate for poor peer support or transfer design. This conception is consistent with the basic tenets of systems theory, which hold that multiple configurations can be effective.

Alternatively, a fit perspective might be more appropriate whereby certain cultures will require certain elements of a transfer system to be stronger than in other cultures. This perspective would explain why supervisor support is essential in a bureaucratic structure (such as a government agency), but peer support is less salient. Unlike the normative or constellation perspectives, this perspective suggests that other factors in the transfer system would not be able to substitute in a particular organization. Thus there is an optimal level for a given organization with a specific culture.

This suggests that the LTSI is best used to search for *leverage points* for change. It seems likely that the particular factors in an organization's transfer system that are optimal for intervention will vary widely. The leverage point is likely to be a function of the absolute level of a particular factor and its salience in a particular organization's culture. Most organizations would like to see a simple decision rule, say, "If supervisor support is less than 3.0, an intervention is needed." This is too simplistic. Raising a value of 2.5 on the supervisor support scale might be a critical leverage point in the government agency, but the same 2.5 found in a team-based organization might not indicate a leverage point because the supervisor is less important.

The LTSI authors expect to develop validated procedures to test this premise. For now, practitioners are advised to use a qualitative process to analyze LTSI results. Lower scores should be seen as candidates for intervention, then assessed through a second screen asking which of the factors are most important in that organization's culture. Low scores on factors important in an organization's culture are leverage points for change.

A Case Study

A mid-size specialty manufacturing company decided to completely revamp its sales training programs in an effort to substantially improve performance of the sales force. The LTSI was administered to the salespeople at the end of training with the results shown in Table 4.2. For ease of interpretation, the scores have been placed into five possible categories: Extremely positive (4.1—5.0); positive (3.5—4.0); neutral (2.5—3.4); negative (2.0—2.4); and extremely negative (1.0—1.9).

Table 4.2. LTSI Results for Case Study.

	Extremely Negative	Negative	Neutral	Positive	Extremely Positive
Ability					
Personal Capacity for Transfer			3.2		
Perceived Content Validity			3.0		
Transfer Design				3.7	
Opportunity to Use Learning				3.7	
Motivation					
Motivation to Transfer Learning					4.1
Transfer Effort— Performance Expectations				3.9	
Performance— Outcomes Expectations				3.7	
Work Environment					
Personal Outcomes— Positive			3.1		
Personal Outcomes— Negative			3.3		
Peer Support					
Supervisor and Manager Support				3.6	
Supervisor and Manager Sanctions				3.9	
Openness to Change			3.4		
Feedback and Performance Coaching				3.5	
Trainee Characteristics					
Learner Readiness			3.0		
Performance Self-Efficacy				3.9	

Table 4.2 shows that this organization has a lot of strength in its transfer system. However, it highlights a few key areas that may be barriers to transfer:

- The score on content validity (3.0) indicates that learners did not perceive the content to fit their jobs. Clearly, without content that fits job needs, transfer is not likely to occur. This often occurs when subject matter experts have not been as closely involved in the training design as they should have been. Alternatively, it could be that the new learning was not clearly demonstrated to have sufficient job fit, even if it was exactly what the learners actually need.
- Personal capacity for transfer is also rated somewhat low (3.2). This usually indicates that learners are already so busy that they aren't sure they will have time or energy to do things a new way that will slow them down and take more effort in the short run.
- The scores on positive and negative personal outcomes (3.1 and 3.3, respectively) suggest that trainees do not perceive consequences will occur if they use this training. Frequently this indicates that organizational reward systems (formal and informal) are not linked to learning transfer. If learners see no payoff from using the learning, they are not likely to use it. In this case, it is also likely that the scores reflect the low content validity. Salespeople typically have compensation systems that contain contingent rewards, so good training that will improve their sales performance will be rewarded. But if the content is not appropriate for their jobs, little reward will occur.
- Learner readiness is also fairly low (3.0). This indicates that learners were not very involved in the design of the program, were not prepared with goal setting beforehand, and thus were not as prepared as they could have been. Typically this reduces transfer.
- Finally, the learners do not report a high level of openness to change (3.4). This suggests that trainers will need to sell the new methods harder to this group to convince them to use the learning.

The results do convey some good news:

- Motivation to transfer is high.
- Supervisor support is reasonably strong.
- The learning was designed well for transfer.
- The learners believe they can change their performance through learning.

As you can see, this instrument gives a quick pulse-check on the learning transfer system at a point where problems can still be fixed. By administering this instrument at the end of training, management was able to identify potential barriers and take action to show trainees how the content really did fit their jobs, make adjustments in their workloads to give them time to try it out, and show them how the learning would improve their sales and thus their rewards.

Quick Assessment Using the LTSI Audit Format

While we would usually argue that an assessment using the validated LTSI instrument is well worth the small investment of time and effort, we are also sensitive to the time demands of learning professionals. Exhibit 4.1 presents an audit checklist version of the LTSI (Swanson & Holton, 1999). These questions were derived directly from the items on the LTSI instrument. While not as good as the psychometrically valid instrument, the constructs and the questions were derived directly from the validated format, and hence offer a reasonably valid approach to quick analysis of learning transfer systems.

Exhibit 4.1. Audit Questions Based on the LTSI.

Able to Use Learning?

Opportunity to Use Learning	☐ Do workers have opportunities on the job to apply their knowledge and expertise?
	☐ Do they have the resources needed to use their learning (equipment, information, materials, and supplies)?
	☐ Are there enough funds to apply learning?
	☐ Are there enough supporting people to allow workers to implement their learning?
Personal Capacity for Transfer	☐ Are workers' workloads adjusted for practice of their expertise?
	☐ Do workers have the personal energy to devote to new methods?
	☐ Are workers' stress levels already so high they can not cope with more change?

Exhibit 4.1. Audit Questions Based on the LTSI, Cont'd.

Perceived Content Validity	☐ Are the skills and knowledge taught similar enough to performance expectations to be viewed as credible?
	☐ Are they what the individuals need in order to perform more effectively?
	☐ Are the instructional methods, aids, and equipment used similar to those used in the work environment?
Transfer Design	☐ Is the learning designed to clearly link it to on-the-job performance?
	☐ Do examples, activities, and exercises clearly demonstrate how to apply new knowledge and skills?
	☐ Are the teaching methods used similar to the work environment?

Motivated to Use Learning?

Motivation to Transfer Learning	☐ Do learners feel better able to perform?
	☐ Do they plan to use their knowledge and expertise?
	☐ Do workers believe their learning will help them to perform more effectively on the job?
Transfer Effort— Performance Expectations	☐ Do workers believe that applying their knowledge and expertise will improve their performance?
	☐ Do workers believe that investing effort to use new learning has made a difference in the past?
	☐ Do workers believe that doing so will affect future productivity and effectiveness?
Performance— Outcomes Expectations	☐ Do workers believe the application of knowledge and expertise learned will lead to personal recognition that they value?
	☐ Does the organization demonstrate the link between development, performance, and recognition?
	☐ Does the organization clearly articulate performance expectations and recognize individuals when they do well?

Exhibit 4.1. Audit Questions Based on the LTSI, Cont'd.

☐ Are individuals rewarded for effective and improved performance?

☐ Does the organization create an environment in which individuals feel positive about performing well?

Work Environment a Catalyst for Learning Transfer?

Supervisor Feedback and Performance Coaching	☐ Do individuals receive constructive input and assistance when applying new abilities or attempting to improve work performance?
	☐ Do they receive informal and formal feedback from people in their work environment (peers, employees, colleagues)?
Supervisor and Manager Support	☐ Do managers clarify performance expectations after HRD experiences?
	☐ Do they identify opportunities to apply knowledge and expertise?
	☐ Do they set realistic goals based on new learning?
	☐ Do they work with individuals on problems encountered while applying new learning?
	☐ Do they provide recognition when individuals successfully apply new learning?
Supervisor and Manager Opposition	☐ Do managers oppose the use of new knowledge and expertise?
	☐ Do managers use techniques different from those learned by workers?
	☐ Do they provide negative feedback when individuals successfully apply new learning on the job?
Work Group Support	☐ Do peers mutually identify and implement opportunities to apply new knowledge and expertise?
	☐ Do peers encourage the use of or expect the application of new learning?
	☐ Do peers display patience with difficulties associated with applying new learning?

Exhibit 4.1. Audit Questions Based on the LTSI, Cont'd.

	☐ Do peers demonstrate appreciation for the use of new expertise?
Openness to Change	☐ Do work groups actively resist change?
	☐ Are they willing to invest energy to change?
	☐ Do they support individuals who use new techniques?
Positive Personal Rewards	☐ Does use of new learning lead to rewards such as increased productivity and work effectiveness, increased personal satisfaction, additional respect, a salary increase or reward, the opportunity to further career development plans, or the opportunity to advance in the organization?
Negative Personal Outcomes	☐ Does use of new learning lead to negative outcomes such as reprimands, penalties, peer resentment, too much new work, or the likelihood of not getting a raise if newly acquired expertise is used?

Learners Ready to Transfer?

Learner Readiness	☐ Did individuals have the opportunity to provide input prior to the learning intervention?
	☐ Did they know what to expect?
	☐ Did they understand how training was related to job-related development and work performance?
Performance Self-Efficacy	☐ Do workers feel confident and self-assured about applying their abilities in their jobs?
	☐ Can they overcome obstacles that hinder the use of their knowledge and skills?

This audit checklist can be applied in a variety of ways inside organizations:

- As a preliminary analysis for organizational triage to see whether a complete assessment is warranted.
- As questions to direct a focus group or interviews about the learning transfer system.
- As a training aid in workshops for managers or learning professionals.
- As talking points to help executives understand learning transfer systems so they will support interventions.
- As discussion points for workgroups embarking on significant training processes.

In short, it is most important that you think systemically about learning transfer. When you can't do a complete assessment (which ensures a systemic analysis), the audit checklist provides a sound guide that will force systemic thinking about learning transfer. If your organization is not thinking systemically and you can't afford to invest in a full assessment, then start with the audit format and move up to the full LTSI later.

Conclusion

The beginning of this chapter suggests that organizations should work toward understanding their transfer system and intervene to eliminate transfer barriers. The instrument provides an easy, economical, and sound diagnostic inventory to identify intervention targets. As a psychometrically sound diagnostic tool, it is valuable to both researchers and practitioners. Considering the wide range of interventions that are available to influence transfer, it is clear that the wrong intervention could be easily chosen without sound diagnostic data.

References

Baldwin, T. T., & Ford, J. K. (1988). Transfer of training: A review and directions for future research. *Personnel Psychology, 41,* 63–105.

Bates, R. A., Holton, E. F., III, & Seyler, D. L. (2000). The role of interpersonal factors in the application of computer-based training in an industrial setting. *Human Resource Development International, 3,* 19–42.

Bookter, A. (1999). *Convergent and divergent validity study of the Learning Transfer Questionnaire.* Unpublished dissertation, Louisiana State University.

Broad, M. L., & Newstrom, J. W. (1992). *Transfer of training: Action-packed strategies to ensure high payoff from training investments.* Reading, MA: Addison-Wesley.

Cummings, T. G., & Worley, C. G. (1998). *Organizational development and change* (7th ed.). St. Paul, MN: West.

Facteau, J. D., Dobbins, G. H., Russell, J.E.A., Ladd, R. T., & Kudisch, J. D. (1995). The influence of general perceptions of the training environment on pretraining motivation and perceived training transfer. *Journal of Management, 21,* 1–15.

Ford, J. K., Quinones, M. A., Sego, D. J., & Sorra, J. (1992). Factors affecting the opportunity to perform trained tasks on the job. *Personnel Psychology, 45,* 511–527.

Ford, J. K., & Weissbein, D. A. (1997). Transfer of training: An update review and analysis. *Performance Improvement Quarterly, 10,* 22–41.

Gist, M. E. (1987). Self-efficacy: Implications for organizational behavior and human resource management. *Academy of Management Review, 12,* 472–485.

Holton, E. F., III (1996). The flawed four-level evaluation model. *Human Resource Development Quarterly, 7,* 5–21.

Holton, E. F., Bates, R. A., & Ruona, W.E.A. (2001). Development of a generalized learning transfer system inventory. *Human Resource Development Quarterly, 11*(4), 333–360.

Holton, E. F., III, Bates, R., & Seyler, D. (1996). Construct validation of a transfer climate instrument. In E. F. Holton III (Ed.), *Proceedings of the 1996 Academy of Human Resource Development Annual Conference.* Bowling Green, OH: Academy of Human Resource Development.

Holton, E. F., III, Bates, R., Seyler, D., & Carvalho, M. (1997). Toward construct validation of a transfer climate instrument. *Human Resource Development Quarterly, 8,* 95–113.

Huczynski, A. A., & Lewis, J. W. (1980). An empirical study into the learning transfer process in management training. *Journal of Management Studies, 17,* 227–240.

James, L. R., & McIntyre, M. D. (1996). Perceptions of organizational climate. In K. R. Murphy (Ed.), *Individual differences and behavior in organizations* (pp. 416–450). San Francisco: Jossey-Bass.

Mathieu, J. E., Tannenbaum, S. I., & Salas, E. (1992). Influences of individual and situational characteristics on measures of training effectiveness. *Academy of Management Journal, 35,* 882–847.

Noe, R. A., & Schmitt, N. (1986). The influence of trainee attitudes on training effectiveness: Test of a model. *Personnel Psychology, 39,* 497–523.

Rouillier, J. Z., & Goldstein, I. L. (1993). The relationship between organizational transfer climate and positive transfer of training. *Human Resource Development Quarterly, 4,* 377–390.

Ruona, W.E.A., Leimbach, M., Holton, E. F. III, & Bates, R. A. (in press). The relationship between learner utility reactions and predicted learning transfer among trainees. *International Journal of Training and Development.*

Seyler, D. L., Holton, E. F., III, Bates, R. A., Burnett, M. F., & Carvalho, M. A. (1998). Factors affecting motivation to use training. *International Journal of Training and Development, 2,* 2–16.

Smith-Jentsch, K. A., Jentsch, F. G., Payne, S. C., & Salas, E. (1996). Can pretraining experiences explain individual differences in learning? *Journal of Applied Psychology, 81,* 110–116.

Swanson, R. A., & Holton, E. F., III (1999). *Results: How to assess performance, learning and perceptions in organizations.* San Francisco: Berrett-Koehler.

Tannenbaum, S. I., & Yukl, G. (1992). Training and development in work organizations. *Annual Review of Psychology, 43,* 399–441.

Tracey, J. B., Tannenbaum, S. I., & Kavanaugh, M. J. (1995). Applying trained skills on the job: The importance of the work environment. *Journal of Applied Psychology, 80,* 239–252.

Tziner, A., Haccoun, R. R., & Kadish, A. (1991). Personal and situational characteristics of transfer of training improvement strategies. *Journal of Occupational Psychology, 64,* 167–177.

Warr, P., & Bunce, D. (1995). Trainee characteristics and the outcomes of open learning. *Personnel Psychology, 48,* 347–375.

Xiao, J. (1996). The relationship between organizational factors and the transfer of training in the electronics industry in Shenzhen, China. *Human Resource Development Quarterly, 7,* 55–86.

CHAPTER 5

Managing Transfer Before Learning Begins

The Transfer-Ready Learner

Sharon S. Naquin
Timothy T. Baldwin

Recent models of the learning process identify learner characteristics and pretraining conditions as among the most important influences on transfer outcomes. Nonetheless, most transfer interventions have focused largely on the design and aftermath of development experiences. In this chapter, we explore why learner characteristics have not been more actively assessed and managed in organizations, and argue that identifying and nurturing transfer-ready learners is a potentially fruitful avenue for improving transfer outcomes. We particularly highlight two learner characteristics, motivation to improve work through learning (MTIWL) and learning agility, which we believe are critical antecedents of transfer. We conclude with some principles for creating the pretraining conditions that will help identify and prime transfer-ready learners.

We need reminding that trainees do not just fall out of some great trainee bin in the sky. They probably have rather long and varied organizational histories, which have created certain attitudes, values and behaviors relative to specific training experiences.
        —J. P. Campbell, "The Agenda for Theory and Research."

I managed good, they just played bad.
        —Casey Stengel, former coach of the N.Y. Mets

Transfer of learning, by definition, can occur only after a learning experience. Not surprisingly, then, the majority of traditional efforts to enhance transfer have focused either on the nature of the training event itself or on the post-learning context. The impetus for this chapter was our belief that the people who enter organizational learning experiences, and how they enter, are among the most important predictors of transfer outcomes. While not discounting the potential importance of learning design and post-training factors, we concur with Coach Stengel's diagnosis that the players (that is, learners) really do matter.

Of course, that idea is hardly new. Virtually all recent models of the learning and transfer process (such as Baldwin & Ford, 1988; Mathieu & Martineau, 1997; Colquitt, LePine, & Noe, 2000) include learner characteristics as important antecedents of transfer. Moreover, the notion that performance, in any setting, is determined by a combination of an individual's motivation and ability has been one of the most enduring conceptualizations in industrial-organizational psychology. Nonetheless, neither identification of the individual characteristics most conducive to high transfer nor the creation of pretraining conditions to help induce such dispositions have generally been actively managed. We contend that this helps account for the consistently dismal estimates of transfer yield (for example, often as little as 10 percent) so ubiquitous in the training literature.

The lack of organizational attention devoted to learner assessment has at least three causes. First, for many, learning experiences are a fundamental right of employment, or an entitlement, and certainly not an appropriate focal point for the differentiation of employees and the creation of any kind of meritocracy. The idea of actively assessing and selecting certain individuals, rather than allowing self-selection and more egalitarian forces to prevail, would represent a significant culture change in many organizations and is repugnant to some learning advocates.

Second, while a number of studies of individual differences in learning contexts have been conducted, there is little existing synthesis of that research in a way that makes clear just what the profile of a "transfer-ready" candidate might look like. Questions such as What is an optimal transfer-ready profile? How do you identify such a profile? and, most important, How do you help someone become more transfer-ready? warrant careful consideration. Therefore, prerequisite to effective learner assessment in an organization is some consensus about what might be thought of as the "right stuff" for transfer, and such a profile has been heretofore lacking.

Third, and consistent with the overall impetus for this SIOP volume, there is a disconnect between the concept of identifying a profile for high-potential transfer candidates and actual prescriptive guidance for learning professionals interested in designing interventions to improve transfer. As noted, it is hardly provocative to suggest that some learner characteristics are likely to predict transfer. The more pragmatic issues relate to how the knowledge of individual characteristics might be used and how such characteristics might be fostered through the management of pretraining conditions.

The objective of this chapter is to address each of these three issues, and the sections are organized accordingly. First, we highlight research evidence showing that learner characteristics are important predictors of transfer outcomes and make the case that the assessment and development of those characteristics is therefore not only appropriate but essential to achieving better transfer outcomes.

Second, we selectively review the existing literature with the goal of synthesizing a preliminary profile of the transfer-ready learner. Key to this section is our shift of focus away from traditional and limiting conceptions of learner motivation (that is, motivation to learn) and ability (cognitive aptitude) and toward two broader variables (that is, motivation to improve work through learning and learning agility), which we think hold great promise for increasing our ability to predict who transfers learning and why.

Third, we discuss several implications of learner assessment and how learning professionals might use learner profiling to more actively manage the learning process and ultimately create pretraining conditions that induce greater transfer readiness. Given that widespread assessment and selection of learners is unlikely to be broadly applied for a variety of reasons, we offer four principles for creating a pretraining context most conducive to helping foster transfer among all learner profiles.

First Who—Then What

The success of any organization is largely contingent on its ability to unleash and maximize the talents and abilities of its workforce. To enhance the productivity and profitability levels of an organization, employees are often required to learn new methodologies and more efficient processes. It logically follows, then, that employee development programs are among the most important activities of any organization. In fact, Pfeffer (1994) asserted that effective employee development is perhaps the key to success in today's global economy. Empirical evidence generally supports that contention and indicates that comprehensive learning and development activities produce beneficial organizational outcomes (Bartel, 1994; Swanson, 1998).

At the same time, as noted many times throughout this volume, estimates of the transfer stemming from the enormous organizational expenditures on learning continue to be abysmal. Although U.S. corporations annually spend billions on employee training, most evaluation reports suggest that at least 50 percent (and many go as high as 90 percent) of those training dollars are wasted because trainees never use the trained skills back on the job (Broad & Newstrom, 1992). Even much more conservative estimates of the lack of transfer indicate a staggering waste of organizational resources. Moreover, when trainees fail to use training, organizations experience a double loss, both of the direct investment made in training and of the opportunity cost of passed-over alternative investments that could have contributed to organizational objectives and outcomes.

Our thesis is that the effectiveness of organizational training and development efforts is heavily dependent on the characteristics of the learning participants. In his recent landmark study of those organizations that were able to make the jump from good to great, Collins (2002) attributed those firms' sustained excellence in part to their concerted focus on first identifying and deploying the right people, and only later on vision, strategy, and tactics. We think that tenet is an apt prescription for learning contexts as well.

More specifically, research clearly indicates that people benefit differentially from educational experiences, both formal and otherwise. Some learn new perspectives and behaviors effectively from courses, life, and work, and others do not. For example, studies by the Center for Creative Leadership (see McCall, Lombardo, & Morrison, 1988) found that successful managers had a strong and similar pattern of learning from key job assignments. Derailed managers, on the other hand, had virtually no pattern of learning from jobs. Further, personal learning blocks were among the key reasons for their derailment. Outsider descriptions of these derailed managers found that they (the managers) thought they were infallible, could not make the transition to a different job or way of behaving, and had essentially quit learning. They relied on what had gotten them to where they were, ironically becoming victimized by their past successes. They became locked into standard ways of thinking and acting that didn't really meet the new demands (McCall, Lombardo, & Morrison, 1988).

In their seminal work over forty years ago, McGehee and Thayer (1961) identified person assessment as a key precursor to effective training. Their notion then, and one since substantiated by considerable research, is that even when learning opportunities, methods, and contexts are held constant, some learners will transfer more than others. And as training becomes more complex, costs more, takes longer, and occurs in many ways beyond classroom learning, focusing on the learner will be increasingly important. The goal is to maximize the levels of motivation and ability that learners bring to development experiences.

To be clear, our intent is not to discount the potential importance of learning design and transfer climate—they are unquestionably important influences on transfer. Rather, our point is simply that questions of who (the learners) should be considered—and generally considered before—those of learning context. Our experience is that the "person assessment" element prescribed by McGehee and Thayer has generally been haphazard and unsystematic and often entirely neglected. In fact, we suspect that it is the rare development activity in organizations today where sponsors could produce even a rudimentary profile of the participants and their likelihood of achieving positive transfer from that experience.

The "Right Stuff" for Transfer

So what does constitute an optimal "transfer-ready" profile? At a general level, the maxim that learning outcomes will be a function of learner motivation and ability is unassailable (Noe, 1986; Pintrich, Cross, Kozma, & McKeachie, 1986). However, using the conventional definition of transfer as the application of learned skills to the workplace, our contention is that the ways in which learner motivation and ability have been conceptualized are too narrow and too bounded in the learning (not work) context to fully predict such outcomes. We believe that the combination of two recently introduced constructs—motivation to improve work through learning (Naquin & Holton, 2002) and learning agility (Lombardo & Eichinger, 2000)—can provide a fuller profile of the potential of any given individual to achieve high transfer of learning.

The Motivation to Improve Work Through Learning

While research linking intelligence to learning outcomes has a strong and robust history, only recently have researchers turned their attention to training motivation. In a recent meta-analytic review, Colquitt et al. (2000) concluded that dispositional and situational factors do explain significant incremental variance in learning outcomes (including transfer) over and above cognitive ability. From a practical standpoint, the challenge is to synthesize the confusing array of dispositional variables into a composite that might be interpretable and useful to training professionals.

For any who have been involved even casually in organizational learning contexts, motivation to learn is an intuitively important precondition for learning. Individuals who are motivated when they approach a learning situation clearly seem to have a higher likelihood of achieving positive outcomes than those with a lower level of motivation (Goldstein, 1992). In support of that supposition, Noe and Schmitt (1986), Hicks and Klimoski (1987), and Mathieu, Tannenbaum, and Salas (1992) found a positive relationship between scores on learning measures and an individual's motivation to learn (Goldstein, 1992). Ryman and Biersner (1975) studied a Navy school for divers and found that trainees who strongly agreed with training-confidence scale items were more likely to graduate.

Warr and Bunce (1995) extended existing conceptions of motivation to learn and introduced the notions of distal and proximal motivation. In distal terms, "individuals vary in the favorability of their attitudes to training as a whole. More proximally, those general attitudes are reflected in specific motivation about a particular set of training activities" (p. 349). They studied 106 junior managers over a seven-month period and found significant relationships between managers' learning scores and both distal and proximal motivation.

As these studies illustrate, explorations of motivation in learning contexts has been largely limited to constructs of motivation to learn (or motivation to train) within the boundaries of the learning experience or experiences. However, any learning professional can convey stories of employees with a great thirst for learning (perhaps just as an alternative to working) but little real interest in using the learning in a way instrumental to their organization's goals. Further, conventional descriptions of motivation to learn are almost all in the context of formal or structured classroom learning. Yet in today's business reality learning might take the form of a challenging job assignment, a quick search of the Internet, or a dialogue with a coach or mentor.

If our interest is in transfer, and transfer from the full range of learning opportunities that exist in our organizations today, then we contend that conceptions of motivation have to expand to be consistent with those realities. To be sure, unlike college or other academic courses, the primary desired outcome of organizational learning initiatives is not just learning but improvement in work outcomes or productivity. The process of improving work through learning involves an employee's willingness to transfer any knowledge acquired through such learning back to the real work context.

Here again, this notion is not new; others have previously acknowledged the importance of motivation to transfer (Noe, 1986). Mathieu and Martineau (1997) developed a conceptual framework extending the concept of learner motivation to multiple training criteria. As they stated, "participants enter and leave training with varying levels of motivation that will likely influence how much they learn, whether they transfer learning to the job, and ultimately how successful the program is." Wlodkowski (1985) noted, "When we talk about transfer, we are usually concerned with how well adults can apply what they have learned to their life, community, or workplace" (p. 331). Nonetheless, the measurement and empirical test of learner motivation beyond the learning context itself has received little traditional research attention.

Mindful of that gap in the literature, Naquin and Holton (2002) incorporated both the motivation to train and motivation to transfer into a higher-order construct they labeled the Motivation to Improve Work Through Learning (MTIWL). Individual motivation to improve work through learning is a function of motivation to train and motivation to transfer.

Because organizations have an appropriate interest in something more than just learning for learning's sake, the MTIWL construct focuses on motivational influences that will lead to improved work outcomes from learning. MTIWL is defined as the motivation to improve work outcomes by engaging in training or learning activities and using what is learned to perform job functions differently. This construct is potentially a more powerful motivational construct because it incorporates both dimensions of motivation critical to achieving transfer outcomes.

Using structural equation modeling techniques to better understand the antecedents of MTIWL, Naquin and Holton (2002) found that extroversion, positive affectivity (an individual's tendency to experience high levels of positive emotional states), and work commitment attitudes directly affected MTIWL. Further, they found that other personality dimensions, conscientiousness and agreeableness, indirectly affect the construct through work commitment. Four scales were selected to measure this new construct—attitudes toward training and motivation to train, both from the START instrument (Weinstein et al., 1994), and motivation to transfer and performance outcomes expectations from the LTSI instrument (Holton, Bates, & Ruona, 2001).

The four scales loaded on one latent construct, identified as motivation to improve work through learning. Each of the separate scales selected had evidence of initial content validity. Construct validity and criterion validity were also evident because a significant portion of the variance in the construct was predicted ($r = .59$). Finally, the fact that certain other constructs related to training proficiency (that is, openness to experience) were not related to this one suggests discriminant validity between MTIWL and motivation to learn.

In short, the MTIWL variable is a composite of several dispositions previously shown to influence learning outcomes. It is conceptually distinct from more narrow motivation to learn and, we believe, one key element of a transfer-ready profile.

Learning Agility

As noted earlier, cognitive ability has a long and robust research history in the training literature and has been found to be a determinant of training success (though rarely using transfer outcome criteria) across a wide variety of contexts (Ree & Earles, 1991). Although there is debate about its underlying causes (that is, genetic versus environmental), it is clear that individuals differ in terms of basic information processing capacities and their levels of cognitive resources.

However, just as we argued that conceptualizations of motivation need to move beyond "motivation to learn," we similarly believe that a conceptualization of intelligence as strictly cognitive aptitude is too limiting to predict transfer. Such notions are not novel in that several research streams challenging the primacy of cognitive aptitude have emerged in the past decade, including those related to multiple intelligences (Gardner, 1999), emotional intelligence (Goleman, 1995), and practical intelligence (Sternberg, 1996). Yet, until recently, little attention has been devoted to identifying the specific aptitudes most predictive of transfer.

In two studies designed to determine the characteristics of those most able to learn from experience and stay on track in organizations, Lombardo and Eichinger (2000) identified four types of agility (people, results, mental, and change), which they collectively labeled *learning agility*. People agility involves seeking and getting feedback (from self and others) on what is needed to improve, learning from experience, and treating others constructively. Results agility describes getting results under tough conditions, inspiring others to perform beyond normal, and exhibiting the sort of presence that builds confidence in others. Mental agility describes thinking through problems from a fresh point of view and being comfortable with complexity and ambiguity and capable of explaining one's thinking to others. Change agility involves curiosity, a passion for ideas, willingness to experiment with test cases, and proactively engaging in skill-building activities.

In that study, the four elements of learning agility correlated with high-potential rankings and the pattern of relationships was consistent across gender, age, level and type of position (line or staff), and company. In short, learning agility varies rather significantly among people and those with a high degree of such agility can be expected to show higher rates of transfer, particularly in those situations where the learning situations are work-based or require a propensity to learn from experience.

Managing Learner Assessment and Pretraining Conditions

The recognition of differences in transfer readiness points to several potential implications for learning professionals. First, the idea of including learning profiles as part of the criteria for selection into an organization is appealing. Given rapidly changing corporate environments and the importance of continuous learning to firm competitiveness and survival, a focus on identifying and hiring the most agile and motivated learners would seem valuable.

A second, and related, possibility is to use learning profile information as a form of "tie-breaker" in selection for challenging assignments. Given several qualified candidates, determining who would be likely to learn the most from a premium learning program or challenging job assignment could help narrow the candidate pool.

A third possibility is to use learner profile information to gauge the level and intensity of other transfer support. For example, those who come to learning experiences with high levels of motivation and agility will probably require less than others in terms of active transfer management throughout the process. While they may still benefit from such interventions, in climates of scarce resources learning professionals will want to allocate their resources in ways that make the most difference.

While we suspect that the prospect of these various forms of "selecting for transfer" will be enticing to those who have wrestled with the transfer problem, we also acknowledge the reality that such selection is not likely to gain widespread application. As with any process of differentiation in organizations, the demands for discipline and consistency would be high. Those not favorably assessed will undoubtedly feel some anxiety and pressure. There may well be some discontent from those passed over for prime development opportunities, and the culture of many organizations includes antibodies against any wholesale assessment of the workforce.

Moreover, the current state of readiness measurement (largely self-reports) makes it difficult to support the assertion that we can always reliably distinguish between those high and low in motivation and agility. Finally, even if we could reliably isolate those with the most transfer-ready profiles, the pool of such individuals is undoubtedly small; no organization of any size can realistically aspire to select only those with such high profiles.

With that in mind, we contend that a more widely applicable approach for intervention related to transfer readiness is to focus on establishing those pretraining conditions that can influence it. Although some of the principles for priming learners may prove superfluous for those with high transfer-ready profiles, the reality is that many organizational learners will not be in that category. The principles outlined here reflect our belief that learning stems from a need to know and transfer from a need to perform. In some cases, those motives may emanate from intrinsic or internalized sources. In many others, however, they will likely require some active stimulation or push. These four principles are designed to induce greater transfer readiness:

Principle 1: *Set explicit, public training goals. And have them set by management rather than by training designers or instructors.*

The relationship between specific, challenging goals and higher performance is among the most robust findings in the social science literature. Although learning objectives have long been part of instructional design, only recently have learning researchers begun to explore the effects of assigned goals from managers (or other organizational representatives) as a mechanism for enhancing training outcomes. For example, Dixon (1993) found that a strategic training objective set by the CEO or other top-level manager had a powerful effect on reported trainee motivation. Similarly, Cohen (1990) found that trainees with goals entered training with higher levels of motivation to learn.

The research, then, supports the prescription that managers should work with trainees prior to their attendance at training programs and set goals for learning and transfer. That may sound simple enough, but our experience suggests that this principle may be among the least practiced. The lack of attention to the development and evaluation of specific accountabilities may be attributed in part to a lingering bias that learning is a "delicate flower" that cannot be forced or even aggressively managed. Although challenging goals and incentive compensation are now commonplace in other areas of organizational life, there has been a curious reluctance to implement such strategies in conjunction with learning activities.

Trainers and others can and should also set goals, but the research suggests that the most powerful source for transfer is the manager. Organizational life is generally hierarchical and the review and rewards under the control of one's boss are often the most powerful influences on employee behavior. There is no reason to believe that such powerful influences will not be operative in learning contexts.

Principle 2: *Do not assume that learners believe that they can master the training content and transfer it to their work. Find ways to instill confidence in trainees that they can succeed in the learning activity and try to frame learning activities as opportunities rather than threats.*

While general intelligence and past experiences are clearly important for affecting an individual's readiness to learn, our focus here is on the psychological states that are more amenable to interventions. And, because admitting to a lack of confidence is so socially undesirable, we suspect that a lack of confidence is more prevalent than it may appear. Attention to trainee readiness is time well spent.

Trainees' confidence in their ability to succeed in training is a function of how they have interpreted past training successes and failures. Research suggests that those who believe they can improve and attribute learning outcomes to internal, changeable, and personally controllable factors are likely to be motivated to learn.

The challenge is to explicitly shape trainees' attributions to enhance confidence, motivation, and subsequent learning. Such efforts encourage trainees to move to make more constructive attributions, leading them to exert more effort and use more creative learning strategies. For example, Stevens and Gist (1997) found that improving trainee perceptions that they were in control of their learning led to better performance two weeks after the training program. Marx's relapse prevention application (described in Chapter Eleven) is a good example of attribution shaping in the post-training period. In a study on negotiation training, Weissbein (2000) showed that trainees given attributional reframing were more motivated to learn than were trainees who did not receive the intervention prior to training.

Other researchers have reported some success with methods of explicitly framing learning experiences as opportunities instead of threats. Feelings of threat are often associated with the arousal of anxiety and evidence is clear that high levels of anxiety are negatively related to pretraining self-efficacy, motivation to learn, and learning (Colquitt et al., 2000). For example, Warr and Bunce (1995) found a negative relationship between task anxiety and motivation to learn in their sample of junior managers. In a study of computer skills training, Martocchio (1992) found that labeling the training context as an opportunity resulted in lower computer anxiety and greater learning than a neutral context did. These findings are consistent with the power of labeling documented by Eden and others in their work on the Pygmalion effect (Eden & Ravid, 1982). Results showed that conveying high expectations to both trainer and trainee could lead to the development of stronger efficacy, more positive outcome expectations, and higher transfer.

Principle 3: *Demonstrate support for forthcoming learning initiatives in ways that really matter in organizations. That means*

- *Do not simply pronounce the importance of learning (permission). Rather, show behavioral support by having managers participate in and lead training.*
- *Find a way to link learning performance to any meaningful organizational reward (for example, performance evaluation, pay, career development).*
- *Find a way to link managers' rewards to the learning outcomes of their subordinates.*

Ubiquitous in discussions of successful organizational interventions is the notion of management support. In a study across five organizations, Cohen (1990) found that trainees with more supportive supervisors entered training with stronger beliefs that training would be useful. Baldwin and Magjuka (1991) found that trainees who entered training expecting some kind of supervisory follow-up reported stronger intentions to transfer what was learned to the job.

Organizations today generally announce that training is vital to their mission and future, and development expenditures have certainly risen dramatically in recent years. But Baldwin and Magjuka

(1991) also found that organizational employees might make a distinction between management "permission" and more meaningful management support. Management spends money and allocates employees' time, but that is not viewed as support. According to survey respondents, if managers devoted their time to kick off the program, attended sessions, agreed to lead some sessions, committed to set goals (as described earlier), and followed up with participants, then training was being truly supported.

This is a principle that is simple to state and yet daunting to implement. Creating a pretraining climate that maximizes support generally requires the breaking down of any of a number of explicit and implicit disincentives. Unfortunately, supportive reward systems such as pay for performance, promotion from within, skill-based pay, and rewards for managers who encourage employee development are often the exception rather than the rule. Given that considerable organizational research has pointed to the power of those reward systems as salient signals of organizational importance, we suspect that learners frequently perceive that they have "permission" to participate but not really support.

Principle 4: *Seek ways to require learners to make a significant public (and ideally written) commitment of their intention to transfer their learning.*

Psychologists have long understood the power of the consistency principle to direct human action (see Festinger, 1989). As humans we have a nearly obsessive desire to be (and to appear) consistent with what we have already done. Once we have made a choice or taken a stand (for example, to apply skills from a learning activity) we will encounter personal and interpersonal pressures to behave consistently with that commitment. Those pressures will cause us to respond in ways that justify our earlier decision. Further, persons who go through a great deal of trouble or pain to attain something tend to value it more highly than persons who attain the same thing with a minimum of effort.

Those findings have potentially powerful implications for framing training in maximally motivating ways. Rather than view the learner as just a consumer, with the transfer pressure on the designers, we need to induce a sense of personal ownership of transfer goals and to directly challenge those learners to apply learning. The more that we can make the transfer of learned knowledge and skills part of a learner's felt need to be consistent with an earlier commitment, the higher the probability that we will see motivated behavior in that direction.

Conclusion

Of the three categories of transfer influences originally proposed by Baldwin and Ford (1988), trainee characteristics have received the least attention in terms of interventions. The premise of this chapter is that successful outcomes will be significantly influenced by the transfer readiness learners bring to development experiences.

Indeed, given the dearth of active transfer interventions in organizations, we would submit that, where positive transfer has been observed, it has often been a function of highly motivated and learning-agile individuals succeeding in relatively unmanaged and unsupportive transfer conditions.

Evidence of what constitutes transfer-ready profiles is emerging, and knowledge of individual profiles may in some cases enable employers to be more proactive in selection and placement of transfer-ready learners. Perhaps most important, a more explicit recognition of the importance of transfer readiness should help learning professionals to more actively and confidently manage pretraining conditions that will maximize it.

Unfortunately, our experience suggests that too many learning activities begin already set up to fail. Greater positive transfer will depend on how well managers and learning professionals succeed in framing learning experiences in ways that prime the motivation and agility of their learners. We hope the principles presented here will be useful to that cause.

References

Baldwin, T. T., & Ford, J. K. (1988). Transfer of training: A review and directions for future research. *Personnel Psychology, 41,* 63–105.

Baldwin, T. T., & Magjuka, R. J. (1991). Organizational training and signals of importance. Linking pre-training perceptions to intentions to transfer. *Human Resource Development Quarterly, 2,* 25–36.

Bartel, A. (1994). Productivity gains from the implementation of employee training programs. *Industrial Relations, 33,* 411–425.

Broad, M., & Newstrom, J. (1992). *Transfer of training: Action-packed strategies to ensure high payoff from training investments.* Reading, MA: Addison-Wesley.

Campbell, J. P. (1989). The agenda for theory and research. In I. L. Gold-
stein (Ed.), *Training and development in organizations* (pp. 177–215).
San Francisco: Jossey-Bass. This material is used by permission of
John Wiley & Sons, Inc.

Cohen, D. J. (1990). What motivates trainees. *Training and Development
Journal, 36,* 91–93.

Collins, J. (2002). *Good to great: Why some companies make the leap and others
don't.* New York: HarperCollins.

Colquitt, J., LePine, J., & Noe, R. (2000). Toward an integrative theory of
training motivation: A meta-analytic path analysis of 20 years of
research. *Journal of Applied Psychology, 85*(5), 678–707.

Dixon, N. M. (1993). Developing managers for the learning organization.
Human Resource Management Review, 3, 243–254.

Eden, D., & Ravid, G. (1982). Pygmalion vs. self-expectancy: Effects of
instructor and self-expectancy on trainee performance. *Organizational Behavior and Human Performance, 30,* 351–364.

Festinger, L. (1989). *Extending psychological frontiers: Selected works of Leon
Festinger.* S. Schachter & M. Gazzaniga (Eds). Sage: New York.

Gardner, H. (1999). *Intelligence reframed: Multiple intelligences for the 21st
century.* New York: Basic Books.

Goldstein, I. L. (1992). *Training in organizations* (3rd ed.). Pacific Grove,
CA: Brooks/Cole.

Goleman, D. (1995). *Emotional intelligence.* New York: Bantam Books.

Hicks, W., & Klimoski, R. (1987). The process of entering training programs and its effect on training outcomes. *Academy of Management
Journal, 30,* 542–552.

Holton, E. F., III, Bates, R. A., & Ruona, W.E.A. (2001). Development and
validation of a generalized learning transfer climate questionnaire.
Human Resource Development Quarterly, 11(4), 333–360.

Lombardo, M. M., & Eichinger, R. W. (2000). High potentials as high
learners. *Human Resource Management, 39,* 321–329.

Martocchio, J. J. (1992). Microcomputer usage as an opportunity: The
influence of context in employee training. *Personnel Psychology, 45,*
529–552.

Mathieu, J. E., & Martineau, J. W. (1997). Individual and situational influences on training motivation. In J. K. Ford, S.W.J. Kozlowski,
K. Kraiger, E. Salas, & M. S. Teachout (Eds.), *Improving training effectiveness in work organizations,* pp. 193–221. Mahwah, NJ: Erlbaum.

Mathieu, J. E., Tannenbaum, S. I., & Salas, E. (1992). Influences of
individual and situational characteristics on training effectiveness
measures. *Academy of Management Journal, 35,* 828–847. McCall,
M., Lombardo, M. M., & Morrison, A. (1988). *Lessons of experience.*
Lexington, MA: Lexington Books.

McCall, M., Lombardo, M. M., & Morrison, A. (1988). *The lessons of experience.* Lexington, MA: Lexington Books.

McGehee, W., & Thayer, P. (1961). *Training in business and industry.* New York: Wiley.

Naquin, S. S., & Holton, E. (2002). Motivation to improve work through learning in human resource development. *Human Resource Development International, 5,* 1–16.

Noe, R. A. (1986). Trainee attributes and attitudes: Neglected influences on training effectiveness. *Academy of Management Review, 11,* 736–749.

Noe, R., & Schmitt, N. (1986). The influence of trainee attitudes on training effectiveness: Test of a model. *Personnel Psychology, 39,* 497–523.

Pfeffer, J. (1994). *Competitive advantage through people.* Boston: Harvard Business School Press.

Pintrich, P. R., Cross, D. R., Kozma, R. B., & McKeachie, W. J. (1986). Instructional psychology. *Annual Review of Psychology, 37,* 611–651.

Ree, M. J., & Earles, J. A. (1991). Predicting training success: Not much more than g. *Personnel Psychology, 44,* 321–332.

Ryman, D. H., & Biersner, R. J. (1975). Attitudes predictive of diving success. *Personnel Psychology, 28,* 181–188.

Sternberg, R. J. (1996). *Successful intelligence: How practical intelligence and creative intelligence determine success in life.* New York: Penguin.

Stevens, C., & Gist, M. (1997). Effects of self-efficacy and goal orientation training on negotiation skill maintenance: What are the mechanisms? *Personnel Psychology, 50,* 955–978.

Swanson, R. A. (1998). Demonstrating the financial benefit of human resource development: Status and update on the theory and practice. *Human Resource Development Quarterly, 9,* 286–295.

Warr, P., & Bunce, D. (1995). Trainee characteristics and the outcomes of open learning. *Personnel Psychology, 48,* 347–375.

Weinstein, C. E., Palmer, D. R., Hanson, G. R., Dierking, D. R., McCann, E., Soper, M., & Nath, I. (1994, March). Design and development of an assessment of readiness for training: The START. Paper presented at the annual conference of the Academy of Human Resource Development, San Antonio, TX.

Weissbein, D. (2000). Factors impacting trainee attributions: Impact on trainee motivation and transfer skills. Unpublished Ph.D. dissertation, Michigan State University.

Wlodkowski, R. J. (1985). *Enhancing adult motivation to learn.* San Francisco: Jossey-Bass.

CHAPTER 6

Managing the Organizational Learning Transfer System

A Model and Case Study

Mary L. Broad

This chapter presents a detailed procedural model of learning transfer for performance improvement professionals to consider as they
address performance issues and projects in the organizations they
serve. The model integrates key concepts from other chapters, and
can be useful to those inside an organization as well as those who
provide expertise and services on a consulting basis. Steps in the
model present actions for the practitioner throughout the performance improvement process, from identifying performance and
learning requirements to implementing and evaluating the project.
Every step shows how the involvement of key stakeholders is critical
to ensure transfer of learning to full application in the workplace.
The final steps in the model address stakeholder accountability for
support strategies and full reports to stakeholders at all levels,
emphasizing the value of stakeholders' transfer support in achieving
success. The chapter also presents a detailed case study of the model's
application, involving leadership development at the former GTE,
now merged into Verizon. This gives the background of a learning
requirement in a leading high-tech company, and shows how the
model played out in a challenging and turbulent environment. Careful attention to assessment of needs, strong focus on performance

> improvement and rigorous evaluation, and full involvement by a range of important stakeholders resulted in significant achievement of desired organizational outcomes.

The goal of transfer is the full application of new knowledge and skills to improve individual and group performance in an organization or community. This chapter's first purpose is to suggest a procedural model for practitioners to apply learning transfer principles to support improved performance. The model presents important actions by a learning project manager and other stakeholders to support transfer of new knowledge and skills, and incorporates major transfer issues from preceding chapters. It can be adapted to specific learning challenges in any organizational context. The model also provides guidance to learning project managers and their clients to maximize the impact of learning investments. (Of course, the model is applied only after a performance analysis has identified *learning* as an appropriate intervention to improve performance.)

The chapter's second purpose is to present a case study illustrating application of the model. It describes a recent organizational learning project that actively managed learning transfer principles and reached successful outcomes.

Focus on Performance

Our growing sophistication about necessary stakeholder support for transfer comes from recognition that effective performance depends on several essential organizational factors. Only one of these is the knowledge and skill level of performers, which learning activities provide. Learning activities (for example, training) are almost never sufficient to support development of necessary skills and knowledge. Almost always, other organizational factors are also missing or inadequate. Key stakeholders must take action to ensure that the other factors are provided.

Rummler and Brache (1995) present a useful model of the organizational factors affecting performance at the job performer level, which is shown (adapted) in Exhibit 6.1. The stakeholder responsible for ensuring that each factor is fully in place is also identified.

Exhibit 6.1. Factors Affecting Performance at the Job Performer Level, with Responsible Stakeholders.

Factor	Responsible Stakeholders
1. **Clear performance specifications** Standards for performance and output	
2. **Necessary support** Procedures, time, tools, information, recognized responsibility, and the like	Manager of Performers
3. **Appropriate consequences** Meaningful to performer, timely	
4. **Useful feedback** Relevant, timely, specific	
5. **Individual capacity** Physical, mental, emotional competence for the performance	
6. **Necessary skills and knowledge** Based on experience or learning	Manager of Performers and Learning Professional

Source: Adapted from Rummler and Brache, 1995.

Please note that the term *learning professional* is used here to denote the learning specialist (or performance improvement professional) who carries out one or more of the following tasks:

- Analyze performance requirements.
- Design an appropriate learning activity.
- Evaluate the learning activity.

(The more traditional term *trainer* is now often used for the one who delivers training, but who may not be involved in performance analysis, design, and evaluation.)

The *managers of performers* are fully responsible for five of the factors affecting performance: specifying the desired performance; providing necessary support, consequences, and feedback for the performance; and ensuring that those selected as performers have the necessary capabilities. *Learning professionals* are responsible for designing, developing, and evaluating appropriate learning activities. Thus they share responsibility for the sixth factor, provision of skills and knowledge, with the performers' managers, who must approve and fund the learning activities.

However, learning professionals are almost always the only stakeholders who recognize the critical importance of collaborative stakeholder actions to support performance. Therefore, they have an additional responsibility, to help other stakeholders understand their responsibilities and identify useful strategies to support the desired performance. Learning professionals must become *learning transfer managers* to ensure that the emphasis on transfer is shared and implemented by all stakeholders.

Learning transfer (LT) managers must help all stakeholders learn the six factors supporting performance (Exhibit 6.1), since all the factors are important and together they form the basis for all strategies to support transfer. The performers, their managers, learning professionals, and other stakeholders should be able to refer to these factors in discussions about, plans for, and assessments of improved performance.

In some situations, of course, performers already have necessary knowledge and skills but are prevented from performing effectively by lack of one or more other factors. Here too, stakeholder strategies must provide those factors, even when learning new knowledge or skills is not required.

The focus on achieving performance and the six factors necessary to support performance are essential to avoid the temptation to throw only *training* at any performance problem. When learning activities are necessary, we know learning has transferred when we see the desired new performance in the workplace. LT managers must include, as part of their management responsibilities, the education of stakeholders (managers, performers, coworkers, others) about the factors affecting performance, and the oversight and tracking of those stakeholders' transfer strategies (Broad, 2002).

A Model for Managing Learning Transfer

The comprehensive model for managing learning transfer (Figure 6.1) is integrated into the implementation steps of a learning project. It emphasizes stakeholder strategies to support full transfer of learned knowledge and skills to job performance (Broad & Newstrom, 1992).

Figure 6.1. A Model for Managing the Organizational Learning Transfer System.

Note: The LT Manager shares steps 2a through 6b with client and other stakeholders.

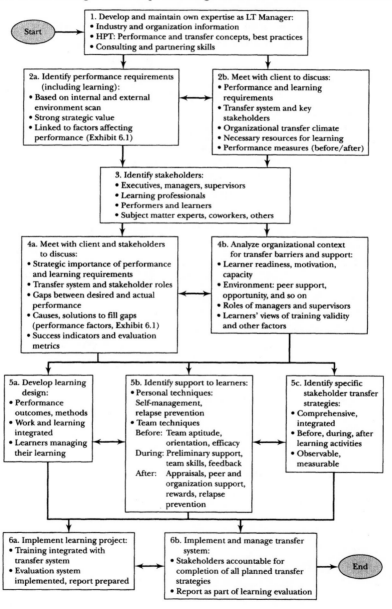

The model reflects the perspective and actions of the LT manager internal or external to the organization. (It does not go into detail on the performance analysis, design, development, delivery, and evaluation of learning projects, since many other resources are available on these topics.) Rarely can the model be applied exactly as shown, with a clear beginning and steady progress through the sequence of actions to the end. Information and insights may come to the LT manager and stakeholders at many points in no predictable order. Steps with the same number (such as 2a and 2b) may occur in reverse order in some situations. The model serves as a checklist for the LT manager to backtrack and fill in as events allow, to achieve the project's goals.

When managing support for learning transfer becomes part of the organization's way of doing business, there are no clear start or stop points for implementing the model. Stakeholder support becomes integrated into an organization-wide "transfer climate," consciously recognized and maintained as continual learning and transfer challenges evolve.

In the model, LT managers share responsibilities and actions in steps 2a through 6b with the client and other stakeholders as partners, to share information, analyses, and decisions. At all costs, the LT manager must avoid becoming a surrogate for managers in dealing with learners. Research indicates that managers and decision makers must demonstrate their own investment of time and effort in leading and monitoring the change effort, not delegating those responsibilities to others (Baldwin & Magjuka, 1991). Without visible involvement by managers, learners do not perceive the behavioral change as strategically important, so they are unlikely to change their performance.

Step 1. Develop LT Manager Expertise

The LT manager needs three main areas of expertise:

- Detailed information on the industry and the organization, including
    Major lines of business
    Market share and competition
    Regulatory and legislative climate
    Industry issues and trends

- Human performance technology (HPT) skills, with emphasis on performance and transfer concepts and best practices:
  Performance analysis, to identify *current performance* and compare it to *desired performance*
  Gap and cause analysis, to analyze the gap between current and desired performance and to identify *root causes* for the gap
  Intervention selection and design, to identify and design appropriate *learning interventions* to close the gap
  Transfer concepts and stakeholder roles, to identify effective *transfer strategies* by stakeholders
  Project implementation, to *manage* the entire learning intervention
  Evaluation, to determine the extent to which the intervention is *successful*
- Consulting and partnering skills:
  Networking
  Identifying and gaining clients
  Communication
  Consulting process

Even *beginning levels* of these areas of expertise can be helpful to organizational clients. Resources for developing these include reading, formal training and education, hands-on projects, and networking with colleagues.

Step 2a. Identify Performance Requirements (Including Learning)

Scanning the organization's external and internal environment helps the LT manager spot potential strategic performance and learning requirements early. Business and industry publications and contact with internal networks can uncover requirements for new or enhanced performance to reach strategic organizational goals. Stakeholders can help identify which factors affecting performance (Exhibit 6.1) may be present or missing, including learning. *Note:* steps 2a and 2b may occur in reverse order.

Step 2b. Meet with Client

Strategically important learning requirements (and other interventions) are discussed with potential clients.

The LT manager meets with a client who has a real stake in the strategic learning requirement. The client should own the business need for improved performance, and may have already identified specific performance requirements. The client should also be able to make decisions on interventions and evaluation methods (Robinson & Robinson, 1995).

When workforce learning is required, the LT manager emphasizes to the client that cohesive, collaborative support by all major stakeholders is essential to ensure learning, transfer of new skills to job performance, and desired organizational results. This discussion should include the following points:

- Performance and related learning requirements with strong strategic value
- Transfer process and key stakeholders
- Organizational transfer climate
- Necessary resources to support a learning and transfer project
- Measures of successful performance after learning, and baseline performance data before learning

Step 3. Identify Other Stakeholders

The LT manager and client identify other major stakeholders, within and outside the organization, who are concerned about strategic goals and performance required to achieve them. These stakeholders may include

- Executives, managers, and performers' supervisors
- Performance consultants and other learning professionals (including the LT manager)
- Performers who are potential learners
- Subject matter experts (SMEs) and performers' coworkers
- Internal or external suppliers and customers
- Other interested parties (for example, union representatives, quality control specialists)

Step 4a. Meet with Client and Other Stakeholders

The client and LT manager meet with all other major stakeholders to discuss the importance of transfer in accomplishing strategic goals. They cover the following points:

- Strategic importance of performance and learning requirements
- The transfer system and stakeholders' roles
- Gaps between desired and actual performance
- Causes and solutions to fill gaps (learning and/or other interventions, based on factors in Exhibit 6.1)
- Success indicators and evaluation metrics

Step 4b. Analyze Organizational Context for Transfer Barriers and Support

The LT manager and client explore the organizational context for the desired performance. Their goal is to use the insights gathered in step 4a to identify factors that may provide support or act as barriers to the transfer process:

- Learners' readiness, motivation, and capacity
- Organizational environment, including
  Peer support
  Opportunity to apply new skills
  Roles of managers and supervisors
  Trainees' views of training's validity and possible positive and
    negative outcomes

All analytical information is shared among LT manager, client, and stakeholders to gain agreement on the intervention and necessary transfer support. (These discussions and those of step 4a can interact, each enhancing and reinforcing the other.)

Step 5a. Develop Learning Design

Based on the preceding steps, the LT manager develops the learning design:

- Desired performance outcomes and learners' methods for achievement
- Real work incorporated into learning exercises and practice
- Learning activities integrated into the workplace
- Learners managing their learning

Step 5b. Identify Support to Learners

The LT manager and learner representatives identify useful learning transfer strategies before, during, and after learning activities. Strategies include personal techniques such as self-management and relapse prevention, plus a variety of team techniques that apply at different points in the process:

- Before: Assessments of team aptitude, orientation to transfer, efficacy in transfer
- During: Advance organizers, team skills training, feedback on training performance
- After: Performance appraisals, support from peers and organization, rewards, relapse prevention

Step 5c. Identify Specific Stakeholder Transfer Strategies

The LT manager helps each stakeholder identify strategies to support learning transfer before, during, and after learning activities. These are integrated with the learning design (5a) and other support for learners (5b), and give learners resources, opportunities for application, incentives, and rewards. The strategies

- Are comprehensive and integrated
- Occur before, during, and after learning activities
- Are observable and measurable

The Transfer Strategies Matrix (Exhibit 6.2) is a tool to list strategies by each major stakeholder, before, during, and after the learning activity. There often are several strategies in each cell, for a total of twenty or more strategies for a learning project. (For an example of a completed transfer matrix, see Exhibit 6.3 in the case study later in the chapter.) In a continual learning environment, these strategies become ongoing rather than timed as "before, during, or after" learning.

Step 6a. Implement Learning Project

The LT manager begins delivery of learning activities and implements the evaluation process.

Exhibit 6.2. Transfer Strategies Matrix.

Stakeholder	Before	During	After
Executive			
Manager			
Supervisor			
Learner			
Learning professional			
Other			
Other			

Source: Adapted from Broad, 1997.

- Training delivery is integrated with the transfer system (6b) including stakeholder strategies applied before, during, and after the program.
- Evaluation data are gathered and a report is prepared for all stakeholders, including descriptions of all transfer strategies and assessments of their effectiveness.

Step 6b. Implement and Manage Transfer System

The LT manager and stakeholders implement all planned transfer strategies (before, during, and after learning activities) and monitor their effectiveness.

- Stakeholders are accountable for completion of all planned transfer strategies.

- The LT manager prepares a report on use and effectiveness of transfer strategies that is included in the evaluation report (described in step 6a).

The final report, with evaluation data, becomes an effective marketing tool to demonstrate the effectiveness of collaborative stakeholder strategies to support transfer.

End

Completion of steps 6a and 6b can be considered the end of the learning transfer project. However, in an actual complex organizational system, improved performance in one area usually leads to requests for improved performance—and transfer support—in other areas.

Case Study: Leadership Development at GTE

GTE Service Corporation in Irving, Texas, was a leading telecommunications provider with one of the industry's broadest arrays of products and services. It merged with Bell Atlantic in 2000, forming Verizon Communications. GTE's 1999 revenues were $25.3 billion. In the United States, GTE provided local service in twenty-eight states and wireless service in eighteen states, as well as nationwide long distance, directory, and internetworking services for residential, business, and Fortune 500 companies. The company also served customers on five continents.

Keegan Calhoun was GTE's Impact and Outcomes Measurement Manager before and after the merger. She has a strong performance orientation from graduate work and previous positions as performance consultant, instructional designer and trainer, and manager. GTE created her position in spring 1998 to build a new measurement process in the Pricing and Performance Group of Workforce Development, as part of a top-level Human Resources initiative to become more measurement and performance oriented.

Calhoun's contributions to a strong measurement system included

- An "HR scorecard" showing outcomes and value for HR contributions to the organization
- Measurement tools: formative and summative evaluation and "internal health diagnostics" (organizational and individual growth, financial accomplishments, customer satisfaction, and processes)
- A performance-oriented approach to new project development and current project maintenance that relies on stakeholder involvement, use of well-planned transfer strategies, and a strong evaluation focus

Leadership Development Series

The first major project for application of the new performance and measurement focus was GTE's Leadership Development Series. This program was originally designed as an educational experience for all of GTE's approximately thirty thousand managers. This included all managers and senior-level individual contributors from every business unit in the corporation, with mandated attendance.

The program was developed to meet new corporate challenges: transforming the fundamentals of GTE's business—new products, technologies, markets and customers, business economics, and knowledge and skill requirements for all hundred thousand employees. An extensive needs analysis process in 1997 defined core competencies and content. Deployment of classroom experiences, and support for continuous learning through technological tools on an intranet platform, began in the second quarter of 1998.

To measure accomplishments from pilot deployments and to structure performance-focused revisions, Calhoun partnered with Boston-based Productivity Dynamics. Results of the evaluation indicated limited transfer of learning, and supported the shift to a strong performance focus to improve the program's organizational impact.

The LD series was refocused. Through collaborative efforts of GTE internal stakeholders, the educational experiences became an organization-wide strategic management tool. The redesigned program, beginning in 1999 and continuing in the merged company, is a continuous learning and performance support system. Participants focus on business priorities and develop action plans to execute business strategies. All business units use the series to further specific business objectives, resolve issues, and build vital links across units and functions. The redesign's high quality and its strategic impact on GTE were recognized by the American Society for Training and Development's Excellence in Practice Award (spring 2000).

Learning activities are vertically integrated, with managers at each level sponsoring sessions at the next lower level. Each session is preceded by a robust assessment of strategic business priorities for the sponsoring organizations. Then business priorities and issues are worked at successive levels to develop and implement operational plans to resolve issues. Top-level sessions are conducted to communicate themes, challenges, and opportunities revealed in lower-level sessions.

Learners use online enrollment and the online Continuous Learning System (CLS), which provides brief articles and required pretraining preparation. Issues identified in these tools are available to each session's faculty for incorporation into class activities.

Classroom experiences range from two to four days. Common tools—building action agendas, developing support coalitions, and After Action Reviews to systematically learn from experience—are emphasized. A Learning Lab presents a real case based on the organization and business units, with actual regulatory, legal, and financial constraints and competitive environment built in.

The postclass process includes online faculty follow-up and consultation to support learners' progress on action agendas. Participants are encouraged to share results of action agendas and lessons learned on the online Center for Lessons Learned, an inventory of both success and failure stories from all business units.

The LD program is aligned with earlier GTE initiatives such as GTE core competencies (leadership, critical thinking, market focus, and continuous improvement) and the Front-Line Core program for hourly (union) employees.

Stakeholders and Strategies

A number of major stakeholders participated in LD revisions, providing critically important support for redesign and continuous improvement:

• *Business Unit Presidents and Senior Leaders* approve the program, provide funding, and review outcomes.
• *The Leadership Development Practice Leader* manages LD implementation and works closely with all stakeholders.
• *The Leadership Development Steering Committee,* made up of representatives of business unit presidents and senior leaders, serves as an advisory board.
• *Vendor Partners (Leadership Development Inc. and Executive Perspectives)* manage design and delivery of mid, higher, and top-level sessions.
• *Learners* include managers at all organizational levels.
• *Impact and Outcomes Measurement Manager (Keegan Calhoun)* measures outcomes and consults on effective instructional design for all LD interventions.
• *Director of Leadership Development and the Program Managers* oversee delivery of lower and mid-level sessions, and revisions based on evaluation data.
• *Leadership Development Faculty,* vendor facilitators, deliver higher and top-level sessions.
• *Training Administration* handles registration and logistics.

A summary of these stakeholder's transfer strategy contributions is shown in the completed transfer matrix, Exhibit 6.3.

Exhibit 6.3. Integrated Transfer Strategies for LD Series.

Stakeholders	Before	During	After
Business Unit Presidents and Senior Leaders	• Approve sessions, provide funding • Schedule sessions with LD Practice Leader • Participate in preparation for higher-level sessions	• Actively participate in higher-level sessions • Support sessions their managers attend • Ensure alignment of higher-level planning, mid-level operationalizing, and lower-level execution planning	• Ensure that business planning and objectives in higher, mid, and lower sessions are followed up • Work with LD Practice Leader to track successes and areas where additional interventions are necessary
Leadership Development Practice Leader	• Works with BU Presidents and Senior Leaders to coordinate sessions • Ensures all arrangements are made through Training Administration • Attends analysis sessions of senior leadership • Ensures funding transfers from business units	• Attends higher-level LD sessions • Works with Vendor Partners to ensure linkage with identified business needs • Ensures sessions run seamlessly	• Works with vendors and BU Presidents and Senior Leaders to ensure integration and implementation of action planning, objective setting, and strategies • Partners with Impact and Outcomes Measurement Manager to communicate evaluation data to stakeholders and business units
Leadership Development Steering Committee	• Oversee full series of LD sessions • Oversee ongoing process improvements and communications with stakeholders		• Assess feedback from Impact and Outcomes Measurements Manager on evaluation data • Take action based on feedback and recommendations • Ensure that business units are satisfied with session outcomes

Exhibit 6.3. Integrated Transfer Strategies for LD Series, Cont'd.

Stakeholders	Before	During	After
Vendor Partners: Leadership Development, Inc. (Boston) and Executive Perspectives (Boston)	• Provide expertise to design and develop the LD series interventions • Work with LD Practice Leader to coordinate sessions with BU Presidents and Senior Leaders • Participate in gathering relevant business data for sessions	• Facilitate or teach higher- and top-level sessions • Ensure relevant business issues and necessary SKAs are linked to session • Deliver feedback to learners on group activities and Learning Lab • Ensure that lecture, group activities, and Learning Lab are part of learning experience • Administer Level 1 and 2 instruments	• Give reinforcement and support to managers • Capture successes, enter into knowledge database (Center for Lessons Learned) • Incorporate lessons learned from After Action Review process (AAR) and evaluation data (Level 1, 2, 3, and 4) to continually improve sessions
Learners	• Enroll in LD sessions and access Continuous Learning System (CLS pre-work: assessments, competitor articles, objective setting worksheet to complete with managers)	• Bring pre-course work to discuss during session • Actively participate in lecture, group activities, and Learning Lab simulation • Complete Level 1 and Level 2 instruments	• Request necessary support and resources from senior management for effective execution of action plans • Transfer and practice SKAs taught in session within one week back on job • Provide timely feedback to faculty and group members on progress
Impact and Outcomes Measurement Manager	• Ensures funding availability for evaluation • Ensures that Level 1 and 2 instruments are ready for use • Ensures that recommendations for improvement are incorporated into sessions • Procures Productivity Dynamics to assist with evaluation process	• Works with LD Practice Leader and Training Administration to ensure administration and collection of evaluation instruments • Partners with Practice Leader to evaluate LD Series as needed	• Actively collects, analyzes, and reports data quarterly to Steering Committee • Works with Practice Leader to ensure evaluation recommendations are integrated into process improvements

Role	Responsibilities
Director of Leadership Development and Program Managers	• Ensure Vendor Partner management of LD Series • Work closely with Practice Leader to integrate business needs, issues, opportunities into curriculum • Attend LD Series • Ensure that LD Series runs seamlessly • Ensure that vendor incorporates feedback and evaluation recommendations into sessions • Work with Steering Committee and LD Faculty to ensure process improvements
Leadership Development Faculty	• Actively engage Leadership to participate in LD sessions • Gather data from Practice Leader and Vendor Partners to incorporate into curriculum • Facilitate or teach lower and mid-level sessions • Ensure all relevant business issues and necessary SKAs are linked to sessions • Deliver feedback to learners on group activities, Learning Lab • Ensure that lecture, group activities, Learning Lab are part of learning experience • Administer Level 1 and Level 2 instruments • Give reinforcement and support to managers after training • Capture successes, enter into knowledge database (Center for Lessons Learned) • Incorporate lessons learned from After Action Review process (AAR) and evaluation data (Levels 1, 2, 3 and 4) to continually improve sessions • Work with managers to ensure effective environment for transfer
Training Administration	• Notifies learner to enroll and complete preliminary work • Arranges locations, logistics, delivery of materials and equipment to training location • Ensures that Level 1 and 2 instruments are provided to faculty • Ensures all materials and equipment are received and ready for learning session • Tabulates Level 1 and 2 data, provides reports to key stakeholders and Impact and Outcomes Measurements Manager

Evaluation Results

Two phases of evaluation data have been collected to assess effectiveness of LD revisions. Phase 1 post-training interviews focused on participants in sessions before 1998 revisions. Phase 2 interviews were conducted with a stratified random sample of participants in postrevision sessions.

Level 1 participant reactions, before and after revisions, rated those programs as excellent or good, and as providing a good return on investment.

For Level 2, participants rated themselves on accomplishment of learning objectives (gaining skills and knowledge). Participants prior to revision gave positive qualitative information but no hard data. Participants in mid-level sessions after revisions agreed or strongly agreed that they had accomplished at least 85 percent of the learning objectives. Participants in higher-level sessions after revisions agreed or strongly agreed that they had accomplished all learning objectives.

For Level 3, skill and knowledge transfer to performance, significantly higher percentages of participants after revision indicated that they had taken planned actions (see Table 6.1).

For Level 4, organizational impact, many participants have observed qualitative business impacts from the LD series (for example, improvement in the work environment, teamwork, and employee participation and morale). Due to good Level 3 results, the organization won't invest in complete Level 4 evaluation in terms of revenue, costs, and customer satisfaction ratings. However, some interviewees have reported tangible quantitative impact (actual and estimated); several instances are summarized in Table 6.2.

Table 6.1. Level 3 Evaluation.

In this course . . .	This percentage of respondents took action:	
	Before revision	**After revision**
LD III (higher level)	87 percent	95 percent
LD II (mid level)	58 percent	84 percent
LD I (lower level)	15 percent	Data not available

Note: Percentage of responding participants who took planned actions before and after revisions to LD I, II, and III.

Table 6.2. Examples of Level 4
Quantitative Business Impact of LD Series.

Program	Case	Quantitative Impact (Actual and Estimated)
LD III (Higher level)	1	• Improvement of 10–15 points in customer service indexes, calculated monthly. • Sales increase of 23.7 percent over preceding year(about $2.5 million). Sales manager is convinced that LD experience was a major factor.
	2	• Improvement of 12 points in wholesale index (tied to productivity measures such as rework, completing work on time). Equivalent to increased revenue of over $132,000 and cost savings of more than $6,000 per year.
	3	• Tangible improvement (5–10 percent increase) in customer satisfaction index. • Reorganization decision estimated to save several millions of dollars in long run.
	4	• Reduction of defects per million due to operational improvements ($2 million savings).
	5	• Gains of 7.5 and 3.5 points in customer satisfaction indexes in first four months of 1999.
	6	• Efficiency improvements estimated to lead to 20 percent cost avoidance over long run, equivalent to several millions of dollars for all group projects.
	7	• Maintenance of group's excellent customer satisfaction indexes.
LD II (Mid level)	8	• Estimated potential cost savings of $3 million annually.
	9	• Estimated cost savings of $240,000 in one project.
	10	• Increase of 15–20 percent in sales, equivalent to $120,000 increased revenue for one sales manager in two-month period.
LD I (Lower level)	11	• Estimated 10 percent increase in sales, equivalent to $2.4 million in annual revenue.

Summary

As the GTE Leadership Development Series redesign and continuous improvement process illustrates, efforts to bring about significant changes in behavior through training may involve many organizational stakeholders. Gaining involvement of key stakeholders is not easy, and persuading them to spend time and effort in transfer strategies can be daunting. The primary leverage for the learning specialist (or performance consultant) is the growing body of research and good practice showing successful results from stakeholder involvement in transfer.

This model of managing a learning transfer project is based on transfer research and experiences of many practitioners in organizations worldwide. The LT manager for the GTE case, Keegan Calhoun, helped shape the model to reflect her experience. Comments and feedback are requested from all readers, to help continue the model's evolution and increase its applicability to emerging and unforeseen transfer challenges and opportunities in all settings. (Contact Mary Broad at marybroad@earthlink.net.)

References

Baldwin, T. T., & Magjuka, R. J. (1991). Organizational training and signals of importance: Linking pretraining perceptions to intentions to transfer. *Human Resource Development Quarterly, 2*(1), 25–36.

Broad, M. L. (2002). The research is in: Stakeholder involvement is critical. In G. M. Piskurich (Ed.), *HPI essentials: A just-the-facts, bottom-line primer on human performance improvement* (pp. 133–151). Alexandria, VA: ASTD.

Broad, M. L., Ed. (1997). *In action: Transferring learning to the workplace.* Alexandria, VA: American Society for Training and Development.

Broad, M. L., & Newstrom, J. W. (1992). Transfer of training: Action-packed strategies to ensure high payoff from training investments. Reading, MA: Addison-Wesley.

Robinson, D. G., & Robinson, J. C. (1995). *Performance consulting: Moving beyond training.* San Francisco: Berrett-Koehler.

Rummler, G. A., & Brache, A. P. (1995). *Improving performance: How to manage the white space on the organization chart* (2nd ed.). San Francisco: Jossey-Bass.

PART THREE

From Knowledge to Performance Capability

CHAPTER 7

Transfer Is Just a Symptom
The Neglect of Front-End Analysis
Richard A. Swanson

This chapter challenges training practitioners and scholars to think more holistically about the organizational performance require- ments and performance requirements that create the demands for training. Training processes committed to understanding the work system and its performance requirements as the basis for perfor- mance improvement interventions will almost automatically ensure training transfer. Training transfer problems are largely system prob- lems, not psychological problems. Thus, up-front analysis or orga- nizational diagnosis is the practitioner's best tool for determining the system components and barriers required for achieving perfor- mance (and training transfer). The data from the up-front analysis phase easily and logically cascades through the remaining training phases without requiring anyone to obsess about training transfer.

When I think of transfer of training, I think of the "building an air- plane in flight" metaphor. To me this has always conjured up a pic- ture of unsystematic and harried action, trying to make something that should already have been taken care of happen before it is too late. That is exactly how I view most of the transfer of training lit- erature: it's worrying about something that should have been taken care of already—something that should have been understood and easily built into the system at the beginning. Transfer of training is not the problem. Improving the performance of the host system is the problem. Holistic and intelligent pursuit of system-level performance improvement dismisses transfer of training as a discrete realm of concern.

I am sure that those fascinated by training transfer would argue just the opposite—that they are being thoughtful and proactive in thinking about and planning for training transfer. I will try to dissect these conflicting views as the chapter unfolds.

The general problem-defining and problem-solving method that Human Resource Development (HRD) follows includes variations on the following five phases: *Analyze* → *Propose* → *Create* → *Implement* → *Assess*. The training arm of HRD typically uses its own five-phase version: *Analyze* → *Design* → *Develop* → *Implement* → *Evaluate* (Swanson & Holton, 2001). For me, everything critical that you need to know about transfer in a particular situation is learned in the analyze phase (performance diagnosis and documentation of workplace expertise) and everything important you need to know about the transfer results is learned in the evaluation or assessment phase. The middle phases are standard "best training practices."

It is important to recognize that most of the transfer of training research addresses subtleties of the training design, develop, and implement middle phases without serious consideration of the performance requirements in light of the mission-related goods or services produced by the host organizational system. When conceptual models of transfer of training finally do reach for performance, they are usually done in context of the individual worker—with little reference to the work group, work processes, or organization performance requirements.

Purpose

The purpose of this chapter is to report on the performance perspective within HRD (including personnel training and development and organization development) and how this approach views the topic of transfer of training. This approach to training is rooted in performance requirements, organizational diagnosis, systematic implementation, and results assessment through processes that automatically embrace the phenomena of transfer of training.

The following two examples serve as an advanced organizer for this chapter. The first illustrates the topic that ignites most discussions and inquiry about transfer of training, while the second shows how the performance approach marginalizes the concern and need for inquiry about transfer of training.

Typical Training Case Giving Rise to the Concern About Transfer of Training

1. Company sales have declined and are not as high as they should be.
2. The sales training manager meets with sales executives and managers.
3. They agree that salespeople need better communication skills to be effective representatives.
4. The sales training manager searches around for good training options and discovers a highly recommended consultant-trainer.
5. The consultant-trainer accepts a contract to deliver a program with some customization.
6. The consultant-trainer obtains company information and cases to make the sales communication training program connect better with the client company.
7. The consultant-trainer delivers the program for two years to hundreds of salespeople.
8. The trainees (sales personnel) rate the program highly.
9. Company sales continue flat, or even decline.

Typical Performance Improvement Case Using Training as a Key Element in Improving Performance

1. Company sales have declined and are not as high as they should be.
2. The sales performance consulting and training (SPC&T) people met with sales executives and managers and agree that the present training is of questionable value.
3. The SPC&T team gains permission to do a thorough performance diagnosis including such things as:
   Interview key stakeholders.
   Visit regional sales offices.
   Review the sales records.

Observe expert and below-average sales managers and sales-people in action with customers.

Interview new and lost customers.

4. SPC&T present management with a performance improve-ment proposal that
   • Involves several components, including a highly targeted performance-based training on sales communication.
   • Uses sales managers as trainers and evaluators of partici-pant expertise.
   • Revises the performance appraisal system so managers rate salespeople on demonstrated expertise developed in train-ing with customers.
   • Applies an on-the-job work-reporting and performance appraisal method that parallels the work process taught in the training.
5. After implementation, performance reporting follows up on sales won and lost, and on sales managers and sales personnel recognized and rewarded.
6. The company sees continuous improvement in sales.

One of the lessons to be learned when a training researcher or trainer makes the shift to the performance approach is to think more critically about the dependent variable. The dependent variable is *performance*—the mission-related outputs of the organization in the form of goods or services produced and their financial worth (Swanson, 2001). The minute that the trainer or researcher takes on the performance perspective, the whole thought process becomes that of an organizational stakeholder or organizational systems expert. In contrast, the transfer of training perspective has *learning* (knowledge and expertise) as the dependent variable and a follow-up scramble to ensure that it transfers somehow and some-where. The performance perspective creates rational performance goals and the matrix of connections of variables and levels within the organization needed to ensure the appropriate actions and performance (see Swanson, 1996). The performance perspective acknowledges that training will almost always be used as a part of a larger change or improvement effort. Also acknowledged is the fact that performance in many situations can be obtained with or without purposeful training or learning experiences.

Performance, With or Without Training

Training that is intelligently and systemically called upon for the purpose of improving performance is not overtly concerned about transfer. In contrast, training called upon simply for the purpose of learning will always need to answer the transfer question as a way of making up for the organizational disconnect inherent in its origins.

In pursuit of performance, the organizational rivals to training are numerous. New technology, outsourcing, reengineering, and incentives are a few. Thus anything as vague as a "learning organization" will ultimately be challenged by the ongoing performance requirements of the host organization. An organization assesses its success by vision and mission components connected to the goods and services it provides to customers. Organizations rarely assess ultimate success on how they get to performance. Such values and process statements—the organization's means to its ends—make for unique organizational cultures and good marketing slogans but inadequate scorecards:

- The company that listens.
- The learning organization.
- Low prices, always!
- Quality is job #1.

For example, does 3M regularly rely on enhanced learning among its workforce to assist in meeting its performance goals? *Yes.* Thus, is 3M a learning organization? *Probably.* Is 3M a Six Sigma corporation? *Probably.* Is 3M a Minnesota-headquartered company? *Yes.* Is 3M a multinational corporation? *Yes.* These features of 3M (and others) can all be considered rivals or roadblocks to performance. The closer any phenomenon or process is to the core processes of an organization, the more it will have a chance to impact end results.

And although there is a great deal of interest in the idea of performance drivers (Kaplan & Norton, 1996), the word *performance* and the focus on performance come before attention is given to the performance drivers. Organizational decision makers must first tend to the business and its organizational performance requirements before talking about the drivers of performance. In contrast, the transfer of learning and training literature reveals attention to learning first and foremost, followed by a concern about transfer and possible performance.

People who study organizations and work in organizations make things happen through understanding the system and building what they want into the system. Up to now, and by its own language, transfer of training has positioned learning apart from the core mission and goal of the organization and its requirement to perform. In contrast, performance-focused training requires analysis of the host organization, an understanding of what it is all about and what it requires to survive and improve. When transfer of training experts do struggle with the idea of performance, they typically cannot get beyond the idea of job-level performance. Much can be said about just this point, but the fact remains that individual workers can perform very well with poor-performing work processes and in poor-performing companies. Performance is much more than individual performance. Deming, the quality expert, noted that 90 percent of the performance problems in the workplace were a result of working in bad systems (1986). He got to this fact by taking on the performance perspective while having great empathy for the well-intentioned worker.

Transfer: We Had It Right and Then Lost It

The trauma of the First and Second World Wars, and the rise of the American labor movement during these periods, provided ample opportunity for training and its leaders to emerge and become central in America's development. I contend that the understanding of core ingredients required for performance-based training (and transfer of training) were understood and implemented during World War II in the United States. I further contend that the postwar influences of psychology and education on organizational training have been instrumental in getting the profession to lose its focus and understanding of the organization.

Channing R. Dooley made profound contributions to the practice and professionalization of personnel training and the fundamental expansion of the field into the contemporary HRD profession (2001 [1945]). Dooley's pioneering contributions, through his oversight of the massive Training Within Industry (TWI) Project during World War II, established the core foci of contemporary

HRD theory and practice. Almost two million TWI certifications of learning and expertise were awarded to supervisors, managers, and senior managers across sixteen thousand production plants. Given the cascade design of this nationwide effort, one might speculate that at least several millions more actually benefited from the nationwide effort. TWI is known for simple and elegant systems for helping individuals and organizations develop and perform.

Ruona (2001) used the following clever introduction to paint the picture of when we understood training as making a fundamental performance difference to the sponsoring organization. She started her article with a job announcement: "Someone actually answered the following call, would you?"

> Independent contractor needed to establish a fully functional and minimally staffed national not-for-profit agency; will benchmark the best of America's companies, and work with them to garner active support for all agency work; will develop and administer training programs to train up to 6000 people per week in varied skills critical to our national safety and prosperity; will assist corporations in hiring and training of supervisors, and in troubleshooting of production problems. Current employer must be willing to financially sponsor your work and applicant must be willing to relocate" [p. 119].

Clearly, the TWI leadership understood that even in the training function, you had to be a businessperson first.

We Found It: World War II

Dooley (2001 [1945]) and his leadership used their World War I experiences to fundamentally shape the history of training when, preceding and during World War II, the War Manpower Commission established the TWI Service.

Training had begun to wane during the Depression years of the 1930s when companies' budgets were tightened. Industrial education was primarily focused on developing skills in the unemployed to improve their personal welfare. Suddenly, World War II demanded fast mobilization of resources and soaring wartime production. Although World War II found many people willing to work after the distress of the Depression, there was once again a significant need for training. TWI's objectives were to help contractors produce efficiently with lower costs and higher quality. Dooley (2001

[1945]) wrote in his retrospective of the wartime effort that TWI "is known for the results of its programs—Job Instruction, Job Methods, Job Relations, and Program Development—which have, we believe, permanently become part of American industrial operations as accepted tools of management" (p. xi).

Indeed, TWI is known for its simple and elegant way of training incredible numbers of people. Each program had a system to support it: limited steps, key words, subpoints, documentation and work methods, and supporting training so as to obtain certification (Torraco & Swanson, 1995). Four programs fostered three key contemporary elements of HRD.

TWI and Performance

The philosophy undergirding the TWI Service was a clear distinction between education and training. Dooley (2001 [1945]) stated, "Education is for rounding-out of the individual and the good of society; it is general, provides background, and increases understanding. Training is for the good of plant production—it is a way to solve production problems through people; it is specific and helps people to acquire skill through the use of what they learned" (p. 17).

The programs of TWI were closely linked to organizational performance. TWI "started with performance at the organizational and process levels and ended with performance at the same levels" (Torraco & Swanson, 1995). The primary measure of success was whether a TWI program helped production, efficiency, and cost-effectiveness.

The Job Instruction Training Program was created for first- and second-line supervisors who would train most employees. The focus of the program was to teach supervisors how to break down jobs into steps and how to instruct using a derivative of the four-step process introduced during World War I. Another program, the Job Safety Program, was implemented to address the crucial need for employees to be safe in the new, unfamiliar industrial environment.

TWI and Quality

TWI also pioneered when it addressed quality issues impeding performance. Two programs are notable. First, the Job Methods Training Program provided a specific method for teaching employees how to address production and quality problems constructively. It encouraged employees to question details of job breakdowns and develop and apply new methods that work better.

Second, TWI partnered with General Motors in 1942 to create the Program Development Method (Swanson & Torraco, 1995, p. 33). This program introduced a four-step process designed to teach employees how to address quality problems and implement improvements:

1. Spot a production problem.
2. Develop a specific plan.
3. Get the plan into action.
4. Check results.

This 1942 method is strikingly similar to the "Plan-Do-Study-Check-Act Cycle" that Deming (1986) brought to the forefront in Japan during the 1950s and in America some thirty years later. These core quality principles introduced by TWI still provide a basis from which many in HRD implement their analyses of work.

TWI and Human Relations

The TWI Service was also one of the first to address human relations issues as important aspects of production success. The Job Relations Training Program trained supervisors in ways to establish good relations with their employees. Job relations training laid important groundwork for the burgeoning of organization development in companies during the 1950s. Clearly, the TWI effort quickly went beyond training and is seen by many as the origin of contemporary HRD as well as a springboard for the human relations perspective of the organization development component of HRD.

Ruona (2001) summarizes the overarching principles that emerged through TWI:

1. Training is a strategic tool to solve production problems and improve organizational performance.
2. Training should produce results and be evaluated accordingly.
3. Training professionals must be business partners and talk the language of business.
4. Employees should be ensured the opportunity to learn their jobs, be treated well, and be rewarded for a job done well [pp. 122–123].

At an operations level, Ruona (2001) summarizes the principles of practice that emerged through TWI:

1. The entire organization should be mobilized and equipped to train and address production and quality problems.
2. Supervisors are the central conduits for training, coaching, and employee performance.
3. Analysis of tasks, work processes, and their "key points" ensures efficiency and effectiveness of training and the operation of the whole.
4. Training should be structured to include ample opportunity for demonstration, intensive individual practice, and feedback.
5. Change one condition and the whole system is affected.
6. Management is ultimately responsible for maximizing the full impact of the training [pp. 124–125].

We Lost It: Post–World War II

The clarity of times surrounding World War II allowed for priorities in principles and practices. The TWI effort is one vivid example. After the war it was a relatively easy and prosperous time in the United States. Strong systems remained intact and took years before they eroded. The most vivid example is the production of U.S. goods. We taught our good systems to other nations, let our own systems erode, and then found that our students became our teachers. In training we had found the performance perspective during World War II and after the war it eroded into a learning perspective. We saw it in goods produced and we saw it in ideas about people in the workplace. Drucker (1986) noted how the human relations movement "freed management from the domination of viciously wrong ideas; but it did not succeed in substituting new concepts" (p. 278). Things do not always get better.

Another national development in the United States following World War II was the establishment of its first-ever standing military. The training system of this new enterprise had minimal interest in the economic performance agenda that was so essential to TWI. During this postwar period the instructional system development model (ISD), primarily driven from the psychological domain, gained support from the military. People falsely assumed that the ISD view of the world was consciously and systemically connected to organizational performance. It was not. It was focused on individuals and learning. ISD military training was massive military training of eighteen-year-old males on highly standardized tasks. There it worked.

The ISD model of training was widely adopted in business and industry as the memory of TWI faded. And when the larger performance infrastructure of business and industry weakened, the postwar ISD model of training became less and less viable in terms of truly identifying and solving core performance problems. This psychology-learning perspective of learning in organizations continues to this day. I contend that the tizzy about transfer is a futile effort to gain what has been lost—the performance perspective.

Individual Stuff Matters, but Organizational Stuff Really Matters

The transfer of training focus has largely been on the internal elements of the training process, and at most, views training as a process that needs to be connected to the larger system at some point for the training of individuals to transfer. In this micro view, the organization is accessed through the perspective of the individual worker and the training process. This is fundamentally different from the larger organization perspective of being focused on performance goals and the system designed to achieve those goals. The organization performance view strategically calls upon training as one means of achieving performance goals.

The transfer view of training starts with training commitments already made (based on minimal analysis) and then concerns itself with the transfer of the training by individual workers to the workplace and the organization. The performance view starts with the organization and its performance requirements and moves on to the use of a performance improvement strategy that might call upon training as part of the intervention. The cases presented earlier in this chapter illustrate these transfer and performance perspectives.

Beyond Psychology and Beyond the Individual

It is quite difficult to deal effectively with transfer of training in organizations from just a psychological lens. Even so, such efforts continue. One of the great shortcomings of personnel training and development is its overreliance on psychological theory (Holton, 2001).

The most widely accepted theoretical foundations of the HRD discipline include and integrate appropriate psychological, economic, and system theories for the purposes of framing and guiding the discipline (Swanson, 2001; Passmore, 1997). Yet organizational psychologists and corporate trainers resist the application of economic and system theories in their work. The propensity of the psychology-only basis for HRD and training yields unlimited subtheories with little evidence of fundamental organizational results. Trainers and industrial psychologists are limited when they simply study people and not the organizations in which they function. Their attention to and understanding of the core of their host organization is generally limited, at best. To function intelligently and strategically in organizations you must also study the organization—the system and the economics of the organization.

Passmore (1997) portrays the discipline of psychology as a "teenager's closet." Pushing too much of that stuff from the closet into the theory and practices of HRD (personnel training and development, and organization development) does not help. It dilutes the holistic theory, models, and practices that will more effectively achieve the goals of the host organization and the people who work in it.

Organizational Performance Perspective of Training Transfer

I contend that the training for performance perspective I am advocating subsumes the construct of training transfer. Table 7.1 further describes the problem from a performance perspective. This grid maps the idea of "required organizational performance" against the idea of "knowledge and expertise required to improve performance" and shows what happens in three varying states for each of the two main ideas: well-defined, ill-defined, and totally unknown.

Call to Action

As noted earlier, the performance approach to personnel training and development is rooted in performance requirements, organizational diagnosis, systematic implementation, and results assessment

Table 7.1. Training Transfer from an Organizational Performance Perspective.

Required Organizational Performance	Knowledge and Expertise Required to Improve Performance		
	Well-Defined	**Ill-Defined**	**Totally Unknown**
Well-Defined	All the ingredients for ensuring performance and transfer are in place.	Need to further document expertise required of workers.	N/A (This can't happen if you have a solid organizational performance diagnosis.)
Ill-Defined	Basis exists for well-defined training content that may or may not be needed. Improve the organizational performance diagnosis to include all elements of the performance improvement intervention.	Improve the organizational performance diagnosis. Then further document expertise if training is still needed.	Improve the organizational performance diagnosis. Then fully document expertise if training is still needed.
Totally Unknown	Basis exists for well-defined training content that is not needed. Do a high-quality organizational performance diagnosis to see if training is needed.	Do a high-quality organizational diagnosis and determine if training is even needed. If yes, improve the documentation of expertise.	Don't waste time thinking about transfer of training.

through processes that automatically embrace the phenomena of transfer of training. What follows is a prescription for embracing this approach:

1. Adopt a definition of training that conceptualizes T&D as a process (versus a department, function, or activity) and connects T&D to performance results. For example, use a statement along the following lines: "Personnel training and development is a process of developing knowledge and expertise in personnel for the purpose of improving performance at the individual, work group, work process, and organizational levels."

2. Adopt a systems worldview of the T&D process within the larger organizational and contextual setting. For example, consider implementing the view illustrated in Figure 7.1.

3. Develop expertise in performance diagnosis that will lead to holistic performance improvement interventions (including training). For example, consider adopting the diagnostic process outlined in Figure 7.2. Table 7.2 sets out the basic questions for each variable at each level.

4. Develop expertise in documenting workplace expertise. For example, see the process sketched in Figure 7.3.

Figure 7.1. HRD in Context of the Organization and Environment.

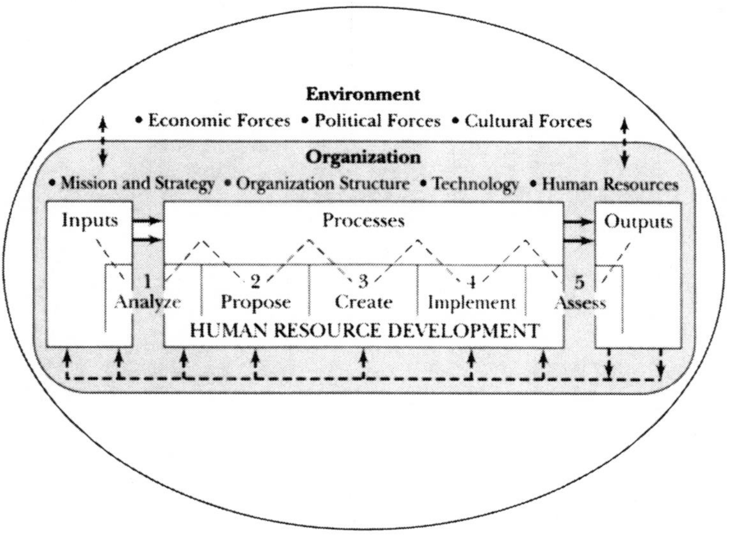

Figure 7.2. Performance Diagnosis Process.

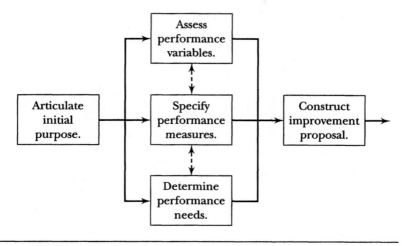

Figure 7.3. Documenting Expertise.

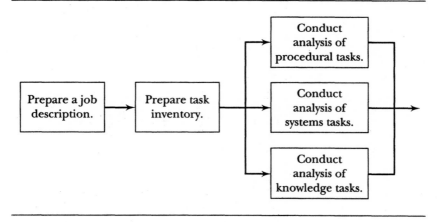

Table 7.2. Performance Diagnosis Matrix.

Performance Variables	Performance Levels		
	Organization Level	Process Level	Individual Level
Mission and Goal	Does the organization's mission and goal fit the reality of the economic, political, and cultural forces?	Do the process goals enable the organization to meet organization and individual missions and goals?	Are the professional and personal mission and goals of individuals congruent with the organization's?
System Design	Does the organization system provide structure and policies supporting the desired performance?	Are processes designed in a way to work as a system?	Does the individual face obstacles that impede job performance?
Capacity	Does the organization have the leadership, capital, and infrastructure to achieve its mission and goals?	Does the process have the capacity to perform (quantity, quality, and timeliness)?	Does the individual have the mental, physical, and emotional capacity to perform?
Motivation	Do the policies, culture, and reward systems support the desired performance?	Does the process provide the information and human factors required to maintain it?	Does the individual want to perform no matter what?
Expertise	Does the organization establish and maintain selection and training policies and resources?	Does the process of developing expertise meet the changing demands of changing processes?	Does the individual have the knowledge, skills, and experience to perform?

5. Maintain high standards in the realms of T&D design, development, and implementation. Standard practices of program and lesson design, the structuring and pilot testing of training materials, and the implementation issues of program management and delivery are simply expected.

6. Develop expertise in assessing performance results of interventions. For example, *system results* can be defined as "units of mission-related outputs in the form of goods or services having value to the customer and outputs that are related to the core organizational work processes, group, and individual contributors in the organization." *Financial results* can then be assessed by converting the worth of the units of outputs in goods and services into money (see Swanson & Holton, 1999; Swanson, 2001).

7. Be totally realistic about the nature of learning in the workplace. Only a portion of the actual workplace learning is consciously taking place to achieve organizational goals, only a portion is systemic or systematic, and only a portion is structured and formal. Many training and learning endeavors do not represent much of an investment and thus do not deserve Cadillac treatment. Any investment in improving such loose practices would be better served by assessing results rather than in tweaking the transfer variables. For example, low-investment training options may in fact be culminating in performance results that well exceed the costs. The recently developed and validated Critical Outcome Technique (Mattson, 2000) is ideal for this inquiry. (See Figure 7.4.)

The Critical Outcome Technique was inspired by Flanagan's (1954) famous Critical Incident Technique, but with a focus on performance outcomes. The new techniques have the ability to—after the fact—identify, verify, and monetize performance outcomes from ill-defined interventions.

Figure 7.4. Critical Outcome Technique Model.

Conclusion

When new learning must be applied in a work setting to achieve desired performances, something like training transfer is happening. Even so, I remain critical of the relative amount of time and effort spent on the topic of transfer of training versus focusing on training within a performance improvement framework.

As Dorner writes in *The Logic of Failure*, "We don't think about problems we don't have" (1996, p. 189). If a professional trainer or manager has to choose up sides as to where to place a big bet—on understanding the work system and its performance requirements or on understanding the workers and how to connect their effort to an ill-defined system—I heartily recommend the former, studying the system and its performance requirements. I am confident that everything fundamental for ensuring performance (and transfer) will reveal itself through a thorough up-front analysis.

I expect that in almost all instances, the transfer that organizations and scholars care about requires more than a training perspective. The larger organizational performance perspective requires performance improvement theory and modeling accompanied by straightforward professional implementation, and followed by an accounting of the results.

References

Deming, W. E. (1986). *Out of the crisis.* Cambridge, MA: MIT Press.

Dooley, C. R. (1945). *The training within industry report 1940–1945.* Washington, DC: Bureau of Training, Training Within Industry Service, War Manpower Commission.

Dooley, C. R. (2001). The training within industry report 1940–1945 (R. A. Swanson, Ed.). *Advances in Developing Human Resources, 3*(2), 127–289. (Reprint of major sections from work published 1945.)

Dorner, D. (1996). *The logic of failure: Recognizing and avoiding error in complex situations.* Cambridge, MA: Perseus.

Drucker, P. F. (1986). *The practice of management.* New York: HarperCollins.

Flanagan, J. C. (1954). The Critical Incident Technique. *Psychological Bulletin, 51*(4), 327–358.

Holton, E. F., III. (2001). Psychology and the discipline of HRD: Contributions and limitations. In R. A. Swanson & R. A. Holton (Eds.), *Foundations of human resource development,* pp. 100–106. San Francisco: Berrett-Koehler.

Holton, E. F., III, Baldwin, T. T., & Naquin, S. S. (Issue Eds.). (2000). Managing and changing learning transfer systems. *Advances in Developing Human Resources, 2*(4) (entire issue).

Kaplan, D. P., & Norton, R. S. (1996). *The balanced scorecard: Translating strategy into action.* Boston: Harvard Business School Press.

Mattson, B. W. (2000). The development and validation of the critical outcome technique. *Human Resource Development International, 3*(4), 465–487.

Passmore, D. L. (1997). Ways of seeing: Disciplinary bases of research in HRD. In R. A. Swanson & E. F. Holton (Eds.), *Human resource development research handbook: Linking research and practice,* pp. 199–214. San Francisco: Berrett-Koehler.

Ruona, W.E.A. (2001). The foundational impact of Training Within Industry project on the human resource development profession. *Advances in Developing Human Resources, 3*(2), 119–126.

Swanson, R. A. (1996). *Analysis for improving performance: Tools for diagnosing organizations and documenting workplace expertise.* San Francisco: Berrett-Koehler.

Swanson, R. A. (2001). Human resource development and its underlying theory. *Human Resource Development International, 4*(3), 1–14.

Swanson, R. A., & Holton, E. F. (1999). *Results: How to assess performance, learning, and perceptions in organizations.* San Francisco: Berrett-Koehler.

Swanson, R. A., & Holton, R. A. (Eds.). (2001). *Foundations of human resource development.* San Francisco: Berrett-Koehler.

Torraco, R. J., & Swanson, R. A. (1995). The strategic roles of human resource development. *Human Resource Planning, 18*(4), 10–21.

CHAPTER 8

Beyond the Classroom

Transfer from Work-Based Learning Initiatives

Lyle Yorks

Contemporary learning and development practice is no longer solely a classroom-based, instructor-focused exercise. Although the traditional classroom-based model is appropriately employed for many learning challenges, the past couple of decades have witnessed the emergence of a variety of learning platforms and delivery vehicles. Work-based learning initiatives such as action learning and communities of practice have become popular forms of such innovations. Both are forms of inquiry focused on actual workplace challenges and take place in groups formed with the intention of learning while addressing these challenges. One can reasonably argue that learning transfer distance is reduced in these programs because the learning is focused on specific workplace issues. Based on experience grounded in both research and practice, action learning and communities of practice are potentially enhancing of learning transfer. However, realizing this potential still requires attention to the learning transfer system. This chapter examines learning transfer challenges associated with action learning and community-of-practice initiatives, challenges that vary somewhat with the design, or form, provided by these initiatives.

Contemporary learning and development practice is no longer a classroom-based, instructor-focused exercise. Although the traditional classroom-based model is appropriately employed for many learning challenges, the past couple of decades have witnessed the emergence of a variety of learning platforms and delivery vehicles. Some of these innovations, such as e-learning applications, have been driven by advances in technology (Driscoll, 2002; see also Eddy & Tannenbaum, Chapter Nine of this volume). Other innovations have been driven by more explicit applications of adult learning theory and a growing awareness of the importance of informal learning in how employees and managers grow and develop their expertise (Marsick & Watkins, 1990; Mumford, 1995). Work-based learning initiatives (Raelin, 2000) have become a popular form of this latter stream of innovation.

Prominent among these work-based learning initiatives are action learning programs (Boshyk, 2002a; Marquardt, 1999; Yorks, O'Neil, & Marsick, 1999a) and communities of practice (Huang, Newell, & Galliers, 2002; Wenger & Snyder, 2000). Although these learning initiatives are distinct in composition and purposes, they also share certain commonalities. Both are forms of inquiry focused on actual workplace challenges and take place in groups formed with the intention of learning while addressing these challenges. One can reasonably argue that learning transfer distance (see Holton & Baldwin, Chapter One of this volume) is reduced in these programs because the learning is focused on specific workplace challenges. Addressing these challenges represents demonstration, not only of learning, but de facto application of this learning to the workplace.

This chapter examines learning transfer challenges associated with action learning and community-of-practice initiatives. These challenges vary somewhat with the design, or form, provided by these initiatives. Specifically, this chapter defines action learning and communities of practice, provides a research-based typology or framework that conceptualizes differences in types of action learning programs that can be related to communities of practice, examines these work-based learning initiatives in the context of what is known about learning transfer, provides some initial evidence regarding learning transfer from these programs, and draws implications for taking action for facilitating transfer.

Action Research and Communities of Practice Defined

Action learning takes actual work as the vehicle for learning. Participants in an action learning program work in small groups to take action on compelling, meaningful challenges in their lives while seeking to learn from having taken this action. Ideally, this involves a cyclical process of taking action, reflecting on that action, drawing conclusions, and taking subsequent action based on these conclusions—in short, putting into practice some variation of what is commonly known as the learning cycle (Kolb, 1984; Mumford, 1995). Many action learning theorists advocate the use of learning coaches to facilitate the effective adoption of this practice through helping participants to question their actions, challenge the assumptions underlying their reflections, conclusions, and actions, and commit to meaningful action. Accordingly, action learning can be defined as follows:

> An approach to working with and developing people that uses work on an actual project or problem as the way to learn. Participants work in small groups to take action to solve their problem and learn how to learn from that action. Often a learning coach works with the group in order to help the members learn how to balance their work with the learning from that work [Yorks, O'Neil, & Marsick, 1999b, p. 3].

Case studies, experiential exercises, simulations, and outdoor adventure exercises are not synonymous with action learning. While each of these learning vehicles has its own unique advantages and limitations, none of them center on a real work problem in real time. Action learning groups can be formed by drawing participants from both within and across organizational boundaries (Dilworth & Willis, 1999).

Communities of practice are naturally occurring or intentionally created groups that share a common identity, membership, and purpose (Wenger & Snyder, 2000). Like action learning groups, these communities can draw members from within or across organizational boundaries. They function as networks of people with common interests (functional, purpose, or across the value chain), drawing upon individual and collective expertise to solve collective problems and enhance organizational knowledge. Communities of practice are collaborative and socially constructed for purposes of developing knowledge and the capacity of their participants to address the challenges that confront them (Brown & Duguid, 1991). The emphasis is placed in these communities on social interaction and collective learning practices for sharing experience-based knowledge and translating tacit knowing into explicit know-how. This extends how knowledge is understood from abstract, formal *know-what* to something that is informal, collective, and situated (Huang et al., 2002; Lave & Wenger, 1991).

There are of course important differences between action learning programs and communities of practice. While participants in communities of practice address commonly shared problems, much of their activities involve knowledge transfer from current experience through storytelling, sharing of cases, and in-depth discussion. Planning for future action is often not part of the community's concern. Each participant must ponder how to translate what is learned in the community back to the workplace. However, such communities are arguably most effective when they operate with principles common to action learning: namely a problem shared by the group, a questioning and reflective process, and a commitment to action and learning (Marsick, 2002).

The Action Learning Pyramid

An analysis of the varieties of action learning practice by O'Neil (1999) identifies four schools of action learning in terms of program structure and processes. Each of these schools of thought represents a cluster of action learning practices, forming a typology that captures some central characteristics of the different ways in which action learning initiatives are organized and implemented. Although the four schools share much in common—including an emphasis on working on actual work-based challenges—each of these schools is also distinguished by different assumptions regarding learning. Consequently each approach designs the learning experience in a different way. Not surprisingly these different designs lead to different learning outcomes, and by extension, to differences in what is potentially transferred to the workplace beyond the learning program itself.

Through further analysis of these programs, Yorks, O'Neil, and Marsick (1999b) have structured the typology into a pyramid model to help practitioners make choices among different programs based on desired outcomes. Essentially, as one goes from the base of the pyramid to the top, each successive level incorporates the primary learning outcomes of the preceding one. However, the level of organizational noise also increases as one goes up the pyramid. By *noise* is meant comments made by participants challenging the program as they are asked to reflect on long-held assumptions, mental models, and issues that have been previously treated as givens, not open to discussion, and other "undiscussables" (Arygris & Schön, 1978). If conceived of as a more general model of work-based learning initiatives, this pyramid also has implications for how communities of practice function (see Figure 8.1).

The Tacit or Incidental School: The Base of the Pyramid

The tacit school is distinguished from the other three by its reliance on informal and incidental learning that occurs as the program focuses on the project itself. The tacit school assumes that significant learning will take place as long as carefully chosen participants are put together, some team building is done, and supporting information is provided by experts (what Revans, 1982, has called "P" for programmed instruction). Foundational skills for the project teams are provided in the early phase of the program through structured team building and other activities designed in conjunction with information transfer and content learning. Participants are placed in project teams working on a strategically driven project that is typically sponsored by a member of the executive team or other senior executive. The project teams may have logistical support from program administrators, but they do not have learning coaches. The learning that occurs is what Marsick and Watkins (1990) have described as incidental. This learning tends to occur around developing strategic thinking among participants on how to address an unfamiliar problem. Working on the project also typically provides for a more generalist or cross-functional understanding of business issues and exposure to senior management thinking. Because formal reflection is not provided for by coaches, these programs tend to reinforce the existing organizational culture and mindset of strong organizational leaders. Tacit programs are appropriate for situations that have strong leader or hierarchical cultures in which management wishes to cultivate strategic thinking within the context of existing organizational norms. The widely publicized corporate action learning programs at General Electric and TRW fit into this category. In the

Figure 8.1. Work-Based Learning Pyramid.

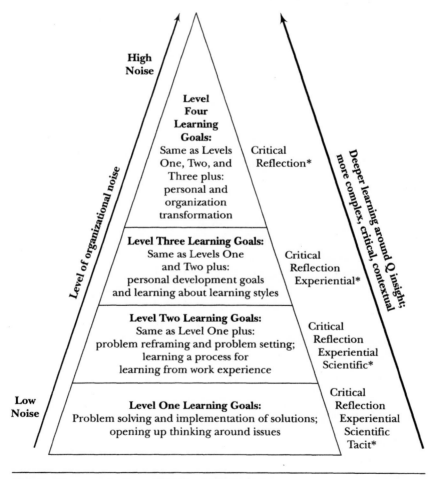

Note: * = Best match of possible AL and CoP choices.

Source: Adapted from Yorks, O'Neil, & Marsick, 1999b, p. 14.

absence of such strong organizational norms the learning is potentially haphazard.

Communities of practice generally provide for informal and tacit learning as participants share experiences through storytelling and discuss how the practices described have been applied in different settings. Such communities typically have a person or group of persons who play a catalyzing role in bringing the group together and designing the experience, but rarely devote time to formal reflection on the lessons learned in terms of personal development or organizational values. Each participant draws private conclusions about ideas and capabilities that can be brought back home. Tacit (that is, informal and incidental) learning about how knowledge might be further shared back in the workplace is largely a function of the participant.

Most studies of communities of practice have conceptualized them as informal groups that evolve naturally within organizations (Huang et al., 2002). As Huang et al. note, little empirical evidence has been collected on how a community of practice can be designed and built as part of a specific organizational development project. However, many organizations are explicitly seeking to construct such communities as a method of knowledge management and management development (Hawkins, 2002). This raises the possibility of more actively facilitated learning by coaches who encourage the use of action learning practices to more systematically capture the incidental learning that is occurring (Marsick, 2002). Such practices might potentially create characteristics in some communities of practice of the other types found in the action learning pyramid, especially the experiential and critical reflection approaches described later in this chapter. Presently, however, communities of practice most commonly function in ways consistent with the tacit school.

The Scientific School: The Second Level of the Pyramid

The scientific school of action learning is rooted in the seminal work of the British physicist Reg Revans (1970). Highly rational, this approach involves applying the classic scientific model to social and workplace problems. Revans describes his approach to management development in terms of three interactive systems: Alpha, Beta, and Gamma (MacNamara & Weekes, 1982; Revans, 1970, 1981, 1982, 1987). System Alpha involves the interplay of a manager's value system, the external system that affects the decisions being made by the manager, and the internal system within which the manager works. System Alpha overlaps with system Beta, which is the negotiation and implementation of the designed strategy that emerges from system Alpha. System Beta has five components:

- *Survey,* in which data for system Alpha are identified
- *Hypothesis,* a trial decision in which one of the alternative designs from system Alpha is selected for experimentation
- *Experiment,* an action stage in which the trial decision is implemented
- *Audit,* during which the observed outcome is compared with the expected outcome
- *Review,* a control stage in which appropriate action is taken on the conclusions reached during this stage

Revans refers to this process by the acronym SHEAR, which he equates with the learning process (1978, p. 14). Heavy emphasis is placed on using data and logical analysis leading to thoroughly researched solutions.

System Gamma involves personal development, referring to the mental predisposition that a manager brings to a presenting problem and its context. Continual checking between expectations and actual consequences from action (experiment, audit, review) identifies discrepancies between the way a problem has been framed and what subsequent action suggests is actually the case. Revans defines learning as the extent to which a manager is able to change perceptions based on this experience of continuing assessment of data and actions. Revans (1982, 1989) emphasizes the importance of asking questions, expressed in the formula: $L = P + Q$ (L = learning, P = Programmed instruction, which is formally codified expert knowledge, and Q = questioning insight, which is "intuition, things crossing the mind, insight") (1989, p. 102). Pedler (1991) refers to Q as asking discriminating questions.

Revans's approach focuses more on solving the problem than on the development of interpersonal and leadership competencies.

This primary emphasis on the project, coupled with a minimalist role for the "supernumerary" (the learning coach), differentiates the scientific school from the two that follow. The scientific approach is appropriate when the desired outcome is the resolution of problems based on a cautious, data-driven approach that emphasizes reformulating the problem. A second hoped-for outcome is incidental learning of how to continue to learn from one's work and experience through application of SHEAR. One can see how this approach, which can also be described as a form of action research, could be adopted in communities of practice. Preston (1977), Casey and Pearce (1977), and Foy (1977) all report on a project using this approach to action learning in General Electric Company.

The Experiential School: The Third Level of the Pyramid

Practitioners working within the experiential school, while accepting Revans's ideas about learning from actual challenges and fostering questioning insight, base their practice on the notion of an experiential learning cycle (Kolb, 1984; Mumford, 1995): namely, having an experience, reflecting on that experience, conceptualizing the experience, and experimenting with the new ideas (Lessem, 1991; McGill & Beaty, 1992; McLaughlin & Thorpe, 1993). In this approach learning coaches actively design practices to help participants implement the learning cycle in their practice and foster questioning insight.

Like the scientific school, the experiential school strives toward problem reframing and problem solving through working on a project or challenge. However, the language of systems Alpha, Beta, and Gamma is jettisoned, and processes of gathering and analyzing data, sense making, and developing action plans follow the learning cycle. Learning methods such as active listening, dialogue, and the ladder of inference are introduced to facilitate the learning process. Additionally, the experiential approach intentionally strives to facilitate personal development by helping participants set personal learning goals and monitor their progress toward these goals. Often participants develop these goals based on a 360-degree appraisal process or some other form of assessment that is also subsequently used for tracking their development.

An example of an action learning program consistent with the experiential school is the food service company ARAMARK (Vicere, 1996). In an ARAMARK program, participants reported increased self-awareness, organizational awareness, collaborative leadership styles, and creative thinking and risk taking. The CEO credited action learning with providing the foundation for the company's growth plan and providing market focus and corporate momentum.

The Critical Reflection School: The Fourth Level of the Pyramid

Practitioners in the critical reflection school generally share the same basic learning theories as those in the experiential school, but differ in how they use reflection. They take reflection to a deeper level by focusing on the underlying premises and governing values in the thinking of managers. Mezirow (1991, 2000) defines critical reflection as a process through which people recognize that their perceptions are filtered through uncritically accepted views, beliefs, attitudes, and feelings that have been socialized through family, school, society, and the organization. This kind of reflection fosters what Argyris and Schön (1978) have termed double-loop learning. Critical reflection also goes beyond the individual participant's underlying assumptions, leading to the examination of taken-for-granted organizational norms (Marsick, 1990; Weinstein, 1995) and shared mental models (Senge, 1990) by seeking to incorporate model II learning norms (Argyris, 1993) into the program, and by extension, to the organization. The goal is personal and organizational transformation.

The extent to which critical reflection can be practiced is dependent on the initial tolerance of participants and the organization culture in which they function. It is essential that any practitioner considering adopting the critical reflection approach understand that such efforts create extensive noise in the form of questioning long-held sacred cows, along with discomfort from those individuals who do not want to change (Weinstein, 1995). There is a need for organizational fortitude during the early phases of the process. Experience suggests that such efforts be approached as organizational development efforts in which members of the larger system agree on the need for generative learning and change, including senior executives who are seeking to learn along with other participants. Such a program can be designed effectively following a search conference and survey feedback interventions pointing toward a broad consensus among key internal stakeholders regarding the need for change and its general direction (Dennis, Cederholm, & Yorks, 1996). It is important, however, to consider the extent to which the organization is prepared to accept critical reflection on core, taken-for-granted values. Often management is interested in having managers think critically about strategic issues confronting the organization without equally critical reflection on how the organization is managed and its traditional values, a desire that Yorks and Marsick (2000) refer to as "bounded critical reflection."

Making Choices in Type of Program and Design

Choosing the right kind of program requires thought; the choice needs to be made in the context of the learning and development goals and the broader organizational system. Yorks, Marsick, and O'Neil (1999) offer a decision-making framework for program choices that revolves around the kinds of outcomes sought by management. Additionally, a number of design choices present themselves within the type of intended program. These include whether the program uses group or individual projects, the selection of participants, and time and spacing of the initiative (O'Neil & Dilworth, 1999). Here are some of the core questions:

- Does the organization face a compelling strategic challenge that has been well articulated in the organization and that provides the basis for meaningful projects? (This is a basic requirement for believable group-focused action learning projects of any model.)
- Is management primarily interested in having learning take place within the context of a strong existing organizational culture? (Consider the tacit model or the scientific model if thoroughness is a criterion of the culture.)
- Are the answers yes to the first three questions, *and* is management seeking to develop bench strength in well-articulated behaviors, competencies, and business capacities? (Consider the experiential model.)
- Is there consensus that the organization has a need for fundamental change, *and* is senior management willing to accept

both a high level of uncertainty about outcomes and a high
level of organizational noise, and to learn from the process?
(Consider the critical reflection model.)

It is beyond the scope of this chapter to explore these issues in
detail. They are, however, important to the question of learning
transfer, to which we now turn our attention.

Transfer of Learning to the Workplace

On the face of it, action learning programs should facilitate learning transfer since a certain degree of transfer is built into the principles of AL, namely experimenting with action on actual workplace
challenges and learning from that action. However, although a limited body of evidence demonstrates the kind of learning that can
take place during action learning programs (Lamm, 2000; Willis,
Deans, & Jones, 1998; Yorks et al., 1998), less is known about the
outcomes of this learning beyond the action learning experience
itself (Willis et al., 1998). Evidence of learning transfer from two
critically reflective programs and an experiential program that
evolved into a critical reflective program demonstrates transfer in
three cases (Yorks, Lamm, & O'Neil, 1999). However, as action
learning gains in popularity and more companies add a project to
their executive development program, sometimes with little cor-
responding logistical and budgetary support and essentially plac-
ing additional work on the plates of already busy managers, we
need to know more about what is being learned by participants in
these initiatives and what is being applied by the learners outside
the program. Even less is known about the dynamics of how knowledge and learning gained in communities of practice is successfully transferred by participants to other settings.

Based on experience grounded in both research and practice,
the following assertion can be reasonably made: *Action learning and
communities of practice are potentially enhancing of learning transfer.* However, realizing this potential still requires attention to the components of what Holton and Baldwin have conceptualized as the
learning transfer system. Specifically, as with any other learning experience that has been formally initiated for purposes of development,
HRD practitioners have to give attention to maintenance of what has
been learned over time, both through subsequent activities on the

part of the learner and through organizational interventions. Additionally, the context of the initiatives is important. The issues associated with these components of the transfer system vary somewhat by the type of program and its design.

Paying attention to the transfer system is not trivial, since a learner may gain new insights and competencies but conclude that applying them in the workplace would be futile. A manager from Singapore commented during an interview conducted as part of research into a critical reflection program, "You shouldn't judge how much I learned from what I do later. I have changed a lot inside in how I view things. It may not show in how I choose to act at work." In this instance, learning transfer, at least in terms of behavior at work, did not happen. In this case, there were issues associated with what is generally thought of as transfer climate that were of concern. Similar issues can happen with communities of practice. A person may self-censor certain ideas as not acceptable in the home situation.

Types of Transfer and Kinds of Learning

Salomon and Perkins (1989) distinguish between *low road transfer*—straightforward application of behaviors learned in one context to another with little modification—and *high road transfer*—application of an explicitly known general principle to a new situation. They further refine high road transfer as *forward reaching*, where "the principle is so well learned . . . as a general principle that it simply suggests itself appropriately on later occasions" (p. 119), and *backward reaching*, which involves the conscious abstraction of a unique situation to guide efforts to reach back to previous experience and learning in a search for relevant connections. Backward-reaching high road transfer has many of the characteristics of what Butterfield and Nelson (1989) conceptualize as *far transfer*—the ability to think and take action in diverse, complex, and uncertain contexts.

Elsewhere in this volume Holton and Baldwin build on the notion of transfer *distance*, describing it as a six-step process. The first three steps involve moving through a *learning process* from "know that" to "know how" and "building performance capability through practice"; the second three steps involve work-based processes of "using learning," "maintaining learning," and "generalizing (far transfer)."

In action learning programs and communities of practice the kind of transfer that is generally desired can be described as far high road transfer. This kind of transfer is embedded in the idea of developing "questioning insight" that can be integrated with existing knowledge to produce learning not only for the specific challenge in question but for application to other challenges as well. The difference between the tacit and scientific school in this regard is the assumption that this ability, and consequently transfer, will occur informally without explicit coaching or methodologies. This raises the question of what is supposed to be transferred.

At minimum, Q learning implies what Cell (1984) calls situation learning—a change in how one interprets a situation. Transfer can be said to have occurred when one effectively acts on this altered interpretation. Viewed as developmental, all action learning programs strive for transfer of this type around the task and hope for it to occur around certain managerial competencies as well, although these may vary from problem-solving and business models to problem-setting abilities and various interpersonal competencies.

In General Electric's programs at the company's Crotonville Center, participants are expected to grasp and apply the basic business models and principles that GE applies in assessing all its varied businesses, and do so with speed, simplicity, and self-confidence— core themes embedded and reinforced throughout the company's culture. In another tacit action learning program, run as a custom program through a major business school with executive education professors providing key programmed instruction supporting the projects, the CEO asked at the conclusion of the program "did they learn what we wanted them to learn," meaning strategic ways of thinking like a business generalist. The expectations around transfer in both of these programs are of the forward-reaching far high road kind. It is expected that the principles of the business models subscribed to by the firm are sufficiently embedded in the participants' way of thinking to be effectively applied in the various contexts that are likely to confront them as they progress in their careers. Additionally, development of conceptual reflection abilities that facilitate backward high road transfer is a bonus.

Moving to the opposite end (top) of the pyramid, backward-reaching far high road transfer is especially sought in action learning programs that place a strong emphasis on reflection (experiential) and critical reflection. The reflective behavior generic to backward-reaching transfer is part of what is intended to be developed in these programs through the action learning experience. This learning is similar to what Cell calls transsituational learning—learning *how* to change one's interpretation of situations, that is, learning to learn.

Perhaps paradoxically, transfer from communities of practice, which are generally organized as tacit or incidental in terms of design, seems to require backward-reaching far high road transfer. Required is the ability for adapting ideas and knowledge shared by people in one practice setting to another setting that can be significantly different in context. Equally important to the codified content knowledge is know-how for making this adaptation to the new setting. It is generally assumed that participants bring this know-how to the community.

The Global Forums on Action Learning, held every year in a different part of the world, provide an interesting merger of action learning and communities of practice (Boshyk, 2002b). Originally conceived by a small group of corporate learning officers working with action learning and organized by Yury Boshyk, this group typically has over a hundred participants from a range of industries and companies. Although the programs are intended to be inclusive, attendance at these three-day events is by invitation, with the focus on practitioners and no selling by consultants. Participants must make a presentation on their applications of action learning and executive development efforts to gain further invitations to the forum. Organized into groupings or sections, the presenters each give a ten-minute overview of their program. People then go into breakout sessions for more intensive discussion around the presentation that most interests them. The emphasis is on sharing and dialogue. Some of the presentations are collected into publications for wider dissemination (Boshyk, 2000, 2002a). Over the past seven years this has evolved into a community of practice of corporate learning officers and academics practicing action learning and related forms of executive development.

One pattern that is obvious from the discussions in the Global Forum is how many of the best practices are context-specific. Whether or not coaches are used in action learning programs, if coaches are internal or external to the organization, spacing and timing of the program all vary by organization. The discussion, while rich, takes the form of know-what—much like a seminar. Informal discussions evolve outside of the formal sessions as relationships are built. Applying the take-aways in the form of new concepts and ideas requires participants to have already developed the capacity to fit what they hear to their own purposes. Casual conversation often reveals the extent to which participants are processing information through their own mental models without reflecting on these models. To date, this rich source of potential learning about the transfer process from this community has not been formally studied.

Returning to Holton and Baldwin's model of transfer distance, although both action learning and communities of practice center learning around actual work, the learning structure is most commonly extra-organizational. There is a need for *bridging* from the learning setting to the actual work processes of the participants.

This point can be most clearly made by considering the most common form used to structure action learning programs regardless of type—participants attend a program and work on projects with the intention of making a recommendation to a group of senior executives. Once this presentation is completed, participants often have little to do with implementing their recommendations. Any learning from action is from the process of developing the proposed recommendations, not from subsequent action on the recommendations. It is the *process of working on the project*—gathering, analyzing, sense making, and testing ideas with others—that constitutes the action from which learning can be transferred. In the case of the tacit school this learning revolves around the experience of grappling with the larger organization and its competitive environment and applying models in forming recommendations. In the experiential school this learning also evolves from developing the group's recommendation, and the learning from personal development goals. In the critical reflection school, the learning potentially encompasses all these factors, as well as using processes of critical reflection for developing one's own continually evolving personal theory of management. In theory, the scientific school requires participants to experiment with their ideas, integrating action learning processes with work processes. Participants are working on *their* challenges, not those sponsored by someone else.

This need for *bridging* from the learning setting to the work setting is also true for communities of practice, where perhaps the most important learning takes place as participants seek to implement ideas and practices from the community.

Implications for Practice

Although much of the transfer literature focuses on training, the extension of this literature into a general model of a learning transfer system (Holton & Baldwin, 2000; see also Chapter One of this volume) has direct implications for the design of action learning programs, communities of practice, and other forms of work-based learning initiatives. It can be argued that linking these programs to a broader model of learning transfer provides a discipline to structuring such initiatives. This discipline is increasingly important in the case of action learning programs. As these programs proliferate, there is a need for paying closer attention to the compromises that are made in terms of budget, timing, and active senior executive support as HRD practitioners strive to take advantage of the best practice of pulling together a group of managers and giving them a real business-based problem or challenge to work on in the hope of demonstrating action learning's potential value. Because action learning principles are so congruent with transfer theory, paying attention to the implications of the latter has direct implications for program design.

More specifically, practitioners would be well advised to consider the following actions:

• *Positioning the program within the context of other preliminary and after-the-fact interventions directly relevant to the focus of the program.* Because action learning programs are very demanding of participants in terms of time, energy, and resources, they need to be positioned in the context of broader organizational strategic initiatives. An often overlooked aspect of programs such as those at GE's Crotonville is that these programs were built around a number of other initiatives, including GE's Work-Outs and change acceleration process (CAP) workshops. Action learning principles (tacit school) were applied in the context of reinforcing a pervasive organizational culture being driven from the top. Until he retired, CEO Welch never missed the final presentation of the action learning program. This is in contrast to another company the author has researched, where the CEO has had last-minute scheduling conflicts and repeatedly missed scheduled meetings, sending other senior executives in his place.

As noted earlier, a successful program oriented toward critical reflection was initiated only after a search conference and a corporate culture survey had built a broad consensus among the executive committee and layers of managers who would provide the participants; they agreed about the need for constructing a global organization and the need for enhanced competencies to support the change. Additionally, projects from the program provided specific input for the structural and systemic change that followed, including the change to a unified corporate-wide profit-and-loss statement and reorganization of the executive team. By contrast, in two other companies studied by the author, participants see little impact from the projects on which they worked. Both preliminary and post linking of action learning programs with broader strategic organizational direction are important as bridging mechanisms. Even when the recommendations from projects are not able to be implemented, follow-up discussions as to why is an important dimension to the learning.

• *Providing participants with clear learning goals that can be followed up after the program.* Where learning coaches are available, they can help participants set learning goals prior to the program. These goals can periodically be the focus of reflection throughout the program. These goals may be instrumental in nature, such as developing a greater capacity for strategic thinking and working the specific levers for enhancing business performance such as pricing strategy, or they can be linked to the participants' personal development plans. In the former case special assignments that draw on the kind of thinking experienced in the action learning program provide reinforcement. At the conclusion of the program, goals for transferring the learning can be set. This personal-level intervention is another important form of bridging.

• *Providing programmed instruction that links to needs of the project.* Rather than providing what one chief learning officer calls a traditional "cavalcade of stars," it's useful to space content learning intermittent with project work in a way responsive to the needs of the participants. A common criticism of some action learning programs is that participants lack the foundational knowledge for addressing the projects. Providing formal learning that is instrumental or process oriented in nature at the teachable moment and coupled with reflection around how the learning applies both in the program and in other settings can support transfer. Depending on the kind of learning needed, it can be supplied to the program by coaches, internal experts, or external experts. In one program, where there was little connection between platform-delivered learning from experts and the project work, interviews with participants revealed that they viewed "the program" as separate from "the project," raising questions of how they were integrating their learning. This suggests the importance of bridging within the design.

• *Spacing meetings across time to allow participants to try new behaviors and test ideas back on the job.* Learning coaches can encourage participants to reflect on their actions back in the workplace and foster dialogue around the experiences at the next meeting. Astonishingly, the fundamental principle of action learning, namely learning from one's actions, is often compromised during programs that become instead traditional task forces. Maintaining this link is perhaps the most powerful bridging mechanism that can be included in the design.

• *Holding reflection and dialogue sessions toward the conclusion of the program that focus on the obstacles to transferring learning from the program more generally to the workplace.* These obstacles can be both organizational and personal in nature, and the reflection can be around developing self-maintenance plans. For these to be effective, they must be linked to deeply held experience from the intensive program. In effect these dialogues can help participants consciously prepare for bridging the gap between the learning setting and the workplace.

These suggestions relate to both design and transfer climate. Management (as opposed to HR) support before, during, and continuing after the program is required, as are projects that have content validity and practices in the program that link to the culture of the organization. Alternatively, an organization needs a wide consensus around transforming itself, along with linkages to performance and development goals of both the individual and the organization.

Many of these suggestions have implications for the functioning of communities of practice as well. In particular, systematically following the experience of various participants over time, hearing the experience of those who have explicitly attempted to modify certain ideas, exploring the obstacles to transferring ideas, and fostering more dialogue around overcoming these obstacles are likely to provide more nuance in the understanding of best practices. As organizations explicitly construct such communities as part of their knowledge management process, learning how to link the communities to the transfer system promises to add to our understanding of transfer dynamics.

One final note: HRD professionals should partner with management in critically assessing what works and coming to a better understanding of how to enhance the learning from both action learning and communities of practice that are created. Learning from experience is an important part of the practice of creating these kinds of learning architectures.

References

Arygris, C. (1993). *Knowledge for action: A guide to overcoming barriers to organizational change.* San Francisco: Jossey-Bass.

Arygris, C., & Schön, D. (1978). *Organizational learning.* Reading, MA: Addison-Wesley.

Boshyk, Y. (Ed.). (2000). *Business driven action learning: Global best practices.* New York: St. Martin's Press.

Boshyk, Y. (Ed.). (2002a). *Action learning worldwide: Experiences of leadership and organizational development.* Basingstoke, England: Palgrave.

Boshyk, Y. (2002b, August 9–14). Global executive learning. Paper presented at Symposium: Building and sustaining networks using action learning; the Academy of Management Meeting, Denver.

Brown, J., & Duguid, P. (1991). Organizational learning and toward a unified view of working, learning, and innovation. *Organizational Science, 2,* 40–56.

Butterfield, E. C., & Nelson, G. D. (1989). Theory and practice of teaching for transfer. *Educational Research and Development, 37*(4), 5–38.

Casey, D., & Pearce, D. (1977). *More than management development: Action learning at GEC.* Hampshire, England: Gower.

Cell, E. (1984). *Learning to learn from experience.* Albany: State University of New York Press.

Dennis, C. B., Cederholm, L., & Yorks, L. (1996). Learning your way to a global organization. In K. E. Watkins & V. J. Marsick (Eds.), *In action: Creating the learning organization* (pp. 165–177). Alexandria, VA: American Society for Training and Development.

Dilworth, R. L., & Willis, V. J. (1999). Action learning for personal development and transformative learning. In L. Yorks, J. O'Neil, & V. J. Marsick (Eds.), *Action learning: Successful strategies for individual, team, and organizational development* (pp. 75–82). San Francisco: Berrett-Koehler.

Driscoll, M. (2002). Web-based training: Designing e-learning experiences. San Francisco: Jossey-Bass.

Foy, N. (1977). Action learning comes to industry. *Harvard Business Review, 77*(5), 158–168.

Hawkins, S. (2002). Using knowledge networks and communities in Skandia. Presentation at the Leveraging Knowledge Across Boundaries Roundtable. J. M. Huber Institute for Learning in Organizations, Teachers College, Columbia University.

Holton, E. F., III., & Baldwin, T. T. (2000). Making transfer happen: An action perspective on learning transfer systems. In E. F. Holton III, T. T. Baldwin, & S. S. Naquin (Eds.), *Managing and changing learning transfer systems* (pp. 1–6). San Francisco: Berrett-Koehler.

Huang, J., Newell, S., & Galliers, R. D. (2002, April 5–6). Inter-organizational communities of practice. Paper presented at the Third European Conference on Organizational Knowledge, Learning, and Capabilities, Athens, Greece.

Kolb, D. A. (1984). *Experiential learning: Experience as the source of learning and development.* Upper Saddle River, NJ: Prentice Hall.

Lamm, S. L. (2000). The connection between action reflection learning and transformative learning: An awakening of human qualities in leadership. Unpublished doctoral dissertation, Teachers College, Columbia University, New York.

Lave, J., & Wenger, E. (1991). Situated learning: Legitimate peripheral participation. Cambridge, England: Cambridge University Press.

Lessem, R. (1991). A biography of action learning. In M. Pedler (Ed.), *Action learning in practice* (2nd ed., pp. 17–30). Brookfield, VT: Gower.

MacNamara, M., & Weekes, W. H. (1982). The action learning model of experiential learning for developing managers. *Human Relations, 35,* 879–902.

Marquardt, M. J. (1999). *Action learning in action: Transforming problems and people for world-class organizational learning.* Palo Alto, CA: Davies-Black.

Marsick, V. J. (1990). Action learning and reflection in the workplace. In J. Mezirow and Associates, *Fostering critical reflection in adulthood* (pp. 23–46). San Francisco: Jossey-Bass.

Marsick, V. J. (2002, August 9–14). Building and sustaining networks through action learning. Paper presented at Symposium: Building and sustaining networks using action learning; the Academy of Management Meeting, Denver.

Marsick, V. J., & Watkins, K. (1990). *Informal and incidental learning in the workplace.* London: Routledge.

McGill, I., & Beaty, L. (1992). *Action learning: A practitioner's guide*. London: Kogan Page.

McLaughlin, R., & Thorpe, R. (1993). Action learning—A paradigm in emergence: The problems facing a challenge to traditional management education and development. *British Journal of Management, 4*(1), 19–27.

Mezirow, J. (1991). *Transformative dimensions of adult learning*. San Francisco: Jossey-Bass.

Mezirow, J. (2000). Learning to think like an adult: Core concepts of transformation theory. In J. Mezirow and Associates, *Learning as transformation: Critical perspectives on a theory in progress* (pp. 3–33). San Francisco: Jossey-Bass.

Mumford, A. (1995). *Learning at the top*. London: McGraw-Hill.

O'Neil, J. (1999). The role of the learning advisor in action learning. Unpublished doctoral dissertation, Teachers College, Columbia University, New York.

O'Neil, J., & Dilworth, R. L. (1999). Issues in the design and implementation of an action learning initiative. In L. Yorks, J. O'Neil, & V. J. Marsick (Eds.), *Action learning: Successful strategies for individual, team, and organizational development* (pp. 19–38). San Francisco: Berrett-Koehler.

Pedler, M. (1991). Questioning ourselves. In M. Pedler (Ed.), *Action learning in practice* (2nd ed., pp. 63–70). Brookfield, VT: Gower.

Preston, P. (1977). Learning how to learn. In D. Casey & D. Pearce (Eds.), *More management development: Action learning at GEC* (pp. 40–44). Hampshire, England: Gower.

Raelin, J. A. (2000). *Work-based learning: The new frontier of management development*. Upper Saddle River, NJ: Prentice Hall.

Revans, R. W. (1970). The managerial alphabet. In G. Heald (Ed.), *Approaches to the study of organizational behavior*. London: Tavistock.

Revans, R. W. (1978). *The a, b, c of action learning: A review of 25 years of experience*. Salford, England: University of Salford.

Revans, R. W. (1981). The nature of action learning. *Omega, 9*(1), 9–24.

Revans, R. W. (1982). *The origin and growth of action learning*. London: Chartwell Bratt.

Revans, R. W. (1987). *International perspectives on action learning*. (Handbook in Manchester Training Handbooks series.) Manchester, England: IDPM.

Revans, R. W. (1989). *The golden jubilee of action learning*. Manchester, England: Manchester Action Learning Exchange, University of Manchester.

Salomon, G., & Perkins, D. N. (1989). Rocky roads to transfer: Rethinking mechanisms of a neglected phenomenon. *Educational Psychologist, 24,* 113–142.

Senge, P. M. (1990). *The fifth discipline: The art and practice of the learning organization.* New York: Doubleday/Currency.

Vicere, A. A. (1996). Executive education: The leading edge. *Organizational Dynamics,* pp. 67–81.

Weinstein, K. (1995). *Action learning: A journey in discovery and development.* New York: HarperCollins.

Wenger, E., & Snyder, W. (2000). Communities of practice: The organizational frontier. *Harvard Business Review, 78*(1), 139–145.

Willis, V. J., Deans, J., & Jones, H. (1998). Verifying themes in action learning: Implications for adult education and HRD. In R. J. Torraco (Ed.), *Academy of Human Resource Development Conference Proceedings* (pp. 497–505). Baton Rouge, LA: Academy of Human Resource Development.

Yorks, L., Lamm, S., & O'Neil, J. (1999). Transfer of learning from action learning programs to the organizational setting. In L. Yorks, J. O'Neil, & V. J. Marsick (Eds.), *Action learning: Successful strategies for individual, team, and organizational development* (pp. 56–74). San Francisco: Berrett-Koehler.

Yorks, L., & Marsick, V. J. (2000). Organizational learning and transformation. In J. Mezirow and Associates, *Learning as transformation: Critical perspectives on a theory in progress* (pp. 253–281). San Francisco: Jossey-Bass.

Yorks, L., Marsick, V. J., & O'Neil, J. (1999). Lessons for implementing action learning. In L. Yorks, J. O'Neil, & V. J. Marsick (Eds.), *Action learning: Successful strategies for individual, team, and organizational development* (pp. 96–113). San Francisco: Berrett-Koehler.

Yorks, L., O'Neil, J., & Marsick, V. J. (Eds.). (1999a). *Action learning: Successful strategies for individual, team, and organizational development.* San Francisco: Berrett-Koehler.

Yorks, L., O'Neil, J., & Marsick, V. J. (1999b). Action learning: Theoretical bases and varieties of practice. In L. Yorks, J. O'Neil, & V. J. Marsick (Eds.), *Action learning: Successful strategies for individual, team, and organizational development* (pp. 1–18). San Francisco: Berrett-Koehler.

Yorks, L., O'Neil, J., Marsick, V. J., Lamm, S., Kolodny, R., & Nilson, G. (1998). Transfer of learning from an action learning program. *Performance Improvement Quarterly, 11*(1), 59–73.

CHAPTER 9

Transfer in an E-Learning Context

Erik R. Eddy
Scott I. Tannenbaum

Recent technological advancements have changed the way training and performance support can be provided. Specifically, technology allows training and other developmental resources to be distributed at a distance—through the use of the computer. Some have heralded e-learning as a solution to the transfer problem. As learning and performance occur almost simultaneously, e-learning might appear to eliminate the gap from learning to application. Can e-learning really overcome the transfer problem? The primary goal of this chapter is to identify ways to maximize transfer through the use of e-learning initiatives. Specifically, the authors identify some of the most common obstacles to transfer of training and explore how various e-learning initiatives (online training and education, performance support, and knowledge management) mitigate these obstacles. Sometimes the technology naturally enhances transfer. Other times, the way the technology is built, implemented, and supported (the human side of the equation) determines the extent to which transfer occurs. Sometimes, no matter how well the technology is supported, transfer problems remain difficult to overcome. Guidelines and tips to support the technological development and implementation of e-learning initiatives are presented, and key learnings are highlighted through the presentation of real-world case examples.

The term *e-learning* refers to sharing organized learning material, presenting information, and supporting the delivery of learning, skills, and knowledge electronically (Henry, 2001; Tyler, 2001). The use of e-learning in training is a relatively new development. Traditionally, training had been provided face-to-face, with trainer and trainees in the same location. The trainees would then leave the classroom and return to the job where they were expected to apply their newly acquired skills and knowledge.

One obstacle to the success of this traditional training process has been referred to in the literature as the "transfer problem" (Michalak, 1981). The transfer problem occurs when what is addressed in training is not applied on the job. Experts estimate that as much as 40 percent to 90 percent of what is trained is not applied on the job (Georgenson, 1982; Saks, 2002). This presents a dilemma for practitioners: How can we best facilitate the transfer of newly acquired knowledge and skill from training to the job?

Recent technological advancements have changed the way training and performance support can be provided. Specifically, technology allows training and other developmental resources to be distributed at a distance—through the use of the computer. Some have heralded e-learning as a solution to the transfer problem. E-learning allows the transportation of knowledge to employees "just-in-time"—so knowledge can be accessed whenever it is needed. As learning and performance occur almost simultaneously, e-learning might appear to eliminate the gap from learning to application. Can e-learning really overcome the transfer problem? This chapter explores transfer in an e-learning context. Specifically, we identify some of the most common obstacles to transfer of training, explore how effective various e-learning initiatives are at mitigating these obstacles, and recommend ways to maximize transfer when using e-learning methods.

E-Learning

Recent surveys suggest that e-learning is growing in popularity. For instance, an International Data Corp. study indicates that the online learning market generated annual receipts of $1.14 billion in 1999 and $2.2 billion in 2000. It is expected to generate more than $10 billion by 2003. According to a 1999 Masie Center study,

92 percent of large organizations implemented some form of online learning ("Fortune On-Line Learning Supplement," 1999). Add to this the fact that Internet usage grew over 1000 percent in the 1990s and it is apparent that this technology is having a substantial impact on the way training is being conducted.

The increase in usage is for good reason, as e-learning has a number of benefits. For example, learners across the globe can have access to the best instruction available; they can set their own pace and schedule; discussions can continue after training using e-mail and discussion groups; and learners can gain access to immediate feedback (Schwann, 1997; Horton, 2000). E-learning can also save organizations time and money. Some research has found e-learning to be 40–60 percent less expensive than training delivered in the traditional classroom setting (Becker, 1999). Additionally, organizations save money used for travel expenses, facilities, and administrative costs.

One of the often-cited benefits of e-learning is the minimization of transfer concerns—users have direct access to the information they need, when they need it (Filipczak, 1996). In theory, transfer of training becomes almost irrelevant. In practice, it may not be that easy.

We know from other technological advances that technology by itself isn't always the answer. A review of some of the more recent technological advancements used by employers, and the reactions associated with these advancements, provides some evidence that technology alone is not a panacea. For instance, organizations implementing a human resource information system (HRIS) looked forward to the cost savings of maintaining employee data in a single, easily accessible location. However, HR was not prepared for the heightened privacy concerns that accompanied the new systems. Employees think, Who has access to my personal information? Will the organization share my information with other companies? These questions had to be addressed before organizations could reap the benefits of this technology (Eddy, Stone-Romero, & Stone, 1999).

Knowledge management initiatives provide another illustration of human reactions to potentially useful technological advances. Knowledge management systems are meant to capture and store individual learnings that can be shared with others within the organization. As these systems are developed, employees may have concerns about the validity of the information. Where did this information come from? Is it accurate? Can I trust that it is correct? Uncertainty regarding the validity of the content contained in the system may decrease system usage (Tannenbaum & Alliger, 2000).

"Employee self-service" (ESS) is a final example of a new people-related technology. With ESS, employees are asked to access centralized kiosks or the company intranet to learn about benefits and other human resource issues. When HR first began implementing self-service initiatives, there was some hesitancy from employees. Employees were used to talking to a person, not a computer, and many wanted a personalized touch often not available in a self-service atmosphere.

There is no question that the proper use of technology can add value to an organization. However, as each of these examples demonstrates, it is impossible to separate technology issues from human issues—there are always two sides to the equation. The same is true for enhancing transfer in e-learning. To ensure value from the technology, the human issues must be addressed. In the case of e-learning, to ensure that e-learning yields maximum transfer, we must understand and address the human elements that facilitate and inhibit transfer.

Terminology

The training and e-learning literatures are replete with jargon. Because there is no universally accepted definition of certain concepts, the following section defines how common terms are used throughout this chapter.

Transfer

There are a variety of definitions for *transfer of training* (Alliger, Bennett, & Tannenbaum, 1995). For instance, cognitive psychologists define transfer in terms of the application of learning from a learned task to a different task (Gick & Holyoak, 1987). Instructional design professionals define transfer as the application of learning in situations different from where the learning took place (Gagne, Briggs, & Wagner, 1992). Therefore, cognitive psychologists and instructional design professionals often measure errors in learning, acquisition rates, and learning as evidence of transfer (Kraiger, 1995).

Our definition of transfer, however, is a very pragmatic one, and is more closely aligned with the industrial-organizational literature (Baldwin & Ford, 1998; Newstrom, 1984; Wexley & Latham, 1981). Specifically, we define transfer as the degree to which employees use newly acquired knowledge and skills to perform their job effectively and enhance organizational effectiveness.

E-Learning

As stated in the introduction, *e-learning* simply refers to sharing organized learning material, presenting information, and supporting the delivery of learning, skills, and knowledge electronically (Henry, 2001; Tyler, 2001). These services are often provided to individuals who are geographically dispersed, are otherwise isolated in space or time, or cannot attend traditional training. E-learning can be provided via the Internet, intranet, e-mail, chat rooms, discussion lists, videotape, interactive television, CD-ROM, virtual communities, and many other technology-based forms of interaction.

There are many types of e-learning initiatives. For the purposes of this chapter, we build on a typology set out by Carliner (1999). Specifically, we break e-learning into three distinct categories. These categories are the focus of our discussion:

- *Online training and education:* Training events where a trainee develops specific knowledge and skills by interacting with a computer. Computer-based training (CBT) and Web-based training are examples of this type of e-learning.
- *Performance support:* Computer-aided support to workers as they perform their jobs. For example, a customer service representative may have a list of diagnostic questions pop up onscreen as a guide during a customer interaction.
- *Knowledge management:* An organization's attempt to capture, store, and organize information from employees, making this information available to others throughout the organization. For example, an organization might develop a safety database, capturing examples of common safety violations and providing guidance on how to resolve these issues.

In his typology, Carliner suggests a fourth type of e-learning, *online collaboration*. This refers to situations where people work together online from different locations. This form of e-learning is especially useful in coaching, mentoring, and tutoring relationships. For example, a senior manager in California and junior manager in New York may chat via the computer for the purpose of helping the junior manager work through a difficult situation. Rather than separating this form of e-learning into its own category, we have decided to integrate the impact of online collaboration into our discussions of online training and education and of knowledge management.

Learning Event

For use in this chapter we have adopted the phrase *learning event* to refer to any training, e-learning, or on-the-job experience specifically intended to build someone's capabilities. Such experiences can be very formal or relatively informal, but learning events are finite activities with a beginning and an end. Naturally, individuals experience a continual series of learning events over time. For example, each time an employee accesses a knowledge management system or attends a training course it can be thought of as a discrete learning event that may or may not result in transfer to the job.

Hurdles to Transfer

For transfer to occur, individuals must overcome many hurdles. They must participate in the learning event, learn something as a result of the event, and then use that learning on the job. The goal is to overcome hurdles along the way and apply newly acquired knowledge and skills to meet job requirements, thereby achieving transfer. However, prior to a learning event an individual may choose not to participate, or may reluctantly agree to participate in the learning event. Similar hurdles exist during the learning event and after the learning event. Any of these hurdles may eliminate or diminish the likelihood of transfer. Figure 9.1 visually depicts these hurdles.

Figure 9.1. Hurdles to Transfer.

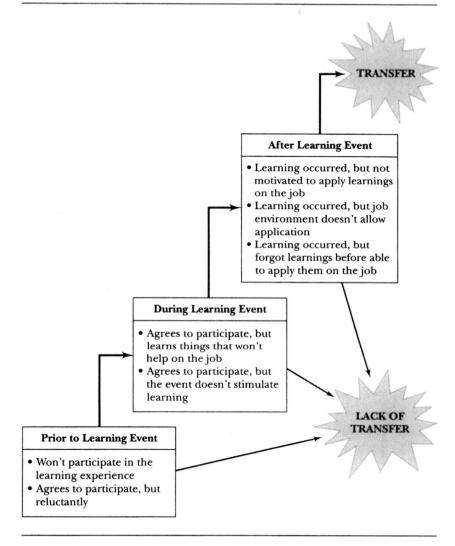

Why do these hurdles to transfer exist? Many factors can inhibit transfer: characteristics of the learning event, attributes of the learner, motivational factors, and characteristics of the work environment can all create obstacles at each stage of the learning process. The following sections identify some of the most common obstacles to transfer and describe when these obstacles might occur in the learning process.

Obstacles to Transfer of Training

Transfer of training occurs when employees use newly acquired knowledge and skills to perform their jobs effectively and to enhance organizational effectiveness. Inherent in this definition is the realization that there are obstacles to the successful application of newly acquired knowledge and skills. In fact, there are a number of well-documented obstacles to transfer of training in the extant literature. Exhibit 9.1 presents a list of some of the more common obstacles.

Exhibit 9.1. Transfer of Training Obstacles.

Trainee Attributes	The Training
• External locus of control • Low self-efficacy • Low need for achievement • Low ability or aptitude	• Lack of perceived relevance to work • Poor trainer capabilities • Lack of feedback • Other poor instructional design issues
Motivational Factors	**Post-Training Environment**
• Lack of job identification • Lack of organizational commitment • Lack of choice to participate • Low perceived instrumentality or value	• Weak continuous learning culture • Lack of follow-up, encouragement, or feedback • Time lag • Situational constraints

In general, obstacles can stem from four sources: trainee attributes, motivational factors, the training itself, and the post-training environment. We do not intend for this to be an exhaustive review of the literature. We merely wish to highlight some of the most common obstacles for use in our discussion of how e-learning might mitigate these obstacles.

Trainee Attributes

Several factors may influence whether a trainee is motivated to attend training, actively participates and learns during training, and applies the training in the workplace. Some of the more common obstacles in this category include external locus of control, low self-efficacy, low need for achievement, and low ability or aptitude.

External locus of control. Locus of control is a generalized expectancy that organizational outcomes are controlled either by an individual's own actions (internal) or by other forces (external) (Rotter, 1966). Individuals with an external locus of control can have lower motivation to attend training and may be less likely to apply new knowledge or skills on the job (Colquitt, LePine, & Noe, 2000).

Low self-efficacy. Self-efficacy is a personal judgment of one's own capabilities to organize and execute courses of action required to attain designated types of performances (Bandura, 1986, p. 391). Individuals with low self-efficacy may be less likely to persevere through training and apply new knowledge or skills on the job (Colquitt et al., 2000; Kozlowski et al., 2001; Warr, Allan, & Birdi, 1999).

Low need for achievement. Need for achievement is demonstrated in employees who treat work seriously, perform actively, and have a high ambition to succeed (Baumgartel, Reynolds, & Pathan, 1984). Individuals with a low need for achievement may be less likely to view training as an opportunity to build their own skills and be more successful. This leads to decreased motivation to learn and apply new learnings on the job.

Low ability or aptitude. Ability or aptitude can influence employees' success on new tasks. Individuals with low ability or aptitude in the area to be trained may be less likely to be successful in training (Ghiselli, 1966; Kozlowski et al., 2001). General intelligence can also impact many facets of the job from training to actual job performance. Research has shown that individuals with lower general intelligence tend to perform more poorly in training (Neel & Dunn, 1960; Colquitt et al., 2000).

Motivational Factors

Several motivational factors may influence whether a trainee is motivated to attend training. Some of the more common motivational obstacles include lack of job identification, lack of organizational commitment, lack of choice to participate, and low perceived value.

Lack of job identification. Job identification is psychological identification with one's career and job (Cheng & Ho, 2001). Individuals with weak career plans and low levels of job involvement may be less likely to be motivated to learn (Mathieu, Tannenbaum, & Salas, 1992) and apply those learnings on the job (Colquitt et al., 2000).

Lack of organizational commitment. Organizational commitment is the relative strength of an individual's identification with an organization (Porter, Steers, Mowday, & Boulian, 1974). Individuals with weaker organizational commitment may not see the value in training both to themselves and to the organization (Carlson, Bozeman, Kacmar, Wright, & McMahan, 2000; Tannenbaum, Mathieu, Salas, & Cannon-Bowers, 1991).

Lack of choice to participate. Sometimes, employees are told to attend training to correct some deficiency. In these instances, training may be viewed as a punishment. In other cases, employees may have greater discretion about which training they attend. Although the finding is not universal, some research has shown that individuals who cannot choose which training to attend demonstrate lower motivation to attend and learn (Baldwin, Magjuka, & Loher, 1991; Hicks & Klimoski, 1987).

Low perceived instrumentality or value. Training may be viewed by trainees as having some potential value or payoff, for example, for enhancing their performance or increasing their career opportunities. Individuals who do not believe in the value of the training they receive may be less likely to apply it in the workplace (Baumgartel et al., 1984; Colquitt et al., 2000).

The Training

Beyond trainee attributes and motivational issues, the training itself may influence whether a trainee is motivated to attend training, learns from the training, and applies the new learnings to the workplace. Some of the more common training obstacles include lack of perceived relevance to work, poor trainer capabilities, lack of feedback, and other instructional design limitations.

Lack of perceived relevance to work. Training should be relevant to the actual work performed by the individual. If the training is not perceived as relevant to the employee's work, the trainee will be less likely to apply the training on the job.

Poor trainer capabilities. An ineffective trainer will inhibit trainee understanding and subsequent learning of the material. This may lead to an inability to apply learning in the workplace.

Lack of feedback. Feedback (or knowledge of the results) occurs when information is provided to individuals about their performance. Improper use of feedback during training inhibits learning and subsequent use of the material (Wexley & Thornton, 1972).

Other instructional design limitations. Poor instructional design may inhibit individual understanding and subsequent learning of the material. This leads to an inability to apply learning in the workplace. For instance, lack of similarity (physical or psychological fidelity) between the training environment and actual work requirements can inhibit learning and subsequent transfer (Underwood, 1951).

Post-Training Environment

Finally, the post-training environment may influence whether a trainee is motivated to attend training or applies the new learnings to the workplace. Some of the more common post-training obstacles include a weak continuous learning environment, lack of follow-up, encouragement, and feedback, time lag, and situational constraints.

Weak continuous learning culture. A continuous learning culture is a pattern of shared meanings of perceptions and expectations by all organizational members that constitutes an organizational value or belief (Tracey, Tannenbaum, & Kavanagh, 1995). If employees believe the organization does not value training, then motivation to attend and subsequent transfer of training will suffer (Bennett, Lehman, & Forst, 1999; Warr et al., 1999).

Lack of follow-up, encouragement, and feedback. Follow-up is a method of ensuring that learning has occurred. Lack of follow-up demonstrates a lack of concern about training impact. Insufficient support from peers (Facteau, Dobbins, Russell, Ladd, & Kudisch,

1992) and supervisors (Marx, 1982) will reduce the likelihood of applying new learnings on the job.

Time lag (no opportunity to apply). The longer the time lag between the actual training event and application on the job, the less trainees retain what they learned (Bennett, 1995). Limited opportunities to apply new skills on the job will contribute to increased skill decay (Noe, 1986).

Situational constraints. Constraints such as lack of time or resources can influence whether individuals apply newly acquired knowledge and skills to the job (Tannenbaum, 1997). Environments with numerous situational constraints reduce transfer because individuals may be unable to apply what they learned. Over time they can lose a sense of efficacy that they will be able to apply new ideas or skills, and thus can lose motivation to participate in subsequent learning events.

Transfer Obstacles and the Stages of Learning

Figure 9.1 suggests that learning involves three stages: preparation before the learning event, learning during the event, and transfer to the job after the learning event (Tannenbaum et al., 1991; Cheng & Ho, 2001). Obstacles can interfere with transfer at each stage in the process. For instance, a lack of input into training decisions may lessen trainee motivation to attend training (Baldwin et al., 1991). Poor practice conditions during the training can inhibit learning (Briggs & Naylor, 1962). A weak continuous learning environment can lessen the extent to which new learnings are transferred from the training to the job (Tracey et al., 1995). Some obstacles can influence multiple stages in the process. For instance, a lack of organizational commitment may decrease motivation to attend training, decrease the effort taken to learn during training, and decrease the probability that the training will be applied on the job. Table 9.1 shows the influence of each training obstacle on the three stages of the learning process. This table suggests that transfer obstacles exist at each stage of the process, and that many transfer obstacles exist throughout the process. This implies that training designers must anticipate potential concerns at each stage of the learning process.

Table 9.1. Impact of Transfer Obstacles
on Stages of the Learning Process.

Transfer Obstacle	Learning Process		
	Prior to Learning Event	During Learning Event	After Learning Event
Trainee Attributes			
External locus of control	✓	✓	✓
Low self-efficacy	✓	✓	✓
Low need for achievement	✓	✓	✓
Low ability or aptitude		✓	✓
Motivational Factors			
Lack of job identification	✓	✓	✓
Lack of organizational commitment	✓	✓	✓
Lack of choice to participate	✓	✓	✓
Low perceived instrumentality or value	✓	✓	✓
The Training			
Lack of perceived relevance to work	✓	✓	✓
Poor trainer capabilities		✓	✓
Lack of feedback		✓	✓
Other instructional design limitations		✓	✓
Post-Training Environment			
Weak continuous learning culture	✓		✓
Lack of follow-up, encouragement, or feedback	✓		✓
Time lag (no opportunity to apply)	✓		✓
Situational constraints	✓		✓

Note: ✓ = Transfer obstacle impacts this phase of the learning process.

Designing E-Learning Initiatives That Maximize Transfer

We have identified some common obstacles to transfer from the training literature, and explored the various points in time when these obstacles may impact transfer. It is important to minimize these obstacles to improve the chances that employees use newly acquired knowledge and skills to perform their job effectively and enhance organizational effectiveness.

Although the focus has been on training obstacles and the extant training literature, we would now like to shift our focus to a broader *learning* event. In fact, learning, and more specifically e-learning, can occur in many instances outside of an actual training program. We can use our knowledge from the training literature, though, to examine the impact of transfer obstacles in an e-learning initiative. Similar to training, e-learning initiatives have a before, during, and after event period. For example, obstacles can inhibit maximum transfer before you access a knowledge management system, while you are accessing the system, and after you have accessed the system. Interestingly, some obstacles from the training literature may not apply in this e-context, while others may be even more important. The goal of this section is to take what we know from the transfer of training literature and apply this to our understanding of how to design e-learning initiatives that maximize transfer.

To accomplish this goal, we explore each type of e-learning initiative (that is, online training and support, performance support, and knowledge management). In our exploration, we identify the good news—areas where the initiative naturally mitigates transfer concerns, identify the bad news—areas of continued transfer concern, and provide tips and guidelines for maximizing transfer.

Enhancing Transfer in Online Training and Education

Online training and education refers to training events where a trainee develops specific knowledge and skills by interacting with a computer.

The Good News

One benefit of online training and education is that the flexibility of when and how to participate makes it easier for employees to participate. With online training and education, employees can choose to log onto Web-based training or load a CD and participate at their discretion. Allowing employees this flexibility can increase motivation, enhancing the chance that they will engage in learning and apply these learnings on the job. However, there is some risk to providing this flexibility. The possibility exists that employees will choose not to participate—thereby missing the opportunity to develop new knowledge and skills. This is more likely to occur in organizations where learning is not considered important for career success.

Once the employee has decided to participate, well-designed online training and education can be structured to ensure appropriate practice conditions and provide appropriate feedback. Of course, this is contingent upon training developers' incorporating good instructional design practices and not just providing "edu-tainment."

Another key transfer obstacle that is mitigated by this type of training is time lag. With online training, the learning event can occur on the job, at the work station. Further, the employee can choose to participate in the learning event just prior to needing the new knowledge or skill, rather than attending a training class weeks or even months before the new skill can be applied on the job. With little or no lag between learning and application, skill decay declines and the chance of transfer is increased.

Areas of Continued Concern

Although online training and education mitigates several of the traditional transfer obstacles, it is not a panacea. A number of critical obstacles must be addressed before this e-learning initiative can have maximum benefit.

It may appear that e-learning takes the trainer out of the learning equation. However, poor trainer capabilities remain a concern in online training. An underlying teacher model is still implicit in online training. For example, some online training systems can assess learner capabilities and progress and adjust the training accordingly, much as effective trainers do. Some online training systems build in reinforcement for learning and teach effective correction strategies, again resembling effective instructors. However, not all online training incorporates effective trainer strategies. Without these trainer strategies in place, the chances for transfer diminish. One way to enhance effective trainer strategies is to provide trainer-facilitated e-learning rather than a simple self-paced opportunity. A trainer-facilitated learning session allows learners to chat with a certified trainer. This provides an opportunity for the learner to ask questions, clarify content, and pursue topics in greater depth.

Learner attributes can also influence the success of online training and education. For example, employees with low need for achievement may not be motivated to engage in the learning; employees with low self-efficacy may not feel confident in their ability to successfully complete an online learning course. Although the technology of online training can provide enhanced access to learning, it is important not to minimize the importance of learner characteristics.

E-learning relies on the learner to initiate the learning process, participate in the learning event, and apply new learnings to the job. However, many factors outside of the learners' control can impact learning transfer. Examples of these factors include a weak continuous learning culture, situational constraints, and lack of support from coworkers and supervisors. If these obstacles are not addressed, the possibility exists that new learnings and skills will not be transferred to the workplace.

Guidelines and Tips to Maximize Transfer

The technology of online training and education can naturally overcome some of the transfer obstacles. However, it is important to address the remaining obstacles. Below, we identify some guidelines and tips for maximizing the transfer of learning in online training and education:

- *Build training that is both relevant and similar to the job.* Employees engaging in e-learning may not have the benefit of an experienced trainer to show them how the training is relevant to the job. Therefore, it is even more important in e-learning to ensure that the training content is on target. This implies an even greater need for a thorough training needs analysis prior to the development of online training.

- *Promote the instrumentality and value of the learning.* Demonstrate how engaging in this particular e-learning initiative will help the employee perform the job more effectively. This is particularly important here because people typically have greater choice to participate. One way to accomplish this is to provide thorough course descriptions so users can accurately identify which course to take. These descriptions can highlight how the training helps make the job easier or increases readiness for career advancement. If you promote the value of the online learning initiative, a greater number of employees may choose to participate, and those that do should be more motivated to learn.

- *Be selective about required courses.* If the culture allows people to pass online tests, then allowing individuals to "test out" of required courses will free their time to participate in courses that will add value to their career. But certain courses can and should be mandated. When used selectively, the "required" label can signal importance. Overuse, however, dilutes its value and can hurt motivation to learn.

- *Build in some intelligent tutoring capabilities.* Intelligent tutoring capabilities allow online training to adjust to the particular trainee. When properly implemented, this feature can enhance individual learning.

- *Prepare computer-phobic individuals to profit from the training.* Many employees remain uncomfortable about their ability to use computers. These computer-phobics must be adequately prepared through preliminary training or coaching before the benefits of online training and education can be realized.

- *Whenever possible, develop the opportunity for practice and feedback.* E-learning shouldn't simply be cool and fun (although that doesn't hurt); it must also incorporate sound instructional design principles to ensure that employees learn and retain information. Building practice and feedback opportunities into the e-learning are two examples of sound instructional design attributes that can facilitate transfer.

- *Build in action planning and other follow-up devices.* Building in action planning capabilities and providing advice about how to follow up after training can help trainees gain support and encouragement from peers and supervisors, while fostering self-monitoring and personal follow-up.

- *Evaluate transfer and usage.* With e-learning, it is helpful to evaluate which courses are being accessed, what is learned from those courses, what is being applied on the job, and where trainees are encountering obstacles to transfer.

Enhancing Transfer in Performance Support

Performance support refers to computer-aided support to workers as they perform their jobs.

The Good News

Performance support systems often reduce or eliminate concerns with job relevance. Of all the e-learning initiatives, a performance support system (PSS) should be the most relevant and most similar to the job because it is built to support actual work processes. In fact, the line between work and support is often blurred with electronic performance support as sometimes a PSS is "baked into" the job—that is, it is a requirement of the job. When the connection between the learning event (using the PSS) and job performance is so clear, transfer can be seamless. Of course, the information in the PSS must be considered credible by the employee for this to be true.

Time lag is another transfer obstacle that is naturally mitigated by this technology. Learning occurs on the job, at the work station or by using a hand-held device. People use it as needs arise, which leads to minimal time lag between learning and application.

In some cases, even lack of encouragement or support from coworkers and supervisors can be overcome by implementing a PSS. In an environment where supervisors are unable or unwilling to spend time advising employees how to address issues, a well-designed PSS can help overcome this lack of support. In essence, the PSS becomes a surrogate advice giver—supporting the employee in lieu of support from others.

Finally, a good PSS can even overcome some employee limitations. The goal of performance support is to provide support and knowledge to employees to help them perform their jobs at a higher level than they could do on their own. Thus, obstacles such as low self-efficacy and low ability or aptitude are targets that performance support systems may attempt to overcome.

Areas of Continued Concern

Performance support systems are built to enhance performance. Someone who doesn't care about the job or is not committed to the organization will probably not be motivated to access the system. With the exception of those cases where the PSS is baked into the job, the system will only support performance for those who choose to access it.

Second, performance support systems do not typically provide feedback to the employee unless there is a practice mode built in. An employee often accesses the PSS and then attempts to apply the advice to real work. If feedback is inherent in the task, it's simple to modify behavior accordingly. However, if the employee cannot tell if the effort is really working, then the PSS may or may not improve performance.

Also, performance support systems are often better at building knowledge than developing skills. For example, the PSS might tell the employee the right thing to do, but that doesn't mean that the employee has the skills to do it properly. Performance support does not override the need for skill development.

Finally, some system design issues must be addressed for a PSS to have a positive impact on knowledge transfer. For example, the PSS must be organized so that the employee can quickly find and apply information, often on a real-time basis. If knowledge organization is poor and information takes too long to access, the system will be abandoned quickly. In essence, the PSS should mirror how people think and work so that it can be easily integrated into the job.

Guidelines and Tips to Maximize Transfer

Performance support systems can naturally overcome some of the transfer obstacles. However, it is important to address the remaining obstacles to enhance learning in this context. Here are some guidelines and tips for maximizing the transfer of learning in performance support:

- *Take time building the PSS.* Spend time up front storyboarding and conducting user testing to ensure that the PSS will be useful to the employees. Throughout the process, ensure that the PSS is relevant to the job, easy to access, and organized so that information can be easily found.

- *Determine what information is "need to know" versus "need to access."*
  Employees must know certain elements of job-relevant information without looking them up. Other information should
  be easily accessible on an as-needed basis. These two types of
  information should be treated differently in the development
  of training and support systems. A thorough needs analysis
  can be useful in identifying "need to know" information,
  which can be conveyed through some form of training, and
  "need to access" information, which can be built into a PSS to
  be obtained when needed. This not only ensures that the
  proper information is contained in the PSS but also that the
  system is not overloaded with irrelevant information.
- *Involve credible sources in the PSS development.* When building the
  PSS, involve both experts and "real people"—people actually
  doing the job in question—in the process. Working with high
  performers from the job you are attempting to support will
  ensure that the PSS is applicable to the job and increase the
  credibility of the system in the eyes of potential users.
- *For high-discretion jobs, allow people to access information in multiple ways.* Some jobs are low-discretion (that is, the employee
  has little ability to alter procedures from day to day). In
  these instances, the PSS can guide the employee through the
  prescribed process in a linear manner. However, for high-
  discretion jobs, such as many professional positions, the PSS
  must be flexible. Allowing employees to access information
  from multiple points of entry and in multiple ways enables
  employees who may approach a problem differently to find
  equally useful advice.
- *Supplement the PSS with training.* Providing some form of orientation on how to use the system and what users will find when
  they get there will enhance the usability of the system.
- *Update the PSS.* An obsolete PSS is less than useless; it can be
  dangerous. Continually update the system with the most
  recent knowledge, support, and information. This process can
  be facilitated by creating a mechanism for soliciting feedback
  from the users about the type of support that is needed but
  not currently available. A well-designed PSS has an administrative capability that allows for easy updating of information.
- *Assess the effectiveness of the PSS.* Through usability testing and
  other methods, ensure that the PSS is effective in supporting

employee performance. One approach is to provide a pilot group with simulated events and determine whether accessing the PSS allows the users to successfully solve problems.

Case Example: Designing a PSS to Maximize Transfer

HR professionals can use gOEbase (http://www.gOEbase.com), a Web-based PSS, for online support for their internal consulting or business partner role. This system can help them work closely with managers, pointing out the right questions to ask to identify business needs and opportunities and assisting with problem diagnosis, innovative solutions, and evaluating success. Traditionally, performance support systems have been designed for low-discretion jobs—where individuals follow a lockstep process to accomplish a task (such as taking an order or troubleshooting a computer problem). This one is different in that it provides support to a high-discretion professional job.

The gOEbase PSS was designed to allow users to access resources in multiple ways. In high-discretion jobs, different people think and work differently. Thus, individual users should be able to find resources in a way that is aligned with their own working style. For instance, users can navigate the system through an "issue definer" based on an expert's model of the job. The issue definer allows users to define their problem and then quickly guides them to the most pertinent resources to address their need. Users can also browse through a "resource library," examining resources clustered by relevant topic areas or by type of resource. Alternatively, they can use a "search" mechanism that allows them to find all resources that contain relevant phrases.

Users of gOEbase can take advantage of its extensive cross-resource linking. This is particularly useful in high-discretion jobs, where users understand the problem they face but may not know the exact name of a tool that they need. They can enter gOEbase through any navigational method and then follow "thought streams," jumping quickly from resource to resource until they see the right tool to address their need.

This PSS is in use at more than forty major organizations. It is often supplemented with training designed to build the skills some users will need to apply the advice contained in the system effectively. The training can also teach any information that users will need to know without accessing the PSS. The content is updated at least monthly based on online user feedback and an analysis of usage patterns. Users receive monthly reminders about updated content to encourage them to access the system.

An analysis of usage patterns reveals that gOEbase's features are working as intended. Each of the navigational methods is used extensively by a subset of the users. Users are able to follow thought streams and find the tools and resources they need quite quickly, suggesting that the organizational schema and cross-resource links are working effectively. Repeat usage levels reveal that the regular updating and reminders appear to be fostering high levels of motivation among users—a critical element, given that system usage is not mandated.

Enhancing Transfer in Knowledge Management

Knowledge management refers to an organization's attempt to capture, store, and organize information from their employees, making this information available to others throughout the organization.

The Good News

As is the case with most e-learning initiatives, the employee typically has discretion about when and how to access the knowledge management system. This discretion can be empowering and build a sense of ownership. This sense of ownership often motivates employees to contribute to the knowledge management system when appropriate, as well as to access the system for guidance.

Another transfer obstacle that can be overcome through the use of knowledge management is time lag. Although perhaps not as direct a relationship as in performance support systems, accessing a knowledge management system occurs on the job (at the work station or via a hand-held device) so the time lag between learning and application is minimized. People use the system as needs arise.

Further, when the right people participate (that is, people dealing with similar issues), the job relevance of information in the system should be high. This can lead to increased system usage, and hopefully to enhanced user performance. In fact, building an online chat capability into the knowledge management system can allow employees to reach knowledgeable coworkers directly. This allows individuals to further explain, clarify, or discuss data contained in the system.

Finally, the opportunity exists for a properly developed and supported knowledge management system to raise the performance level of all employees. For instance, knowledge management systems provide the opportunity for employees with lower self-efficacy or ability to tap into the expertise of more seasoned employees. In some cases, knowledge management can increase job identification, if a successful "community of practice" is formed. Knowledge management systems can't single-handedly overcome a weak continuous learning culture that inhibits sharing of knowledge, but they can help.

Areas of Continued Concern

Although user discretion can be empowering, choice to participate remains a primary concern with knowledge management systems. Individuals can't learn if they don't access the system. Further, impact will be limited if a critical mass of users is not reached. There are many reasons why employees may choose not to access the system. For instance, they may not have time to access it, may view it as additional work, or may be afraid to lose leverage if they share their expertise with others. Therefore, it is essential to motivate employees to access the knowledge management system.

As is the case with much of e-learning, knowledge management systems rely on the employee to initiate the learning process, participate in the learning, and apply new learnings to the job. There remain many factors outside of the employees' control that can impact learning transfer. Examples of these factors include a weak continuous learning culture, situational constraints, and lack of support from coworkers and supervisors. More specific to knowledge management, a culture of sharing must exist for employees to feel comfortable contributing to the system. If these obstacles are not addressed, a strong possibility exists that the system will not be successful.

Users of the knowledge management system must see value in accessing and using the system. Employees need to believe in the value of the content and must see that it is relevant and helps them perform better on the job. The system can actually be a distraction if it is used to focus on trivia or as a place to complain.

A knowledge management system captures, stores, and provides access to knowledge. This doesn't necessarily mean, however, that additional guidance, advice, feedback, and support will be available. Without this, the employee may not know how to apply this new knowledge on the job. Therefore, supportive peers and supervisors remain critical components of a successful knowledge management system.

Guidelines and Tips to Maximize Transfer

Knowledge management systems can naturally overcome some of the transfer obstacles. However, it is important to address the remaining obstacles to enhance learning in this context. Here are some guidelines and tips for maximizing the transfer of learning in knowledge management:

- *Take time building the knowledge management system.* Up-front design work is critical to the development of knowledge management systems. To entice and keep users, the system must be quick and easy to use, contain a logical knowledge structure, and be based on effective knowledge elicitation. One way to ensure this happens is to involve potential users and design experts in the design process.
- *Let people know the system exists.* Many high-quality knowledge management systems are not being used for the simple reason that they are not well publicized. Marketing and promotion are not things you do only to outside customers. Once the system is up and running, it is critical to spread the word about the benefits to employees.
- *Keep people coming back.* Once you have users, keep them. A knowledge management system should contain job-relevant, useful information that employees will want to access. Beyond this, however, create other features that can increase the "stickiness" of the system. For example, post key documents, latest company news, stock information, and other resources to drive traffic up (be careful, though, to avoid the inclination to load every tangentially related piece of information). Next, remind employees to use the system. E-mail notices and other reminders can significantly increase traffic.
- *Reward people for using the system.* Follow-up and encouragement can come from many sources. Advocates of the system can encourage employees to use the system by touting its benefits. Supervisors can encourage usage by driving their subordinates to the system when appropriate (for example, asking, "Did you go to the KM system first?"). Often, accessing a computer system is a drastic shift from more traditional ways of getting answers, and employees who make this shift should be rewarded for their efforts.

- *Consider the use of knowledge managers.* Knowledge managers can perform many functions for the organization. For instance, they can screen content for quality and applicability to the system, they can help avoid information clutter by deleting outdated materials, they can even take the pulse of the users to see what is working and what should be changed. All of these functions can help the system be successful.
- *Assess system usage.* Capture usage trends and other relevant information. For example, identifying which areas are accessed most frequently or identifying common questions can help determine when to modify the knowledge structure or capabilities of the system.

Case Example: Designing Knowledge Management and Training to Maximize Transfer

A large, well-known sales organization had a problem. New territories could not be staffed until newly hired sales professionals were prepared to handle an extremely complex sales job. Sales professionals needed a wide range of knowledge and skills and had to be able to access product and customer information quickly and accurately. Unfortunately, on average it took nearly seven months to prepare a new sales professional—much too long to be successful in a competitive market. Further, if sales professionals were sent out prematurely, the results were unsatisfactory. An analysis of the situation uncovered that part of the problem was that new sales professionals were being asked to learn a tremendous amount of information before going out on their own. In essence, the new sales professionals were being asked to know everything before they could do anything.

The first step to solving this problem was to form a group of credible, respected managers and sales professionals to act as subject matter experts. They helped identify the types of information new sales professionals truly needed to know (that is, what they had to memorize prior to moving into a new territory) and what information could be better defined as "need to access" (that is, information that needed to be readily available but not necessarily memorized). With this information as a guide, an intranet-based KM system was developed to maintain the "need to access" information and a training program was developed to teach sales professionals the "need to know" content and prepare them to quickly access and use the KM system.

The KM system was organized around the sales process—a process that was taught during training and reinforced regularly on the job. This schema allowed users to quickly access information, templates, and advice in a way that was a logical extension of their job.

One question that the subject matter experts were continually asked during the design process was, How will this feature or content help the sales professional succeed on the job? As a result, both the KM system and the training had high job relevance, and their instrumentality for fostering individual success was heavily promoted by the organization's leaders. Users would be rewarded not for simply accessing the system but because by accessing the system they would be more successful.

All new sales professionals were required to complete the self-paced training. Next, they had to demonstrate that they possessed the necessary knowledge and could quickly find information from the KM system to address common needs. Only then would they be allowed to assume field responsibilities.

Results were impressive—new sales professionals responded positively to the system because they were able to assume job responsibilities faster, and both new and existing sales professionals felt they could easily access relevant content as needs emerged. Sales managers liked the system because it allowed them to spend their time coaching their sales teams rather than answering basic content questions. Most important, the organization was able to reduce the time it took to develop fully qualified sales professionals from seven months to just over two and a half months, a significant return on the investment.

Conclusions

It can be a long road from conception to application of an e-learning program. Many obstacles can arise as individuals decide whether to participate in a learning event, learn from that event, and attempt to transfer new knowledge and skills to the job. In conclusion, here are a few lessons learned from this chapter.

E-Learning Initiatives Share a Few Common Advantages

The three types of e-learning we examined in this chapter share a few common attributes. All three help overcome some of the same transfer obstacles. In particular, they all provide increased participant flexibility, allowing individuals greater choices about when and how to participate. This is critical since lack of choice can inhibit trainee motivation. It is difficult to manage enrollments in traditional classroom training while still allowing trainees sufficient flexibility about when to attend. In today's often-chaotic work environments, it can be quite helpful to allow employees to use some discretion about when they participate in a learning event, even allowing for last-minute changes to accommodate sudden work demands. Online training, performance support systems, and knowledge management can be structured to allow that flexibility, whereas traditional classroom training typically cannot. Of course, as noted earlier, flexibility is a two-edged sword. Insufficient uptake or participation levels can undermine an otherwise well-designed e-learning initiative.

The other common, critical advantage of the three e-learning approaches is that they can all be quite effective at reducing or eliminating the time lag between learning and doing. Because employees can participate in online training, access a PSS, or use a KM system when they have an immediate job-related need, the time lag before application is inherently less than we normally see with classroom training. That is not to say that employees won't choose to access e-learning options at the wrong time or for the wrong reasons, or that companies won't mandate usage patterns that create de facto time lags. However, a consistent strength of e-learning initiatives is their ability to reduce skill decay through just-in-time application of learning. Given the clear negative impact of time lag on skill retention, this is an important contribution.

On the other hand, none of the three e-learning approaches inherently address the other post-training obstacles such as lack of follow-up, weak learning culture, and situational constraints. These post-training obstacles, unless they are addressed through other means, can inhibit the effectiveness of any e-learning effort. The three e-learning approaches also show different patterns in their natural ability to address other obstacles such as trainee attributes and motivational factors. None of the three will naturally overcome all or even most of the remaining obstacles without careful design, implementation, and attention to human dynamics issues. Table 9.2 presents a summary of how well the three e-learning initiatives address each of the common obstacles to transfer.

Table 9.2. Relationship Between E-Learning Initiatives and Transfer Obstacles.

Transfer Obstacle	E-learning Initiative		
	Online Training and Education	Performance Support Systems	Knowledge Management
Trainee Attributes			
External locus of control	?	?	?
Low self-efficacy	−	+	+
Low need for achievement	−	?	?
Low ability or aptitude	?	+	?
Motivational Factors			
Lack of job identification	?	−	+
Lack of organizational commitment	?	−	?
Lack of choice to participate	+	?	+
Low perceived instrumentality or value	?	?	?
The Training			
Lack of perceived relevance to work	?	+	?
Poor trainer capabilities	−	?	?
Lack of feedback	?	?	?
Other instructional design limitations	?	?	?
Post-Training Environment			
Weak continuous learning culture	−	?	−
Lack of follow-up, encouragement, and feedback	+	+	−
Time lag (no opportunity to apply)	+	+	+
Situational constraints	−	?	−

Note: + = Transfer obstacle typically mitigated by this form of e-learning initiative.

− = Transfer obstacle rarely mitigated by this form of e-learning initiative.

? = Transfer obstacle may be mitigated depending on the design and implementation of the e-learning initiative.

Not All E-learning Initiatives Are the Same

Although the three approaches share an ability to increase flexibility and decrease time lags, in practice it is better not to think of them as a common, homogeneous set of initiatives. A close review reveals that each has its own strengths and weaknesses, each is better equipped to address certain obstacles, and each requires attention to different details to ensure transfer.

For example, we advocated spending sufficient time during initial project phases, actively encouraging participant usage, and assessing effectiveness for all three initiatives. However, even within these common themes, subtle differences appear.

Although all three initiatives suffer when insufficient time is spent determining needs and designing the solution, the way that time is spent should be different. Online training can incorporate an implicit trainer model, and as a result, effort should be taken to incorporate appropriate instructional design principles (such as practice and feedback) and build in capabilities to emulate effective trainer practices. In contrast, knowledge management systems do not have a formal instructional design element to them. Instead, a key issue during needs analysis and design is building an appropriate knowledge organization, one that allows users to easily and intuitively find information and connect with the right experts and resources. When analyzing user needs for a PSS, a key focal point is teasing out the differences between information that people need to know, and hence must be trained to remember, and information that people can access, and hence can be included in the PSS. Note that all three approaches will rely on expert input for content accuracy and credibility, but the focus of what is needed from those experts is different to address different transfer needs.

We also advocated actively encouraging employees to use the three types of e-learning initiatives. Again, while the general advice is the same, there are subtle differences in the underlying obstacles. For example, with a knowledge management system, a key obstacle to participation is cultural in nature. Unless employees feel that knowledge sharing is acceptable—and that everyone is encouraged to share their expertise with others—the knowledge management system will be underutilized. A primary obstacle is the perceived loss of power that employees may feel if they give away their expertise to others or the perceived risk of looking inept if they pose a "stupid" question to the community of users. Unless these perceived threats are overcome, transfer will be minimized.

With online learning there is often no need for participants to share their expertise with others, so the types of threats that are common with knowledge management systems may be irrelevant. A bigger issue is encouraging people to take the time to participate in online learning modules. As part of the communication and marketing process, employees need to be educated about how the modules can make their jobs easier or help them advance. They need clear descriptions of each module so they can make informed judgments about when to participate. Perceived instrumentality is typically more of an issue with online learning than it is with knowledge management.

Finally, we noted that assessing effectiveness is critical for all three types of initiatives, but yet again, certain differences emerge. With online learning, some of the more traditional evaluation practices can be appropriate, such as assessing knowledge acquisition and retention (knowledge testing) and subsequent transfer (on-the-job performance). However, care must also be taken to examine usage levels. High knowledge retention and strong transfer among participants would be encouraging, but if only a few of the people who need the module are taking it, then the obstacle to transfer lies in the first hurdle, choosing to participate, and changes to the module itself will be unlikely to address the issue.

In contrast, if users are expected to access a PSS when they need information, then it does not make sense to use traditional knowledge recall tests to assess learning. The purpose of the PSS is to allow users to address situations as they arise by accessing advice through the PSS quickly and logically. Therefore, one very effective way of assessing the effectiveness of a PSS is to present users with scenarios and ask them to use the PSS, thinking out loud while they do so, to assess how the PSS may help resolve common problems (or determine what the PSS is missing).

Speed and ease of access are also key requirements for transfer with both a PSS and a knowledge management system. If advice cannot be accessed quickly and easily, people will stop using the applications. Therefore, an evaluation of a PSS or knowledge management system must include a careful assessment of these factors.

In all cases, evaluation is critical because it can reveal remaining obstacles to transfer. However, the appropriate evaluation design and approach will be contingent on the type of initiative.

Each Company Is Unique

Although we highlighted some common themes across e-learning approaches and could distinguish a few typical concerns for each e-learning approach, each e-learning initiative is unique. Research has shown that organizations differ in their environmental readiness for learning, and even within an organization, each e-learning initiative will present some unique challenges. While e-learning can naturally overcome certain obstacles, the use of e-learning technology, will never, in and of itself, assure maximal transfer. Successful transfer in an e-learning environment is contingent upon anticipating and diagnosing key transfer obstacles—before, during, and after learning events—and addressing those obstacles through both technological and nontechnological means.

References

Alliger, G. M., Bennett, W., & Tannenbaum, S. I. (1995, May). *Transfer of training: Comparison of paradigms.* Paper presented at the Tenth Annual Society of Industrial/Organizational Psychology Meeting, Orlando, FL.

Baldwin, T. T., & Ford, J. K. (1998). Transfer of training: A review and directions for future research. *Personnel Psychology, 41,* 63–105.

Baldwin, T. T., Magjuka, R. J., & Loher, B. T. (1991). The perils of participation: Effects of choice of training on trainee motivation and learning. *Personnel Psychology, 44*(1), 51–65.

Bandura, A. (1986). *Social foundations of thought and action: A social cognitive theory.* Upper Saddle River, NJ: Prentice Hall.

Baumgartel, H., Reynolds, M., & Pathan, R. (1984). How personality and organizational climate variables moderate the effectiveness of management development programmes: A review and some recent research findings. *Management and Labour Studies, 9,* 1–16.

Becker, D. (1999). Training on demand. *TechWeek, 11,* 16–22.

Bennett, J. B., Lehman, W.E.K., & Forst, J. K. (1999). Change, transfer climate, and customer orientation: A contextual model and analysis of change-driven training. *Group and Organization Management, 24*(2), 188–216.

Bennett, W., Jr. (1995, July). Factors that influence the effectiveness of training in organizations: A meta-analytic review. *Dissertation Abstracts International, 57–01A,* 0097. Accession no: 1996-95014-163.

Briggs, G. E., & Naylor, J. C. (1962). The relative efficiency of several training methods as a function of transfer task complexity. *Journal of Experimental Psychology, 64,* 505–512.

Carliner, S. (1999). *An overview of on-line learning.* Amherst, MA: HRD Press.

Carlson, D. S., Bozeman, D. P., Kacmar, K. M., Wright, P. M., & McMahan, G. C. (2000). Training motivation in organizations: An analysis of individual-level antecedents. *Journal of Managerial Issues, 12*(3), 271–287.

Cheng, E.W.L., & Ho, D.C.K. (2001). A review of transfer of training studies in the past decade. *Personnel Review, 30*(1–2), 102–118.

Colquitt, J. A., LePine, J. A., & Noe, R. A. (2000). Toward an integrative theory of training motivation: A meta-analytic path analysis of 20 years of research. *Journal of Applied Psychology, 85*(5), 678–707.

Eddy, E. R., Stone-Romero, E. F., & Stone, D. L. (1999). The effects of information management policies on reactions to human resource information systems: An integration of privacy and procedural justice perspectives. *Personnel Psychology, 52,* 335–358.

Facteau, J. D., Dobbins, G. H., Russell, J.E.A., Ladd, R. T., & Kudisch, J. D. (1992). The influence of general perceptions of the training environment on pretraining motivation and perceived training transfer. *Journal of Management, 21*(1), 1–25.

Filipczak, B. (1996). Training on the intranets: The hope and the hype. *Training, 33*(9), 24–32.

Fortune on-line learning supplement. (1999, May 24). *Fortune, 139*(10).

Gagne, R. M., Briggs, L. J., & Wagner, W. W. (1992). *Principles of instructional design* (4th ed.). Fort Worth, TX: Harcourt Brace Jovanovich.

Georgenson, D. L. (1982). The problem of transfer calls for partnership. *Training and Development Journal, 36*(10), 75–78.

Ghiselli, E. E. (1966). *The validity of occupational aptitude tests.* New York: Wiley.

Gick, M. L., & Holyoak, K. J. (1987). *The cognitive basis of knowledge transfer.* In S. M. Cormier & J. D. Hagman (Eds.), *Transfer of learning: Contemporary research and applications* (pp. 9–46). San Diego: Academic Press.

Henry, P. (2001). E-learning technology, content and services. *Education and Training, 43*(4–5), 249–255.

Hicks, W. D., & Klimoski, R. J. (1987). Entry into training programs and its effects on training outcomes: A field experiment. *Academy of Management Journal, 30,* 542–552.

Horton, W. (2000). *Designing Web-based training.* New York: Wiley.

Kozlowski, S.W.J., Gully, S. M., Brown, K. G., Salas, E., Smith E. M., & Nason, E. R. (2001). Effects of training goals and goal orientation traits on multidimensional training outcomes and performance adaptability. *Organizational Behavior and Human Decision Processes, 85*(1), 1–31.

Kraiger, K. (1995). Integrating training research. *Training Research Journal, 1,* 5–16.

Marx, R. D. (1982). Relapse prevention for managerial training: A model for maintenance of behavioral change. *Academy of Management Review, 7,* 433–441.

Mathieu, J. E., Tannenbaum, S. I., & Salas, E. (1992). Influences of individual and situational characteristics on measures of training effectiveness. *Academy of Management Journal, 35*(4), 828–847.

Michalak, D. F. (1981). The neglected half of training. *Training and Development Journal, 35*(5), 22–28.

Neel, R. G., & Dunn, R. E. (1960). Predicting success in supervisory training programs by the use of psychological tests. *Journal of Applied Psychology, 44,* 358–360.

Newstrom, J. W. (1984, August). *A role-taker/time differentiated integration of transfer strategies.* Paper presented at the 1984 meeting of the American Psychological Association, Toronto, Ontario.

Noe, R. A. (1986). Trainees' attributes and attitudes: Neglected influences on training effectiveness. *Academy of Management Review, 11*(4), 736–749.

Porter, L. W., Steers, R. M., Mowday, R. T., & Boulian, P. V. (1974). Organizational commitment, job satisfaction, and turnover among psychiatric technicians. *Journal of Applied Psychology, 59,* 603–609.

Rotter, J. B. (1966). Generalized expectancies for internal vs. external control of reinforcement. *Psychological Monographs, 80*(1), 609.

Saks, A. M. (2002). So what is a good transfer of training estimate? A reply to Kirkpatrick. *Industrial-Organizational Psychologist, 39*(3), 29–30.

Schwann, S. (1997). Media characteristics and knowledge acquisition in computer conferencing. *European Psychologist, 2*(3), 277–285.

Tannenbaum, S. I. (1997). Enhancing continuous learning: Diagnostic findings from multiple companies. *Human Resource Management, 36,* 437–452.

Tannenbaum, S. I., & Alliger, G. M. (2000). *Knowledge management: Clarifying the key issues.* Austin, TX: IHRIM.

Tannenbaum, S. I., Mathieu, J. E., Salas, E., & Cannon-Bowers, J. A. (1991). Meeting trainees' expectations: The influence of training fulfillment on the development of commitment, self-efficacy, and motivation. *Journal of Applied Psychology, 76*(6), 759–769.

Tracey, J. B., Tannenbaum, S. I., & Kavanagh, M. J. (1995). Applying trained skills on the job: The importance of the work environment. *Journal of Applied Psychology, 80*(2), 239–252.

Tyler, K. (2001). E-learning: Not just for e-normous companies anymore. *HR Magazine, 46*(5), 82–88.

Underwood, B. J. (1951). Associative transfer in verbal learning as a function of response similarity and degree of first-time learning. *Journal of Experimental Psychology, 42,* 44–53.

Warr, P., Allan, C., & Birdi, K. (1999). Predicting three levels of training outcome. *Journal of Occupational and Organizational Psychology, 72*(3), 351–375.

Wexley, K. N., & Latham, G. P. (1981). *Developing and training human resources in organizations.* Glenview, IL: Scott Foresman.

Wexley, K. N., & Thornton, C. L. (1972). Effect of verbal feedback of test results upon learning. *Journal of Educational Research, 66,* 119–121.

CHAPTER 10

The Transfer of Team Training

Recommendations for Practice

Janis A. Cannon-Bowers
Eduardo Salas
Laura Martin Milham

Although teams and team training have become commonplace in many organizations, relatively little attention has been paid to enhancing the transfer of team training. This chapter isolates factors unique to team training situations and extends what is known regarding individual transfer to the team level. Several case studies, representing both positive and negative experiences with team training, are presented as a means to frame what is known. And though empirical research support is still modest, the chapter offers twenty-one practical recommendations for enhancing the transfer of team training in organizations.

The use of teams and team-based organizations is becoming more commonplace. Several facts explain this trend. First, teams are believed to be more effective than individuals in performing complex tasks (Hill, 1982), a belief that may or may not be true (see Steiner, 1972). Second, in many cases, the complexity of a task requires the coordination of a number of people working together (Cannon-Bowers & Salas, 1998; Modrick, 1986). Examples here include medical teams, aviation teams, firefighting teams, and military teams, all of which have physical and mental demands that exceed the capacity of a single individual. Finally, the use of teams has become popular as a means to flatten hierarchical structures, increase worker autonomy (as with semiautonomous work groups) and enhance employee involvement and motivation (Ilgen, 1999).

Because teams have become more prevalent in modern industry, developing better team training programs is growing in importance as well. To accomplish this, strategies and methods that maximize both team training efficiency and effectiveness must be identified. The *efficiency* of a training program involves maximizing the utility associated with a given program (for example, minimizing time away from task or maximizing return on investment). Training *effectiveness,* on the other hand, refers to the degree to which desired training outcomes are achieved (Kraiger, Ford, & Salas, 1993). Of these outcomes, the most important—and complex—is the degree to which trainees transfer learned material back to the job. In this chapter we are particularly concerned with this issue, and more specifically, the transfer of team training. Our purpose is to delineate those factors that are unique to team training situations and to describe how those might affect transfer of team competencies. We selected this approach because, whereas much has been theorized and written about the transfer of individual knowledge, skills, and attitudes (KSAs), we find very little in the literature regarding factors that affect the transfer of team competencies. Hence, the goal of this chapter is to leverage and extend work on individual transfer to the team level.

To do this, we present several case studies—representing both positive and negative experiences with team training—as a means to frame what we know about successfully transferring team training. At the conclusion of each section, we include specific recommendations for enhancing team training transfer (and these are also summarized in a table). In most cases, these recommendations are extrapolated from the individual training literature and are in need of empirical verification. Therefore, we caution that these recommendations have not been formally validated; however, in most cases they are the logical extension of what we know about transfer at the individual level or are based on research into team training.

Case Study #1: Rock Climbing and Other Team-Building Exercises

Bob Jones is vice president for human resources at XYZ firm. Recently, the company has undergone a major reorganization around the concept of multidisciplinary product development teams. This new way of doing business hinges on the ability of employees from different parts of the organization to work cooperatively as a team to bring products quickly and successfully to market. Jones is concerned that employees need team training to help them with this transition, and he is considering sending employees to a team training workshop offered by a local vendor.

The program boasts that it builds teams through a series of challenging exercises, many of which involve strenuous physical activities including rock climbing. Before deciding to use the program, Jones decides to call a colleague at a local bank, Paula Mason, who had recently implemented a similar intervention to see what her experience has been. "Well," Mason began, "at first, things seemed to very positive. The trainees returned to work all charged up, and reported that the program had taught them a lot about being good teammates. But after a while it became apparent that nothing had really changed. Team members were having the same coordination difficulties they had before training. When I asked them about this, they said that although the program had helped them in principle, it really didn't teach them any new skills. So when they went back to the job, they knew that they should be better teammates, but they weren't sure how to do it."

The Nature of Team Training and Team Competencies

The story related here is all too common. In an effort to prepare team members, organizations often elect to purchase off-the-shelf training that is not tailored to the particular needs of the team or the team task. Our contention is that the transfer of team training can be optimized only when it is clear what the specific objectives of the training are. Hence, it is crucial to understand the nature of team training and team competencies as a basis for making training decisions. Once this is done, training can be purchased or developed—as long as it is designed to accomplish the specific needs of the task situation and the team.

The first distinction that needs to be made when discussing the nature of team training is the distinction between team training and team building (the confusion of which was the problem in case study #1). According to Salas, Rozell, Mullen, and Driskell (1999), *team building* is an intervention aimed at enhancing team processes and clarifying team member roles and responsibilities (see also Tannenbaum, Beard, & Salas, 1992). In contrast, we define *team training* as a set of theoretically based instructional strategies that create an environment wherein trainees can learn, understand, practice, and receive feedback on required team competencies (Salas & Cannon-Bowers, 1997). These instructional strategies consist of a set of tools for diagnosing, assessing, and remediating team performance; delivery methods that provide a mechanism for imparting targeted material; and appropriate content (that is, the KSAs). We contend that these tools, methods, and content together yield a set of potential strategies that can be implemented to teach teamwork objectives (Salas & Cannon-Bowers, 1997). These strategies can take different formats. Some team training programs consist of similar tools and methods but have very different objectives and content; in fact, a number of strategies have emerged in the literature. These include cross-training (Blickensderfer, Cannon-Bowers, & Salas, 1998), team coordination training (Weiner, Kanki, & Helmreich, 1993), team leader training (Tannenbaum, Smith-Jentsch, & Behson, 1998), and team self-correction (Blickensderfer, Cannon-Bowers, & Salas, 1997; Smith-Jentsch, Zeisig, Acton, & McPherson, 1998). Most of these have been tested and evaluated in simulation environments with very encouraging results (see Cannon-Bowers & Salas, 1998; Salas, Fowlkes, Stout, Milanovich, & Prince, 1999).

In sum, team training can be conceptualized as a set of strategies that create a realistic and relevant context in which team competencies can be practiced, assessed, and learned. Team training is more than just a "feel-good" intervention (like the team-building program described in the case study) and is not simply a one-time event. It is a continuous process of assessing requirements, needs, and deficiencies with strategies or approaches for enhancing teamwork in organizations (Salas & Cannon-Bowers, 1997).

Recommendation 1: Be clear on the goals of
team-level training, and do not confuse team
training with team-building interventions.

Content of Team Training

With respect to content, team training must train appropriate team
KSAs. Therefore, a description of team competencies is in order
as a means to describe what we expect team training programs to
train and transfer. Recently, Cannon-Bowers, Tannenbaum, Salas,
and Volpe (1995) described the knowledge, skills, and attitudes
(that is, competencies) for different kinds of teams and tasks.
According to these authors, team competencies can be held at the
individual or team levels. Further, team competencies can be
generic or specific with respect to the task or team. Team-generic
competencies are applicable to a variety of teams, while team-
specific competencies only apply to a specific set of team members.
Likewise, task-specific competencies are useful only in a particular
task, while task-generic competencies are applicable to a variety of
tasks. According to Cannon-Bowers et al., these factors create four
categories of team competencies—those that are specific to both
the task and team, those that are specific to the team but not to the
task, those that are specific to the task but not the team, and those
that are generic to both the task and team (see Table 10.1).

Context-Driven Competencies

The context-driven category refers to team-specific–task-specific
competencies. When a task involves high degrees of team interaction and interdependence, it most likely demands competencies
specific to both the task and the team. This is because team members must understand how to express their knowledge and skill in
a particular task context and with particular teammates. For example, when team members are unable to communicate as a result of
environmental constraints, they must exercise implicit coordination strategies (that is, coordinating without extensive discussion).
These depend on shared knowledge among team members—with
respect both to the task and to each other. Such shared knowledge
allows team members to anticipate the needs of teammates. It also

Table 10.1. Team Competencies.

Task	Team Specific	Team Generic
	Team	
Task Specific	*Knowledge* • Team member characteristics • Role responsibilities	*Knowledge* • Role responsibilities • Interaction patterns
	Skills • Compensatory behavior • Shared problem model development	*Skills* • Mutual performance monitoring • Compensatory behavior
	Attitudes • Team orientation • Collective efficacy	*Attitudes* • Task-specific teamwork attitudes
Task Generic	*Knowledge* • Team member characteristics • Knowledge of team mission, objectives, norms, resources	*Knowledge* • Understanding of teamwork skills
	Skills • Information exchange • Intrateam feedback	*Skills* • Assertiveness • Information exchange
	Attitudes • Team cohesion • Mutual trust	*Attitudes* • Collective orientation • Importance of teamwork

allows them to compensate for the weaknesses of teammates and to effectively modify their strategy in accordance with task demands.

Task-Contingent Competencies

When team members require competencies that are specific to the task but generic to the team (that is, they hold regardless of who is on the team), these are called task-contingent competencies. This typically occurs when the task is fairly well defined. In such cases, the behavioral discretion—that is, the degree to which team members have discretion in how to accomplish the task—is low (Cannon-Bowers, Salas, & Blickensderfer, 1998). Therefore, it is not important who the team member is—anyone who gets the job will perform it in a similar manner. For example, in highly proceduralized tasks like those found in manufacturing, a team member must learn how to perform a specific role within the context of the task, and this role remains fairly constant regardless of the particular teammates in the current mix.

Team-Contingent Competencies

When team members must be knowledgeable about one another but can apply this knowledge across tasks, they require team-contingent competencies. This would apply to situations where team members are required to work together across a variety of tasks. In this case, having shared knowledge about one another will help team members better communicate and coordinate regardless of the specifics of the task. Various types of semiautonomous work groups, where the team performs several tasks with different roles but with the same team members, would fall into this category.

Transportable Competencies

These refer to team competencies that apply to all tasks and teams. For example, it may be beneficial to have good communication skills regardless of the particular team members or task involved. In such cases, it is expected that such competencies will generalize to a variety of task and team situations.

Deriving Team Competencies

Characteristics of the task and the team must be identified to determine the appropriate competencies and, in turn, content for team training. For example, the degree of behavioral discretion of team members helps to determine the specific nature of team competencies required. As noted, behavioral discretion refers to the degree to which the task allows team members to exercise discretion in how they complete it (Cannon-Bowers, Salas, & Blickensderfer, 1998). We hypothesize, therefore, that when behavioral discretion is low, emphasis on training task procedures will enhance transfer. On the other hand, when team members are relatively free to express their own style in performing the task, transfer will depend on the degree to which team members understand their particular teammates as well as their knowledge of task demands.

Interdependence—that is, the level of task dependency in a team—is also a characteristic of interest. For example, some tasks require team members to work relatively interdependently, with everyone's work heavily dependent on the input or output of another member. The interdependence of a team can be further examined from the perspective of high or low behavioral discretion. Team tasks that require high interdependence and high behavioral discretion (that is, context-driven) may benefit from training in teamwork skills focusing on knowledge about the preferences, style, competencies, and desires of teammates as well as specific training on task factors such as task structure, sequencing, timing, and the like. If there is relatively low interdependence but high behavioral discretion (that is, team-contingent), knowing the characteristics of teammates may allow team members to distribute work according to strengths and weaknesses, since roles are not so well defined as to be restrictive (Cannon-Bowers, Salas, & Blickensderfer, 1998). Conversely, when behavioral discretion is low but interdependence high (that is, task-contingent), knowing the task and role very well will be most beneficial, but knowing specific teammates is less important since the task is performed the same way regardless of who takes the role. If there is low behavioral discretion and low interdependence (transportable), only the most generic teamwork skills may be required for effective task performance.

Team Task Analysis

To determine which team competencies are required in a task environment and to identify how different individuals should contribute to overall team performance, a team task analysis (TTA) is important. Although preliminary guidelines exist for performing TTA (Bowers, Baker, & Salas, 1994), there is not yet a standard methodology, nor do existing methods account for all the observable variables. Major goals of task analysis are to break down the task into components and to identify the KSAs necessary to perform the task. TTA has additional requirements, including determining task structures, role distribution among team members, which competencies are required by which team members, contributions of each team member, and objectives for training. Bowers et al. provided a methodology for identifying tasks that require coordination, then examining the task interdependencies. This approach is a promising first step in specifying the specific KSAs required for a team's task. However, the concepts of behavioral discretion and interdependence (as described earlier) have not been incorporated into team task analytic methods. More development in this area is required.

> Recommendation 2: Conduct a team task
> analysis to determine the nature of team
> competencies required for the task at hand
> using the level of behavioral discretion
> and interdependence as key indicators.

The preceding discussion regarding the nature of team training and team competencies is important because it lays the groundwork for the design of team training and hence transfer. However, our contention is that specifying the appropriate content for team training (that is, by revealing the required KSAs) and designing sound instruction represent a necessary but not sufficient condition for team training to transfer. In addition to these factors, a number of other issues will affect transfer. The following sections delineate such factors, organized according to whether they are related to individual differences, training design, or contextual factors.

Case Study #2: So, Why Do I
Need to Be in a Team at All?

The training manager for a large airline was recently interviewed by a popular industry magazine about the company's experience with crew resource management (CRM) training. The main focus of CRM training is to teach effective teamwork skills among the pilot, copilot, and crew, especially in the face of emergencies. According to the training manager, efforts to successfully implement the training in the early 1990s were slow in gaining traction. "The problem was," she said, "that pilots are not team oriented. They are trained to be self-sufficient, and have developed a culture of fearlessness due to the inherent danger involved in the task. On top of that, many of our pilots are military-trained, which was making the problem even worse. We'd send the crews to training, and the pilots would spend the whole time arguing that they could do it all—we called it the 'Cowboy Syndrome.'" The manager went on to say that they solved this problem by spending time at the beginning of training changing the pilots' attitudes toward teamwork. This was done by presenting a series of case studies and vignettes that dealt with real cases of failures of teamwork in the cockpit, all of which had disastrous consequences. In some cases, she added, "we even had to put the crews in the simulator and show them how vulnerable they were. The good news is that it worked. In fact, the military has since adopted CRM programs too. It's taken awhile, but we have really seen the culture change and now our efforts to train teamwork are much more successful."

Individual and Team-Level Differences in Team Training

Just as individual differences among employees affect the effectiveness of individual training, what the employees bring to the table also affects the success of team training. Some of these differences exist at the individual level (for example, attitudes toward teamwork, as in case study #2), while others are team-level constructs, for example, the team's prior history of working together. Clearly, more research is needed to better understand how various individual and team-level differences affect the transfer of team training. The following paragraphs describe what we know to date in this area and offer some preliminary recommendations for making use of this knowledge. Specifically, team characteristics we discuss include team ability, team history and experience, and team attitudes. Generalizing from the individual level, we can hypothesize that all of these will have an impact on how training is designed—and in turn on how well it transfers.

Team Ability

At the individual level, a trainee's aptitude or ability can affect the quality and depth of learning. In addition, if a trainee is determined not to have requisite competencies, remedial activities can be developed before the training begins. Such remediation is crucial to ensure that desired transfer occurs. By the same token, the initial ability of a team will affect how ready members are to benefit from training. However, little has been written about how to assess a team's aptitude for training. For example, it might be appropriate to measure the ability level of each individual on the team and then sum or average this level to determine the team's ability. In cases where team members are not highly specialized, such an approach might be appropriate. However, when team members require highly specialized knowledge and skill, this approach may not indicate true readiness for training. Here it may be more meaningful to assess the team members' individual aptitude with respect to the particular roles they will play. In addition, no attempts that we know of have been made to assess teamwork skills before training.

The question of how to determine a team's aptitude for training is important because, as at the individual level, remedial activities can be introduced prior to training that can enhance transfer. At the moment, the assertions that we make about team aptitude are based on our knowledge of team training, but they have not been empirically tested. Future research along these lines is needed. Based on this line of thinking, the following proposition applies:

> Recommendation 3: Maximize the transfer of
> team training by ensuring that team members
> have appropriate aptitudes for both the
> taskwork and teamwork aspects of the job.

Team History and Experience

Both team history and experience can affect transfer by helping to identify the nature of the team competencies chosen for training. *Team history* refers to the background that team members have together. The history that team members share will affect how well team members know one another's experience levels and competencies. History is important in some teams, because it influences the ability of team members to anticipate one another's actions and needs in a dynamic task situation. This is crucial in context-driven environments where team members have high degrees of behavioral discretion. For example, teams who have been operating together for a while may not need training designed to learn about each other; rather, the specifics of the task can be the focus of training.

Team history may also differ among team members. For example, if there is a new or novice member on the team, experienced members may provide information, input, or feedback to aid the new member, and may increase their performance monitoring of a new team member. Likewise, a novice team member who knows that another member is highly experienced may be trained to use workload sharing or offloading techniques during periods of high workload.

The experience levels of team members are also important to transfer for the same reasons. *Team experience* level refers to the level of exposure that team members have had to working in a team, or to working on similar tasks. When trainees already have experience working on team tasks, it can be assumed that they have basic team competencies. In such cases, only task-specific aspects of the job need to be emphasized in training.

Given what we have said, two propositions regarding team history and experience can be derived:

> Recommendation 4: When effective
> task performance depends upon
> knowledge of teammate characteristics
> (that is, in context-driven or team-contingent
> tasks), teams with a prior history of
> working together will be better able
> to transfer team training; hence, efforts
> to train and maintain intact teams
> should be made in these cases.

> Recommendation 5: Since transfer of
> team training will be higher for team
> members who have had prior experience
> successfully performing team tasks,
> select team members with prior experience
> for high-priority tasks.

Team Attitudes

Trainee attitudes toward teamwork may also impact motivation to transfer (Tannenbaum, Cannon-Bowers, Salas, & Mathieu, 1993). First, *collective efficacy* is the belief that a team can effectively accomplish a task. Campion, Medsker, and Higgs (1993) suggested that collective efficacy, or potency, was strongly related to effectiveness in work groups; Guzzo, Yost, Campbell, and Shea (1994) stated that it enhances team functioning. Tannenbaum et al. (1993) identified self-efficacy as an important predictor of learning and training performance. Based on these findings, we hypothesize that collective efficacy will enhance transfer in a manner similar to self-efficacy (Gist, 1997). Specifically, if team members enter training with low collective efficacy, it may affect their willingness to learn. Moreover, if training doesn't build collective efficacy early (especially when team members do not know each other at the onset of training), the likelihood of transfer will be reduced. Extrapolating the results from studies on self-efficacy, it seems likely that building collective efficacy can be accomplished by providing success experiences to trainees, demonstrating that the team has the wherewithal to accomplish the task.

Another attitude related to teamwork that can affect transfer is *collective orientation,* or the belief that the team approach is better than an individual one (Driskell & Salas, 1992). A team member holding this attitude may have greater expectations for team training than someone who prefers to work alone would have, and may have a higher motivation to transfer training as well. By the same token, individuals with low collective orientation may not benefit from team training because they do not appreciate being part of a team. It may be appropriate, therefore, to eliminate individuals with low collective orientation. While collective orientation is hypothesized to be an enduring characteristic, a related but more malleable concept is *attitudes toward teamwork* (Helmreich, Foushee, Benson, & Russini, 1986). Put simply, some employees have a negative attitude toward engaging in team tasks, often due to bad experiences in the past. This attitude has been found to affect a team member's willingness to engage in team-related behaviors, and it may have a similar effect on team training. Hence, it may be important to assess attitudes toward teamwork prior to training and, when low, attempt to raise them before team training. Using case studies and examples of teams that failed from lack of teamwork can be an effective method in this case.

Based on what we have said, the following recommendations regarding team attitudes and transfer apply:

> Recommendation 6: Since the initial
> collective efficacy level of the team will
> be directly related to the degree of transfer
> of teamwork to the operational environment,
> attempts to build collective efficacy
> should be made early in training.

> Recommendation 7: Likewise, team training
> strategies that build collective efficacy
> will have a higher degree of transfer, and
> should be employed where possible.

> Recommendation 8: Since individuals low
> in collective orientation are less likely
> to transfer teamwork competencies back to
> the job, collective orientation should be
> measured so that appropriate steps can
> be taken (even if this means excluding
> certain employees from team tasks).

> Recommendation 9: Team members'
> attitudes toward teamwork will affect
> their degree of transfer, and should be
> raised prior to training if necessary.

Case Study #3: Preparing to Prepare

As part of its community preparedness efforts, a local county government had arranged to conduct a large-scale exercise for first responders to prepare for emergency operations. The exercise, which was designed and conducted by a local university, offered a realistic scenario intended to give participants from disparate agencies a chance to practice working together as a team.

At the conclusion of the exercise, a detailed debriefing session was conducted so that participants could give and receive feedback about what happened. During the debrief, participants were asked to comment on their reactions to the training. The fire chief of one of the small municipal fire departments offered the following: "I liked all of the work we did prior to the exercise. In the past, we've just been thrown into a scenario without context or idea of what we were supposed to pay attention to at any given point. This time, the trainers spent time up front preparing us for the exercise and how to get the most out of it. That was very valuable and really made a difference for me." A civil servant from a federal emergency management agency added her observations: "The thing I thought was best was how realistic the scenario was. I mean, I knew that this was just an exercise, but after a while my own stress levels really started to build. I could see the same in my teammates as well." Finally, a paramedic from an area ambulance service said, "The most valuable part for me has been this debriefing session. I got a chance to hear how things went from everyone else's perspective; that really helped me. Now I understand that sometimes I'm misinterpreting the behavior of my teammates—not understanding what they are going through. It's also given us some specific things to work on—like communication procedures that weren't very good."

Several months after the exercise, a series of tornadoes hit the area. In the aftermath of the disaster, the agencies gathered to compile lessons learned from the experience. Among other things, all the participants agreed that the exercise they had all participated in months before had been excellent preparation for the real thing. "Even though we had limited experience together," the fire chief reported, "the fact that we had worked together in the past—and identified and fixed some of our problems ahead of time—was invaluable."

The Design of Team Training

Case study #3 represents a success story in team training. In particular, it highlights the number of factors related to the design of team training that can impact transfer. Obviously, specifying the correct team training content is a crucial element of training transfer, as discussed earlier. However, in addition to content, several training design elements also affect team training transfer, including pre-practice conditions, task and team fidelity, and feedback.

Pre-Practice Conditions

According to Cannon-Bowers, Rhodenizer, Salas, and Bowers (1998), several pre-practice techniques can enhance trainee learning and transfer. The most notable include advance organizers, pre-practice briefs, and metacognitive strategies.

Advance Organizers

Advance organizers are techniques that organize information before practice, allowing trainees to optimize learning during practice (Kraiger, Salas, & Cannon-Bowers, 1995). These techniques provide trainees with a structure for the information provided during training. According to Mayer (1989), advance organizers contribute to practice by indicating relationships between elements, providing organization, and allowing the integration of new information into existing knowledge.

In a team environment, advance organizers can be particularly useful by providing members with graphic cues, outlines, or other illustrative information that promote understanding of the relationships among task elements, team members, and subteams. This is especially true in highly interdependent tasks, where the sequence, timing, and relationship among different members' contributions to the task are complex. The sheer complexity of inputs and outputs among members can be overwhelming to team members without information that explicitly organizes it. In addition, advance organizers can help team members to build accurate expectations for the training.

Pre-Practice Briefs

Pre-practice briefs are another strategy that can be used to target expectations of team members. They give team members an organization of roles and responsibilities, so that people have clear expectations regarding team behaviors. This technique can promote diagnostic and self-regulatory skills by building trainees' mental models of team members and teamwork skills (Cannon-Bowers, Rhodenizer, et al., 1998). Once they have a structure of what behaviors are expected and when, trainees can begin to develop a framework of how to coordinate. In turn, pre-practice briefs can impact expectations of teamwork skills by focusing on their importance in the operational environment and increasing the potential for transfer.

Metacognitive Strategies

Experts commonly use what are called *metacognitive strategies* to track and diagnose their own performance. According to Cannon-Bowers, Rhodenizer, et al. (1998), *metacognition* is a self-regulatory mechanism that involves assessing and adjusting one's own strategy during task performance. By focusing trainees' attention on how they are solving problems, these strategies allow team members to provide feedback to themselves and go over areas that they do not understand. Tannenbaum et al. (1993) suggested that metacognitive skills may affect a trainee's motivation to transfer skills. At a team level, this may entail evaluation and adjustment of teamwork skills.

To date, the concept of metacognition has not been applied directly to the team level. Our hypothesis in this regard is that teams may be able to employ strategies at the team level that are similar to metacognition at the individual level. For example, at the individual level, metacognition helps learners to focus on their current learning state. At the team level, members could be trained to track team performance levels and bring this to the attention of the team. We hypothesize that transfer of team skills would be enhanced in such cases.

To summarize, the following propositions regarding pre-practice conditions and transfer are offered:

Recommendation 10: Include advance organizers that explain complex team and task relationships to help trainees better learn and transfer team competencies.

Recommendation 11: Pre-practice briefs that specify team roles and clarify expectations will help team members to benefit from team training and increase transfer; these should be designed into training where possible.

Recommendation 12: Team-level
metacognitive skills should be developed
in trainees because they will help the team to
monitor its level of mastery during team
training and result in better transfer.

Training Environment Fidelity

Models of transfer often focus on similarity between the training environment and the operational environment. Tulving and Thompson (1973) maintained that remembering will be optimal when the retrieval operations required at learning are duplicated in the operational setting. Based on this theory, Swezey and Llaneras (1997) suggested that training will transfer if the procedures used during training are those required during task performance. Transfer, then, can be increased if the cues provided during training are present in the operational environment.

Fidelity is defined as the degree to which the training environment is similar to the operational environment (Swezey & Llaneras, 1997). Two types of fidelity are task and team fidelity.

Task Fidelity

Task fidelity is the level of similarity between the training environment and the operational task. The training task may have physical fidelity (for example, a medical team trains in a room that looks just like a hospital operating room), response fidelity (for example, the medical team has to perform the same tasks, motions, and communications that they would in the real environment), or psychological fidelity (for example, the medical team is required to make decisions and coordinate in a manner similar to that of the actual environment). As noted earlier, team tasks with high task interdependence will require high task fidelity. Specifically, when the behavior of one team member is dependent on others, transfer will be enhanced if these task relationships are faithfully represented in training.

Team Fidelity

Team fidelity is the degree to which team members in the training environment are the same as those in the actual environment. We hypothesize in this regard that teams with high behavioral discretion and requiring high levels of shared knowledge will benefit from training in intact teams. For these teams, team fidelity is crucial. For example, implicit coordination may be an essential part of the task and require a host of team competencies specific to the particular set of teammates. In this case, team members would benefit from training with their real teams.

Additionally, team fidelity can include the similarity of the team roles and responsibilities between training and the operational environment. Team fidelity would be the extent to which the team roles are simulated in training. For example, in the back of an aircraft, there may be several different team members performing distinct tasks. If training does not include these team members, the team fidelity is low, and trainees may not understand how their role is supported by these other members.

Given what we have said about team and task fidelity, the following propositions apply:

> Recommendation 13: High task fidelity will
> improve transfer of team training for tasks
> that are high in interdependence, and should
> be designed into training in these cases.

> Recommendation 14: High team fidelity
> (that is, real teammates) will improve transfer
> in situations where behavioral discretion for a task
> is high, so it should drive team training
> design in such cases.

Feedback

There are several ways to structure feedback for a team. Measures of performance are important to track the ability of teams to transfer the trained competencies to the operational environment. Outcome measures of performance include how well a team accomplished the mission (for example, quantity of output, time to perform the task, and number of errors). Another way to examine team performance is by measuring *how* a task is accomplished. Process measurement can focus on the degree to which the team used teamwork skills effectively. These measures can be extremely diagnostic, particularly for performance deficiencies, if the observation of team processes is driven by a priori constructs and expectations (Fowlkes, Dwyer, Milham, Burns, & Pierce, 1999). Moreover, process measures provide a basis for feedback (Cannon-Bowers & Salas, 1998). At the individual level, much has been written about feedback (see Vroom, 1964; Ilgen, Fisher, & Taylor, 1979; Nadler, 1979), but at the team level, less is known.

A possible exception here is *intrateam feedback.* This is a process whereby team members monitor their team's performance and process skills, then provide feedback to each other regarding their own or others' examples of team performance (Smith-Jentsch et al., 1998). This serves to call attention to the concept of team behaviors in the environment, to identify those behaviors when they occur, and to assess how performance could be improved.

Team-level feedback may provide team members with realistic expectations of how to exhibit appropriate team behaviors in their operational environment. Further, it may help team members identify how coordination impacts their performance by seeing how the teamwork skills work together. For example, one team member may expect information from another team member and be irritated if it isn't forthcoming. After using a cross-checking technique, however, the team member who needs the information may realize that the other is overloaded and thus incapable of providing the needed information during that time period. Ideally, after going through training with appropriate feedback, team members become aware of the teamwork skills and use self-correction techniques during task performance. Hence, we hypothesize that increased intrateam feedback will increase transfer of team training.

> Recommendation 15: Provide teams with
> the ability to give intrateam feedback,
> which includes mutual performance
> monitoring, in order to enhance
> transfer of team competencies.

Case Study #4: You Get What You Ask (and Reward) For

In an ongoing effort to train sales teams to work better in a new team-based organization, the training department of a large computer company had been conducting team training seminars. The seminars had been developed carefully to highlight areas where employees could combine their expertise to arrive at better outcomes.

At first, things seemed to be going well. Employees were attending the seminars and showing signs of greater cooperation. But suddenly, things changed. Attendance at the seminars began to decline and those employees who did attend seemed to be preoccupied. The facilitator became concerned and asked the few employees who showed up what was going on.

"The training is fine," said one of the employees, "but it's quota time. You know, all of this team stuff is great, but in the end, we are all really competitors. The company gives us each sales goals that we have to reach by the end of the quarter. Then our performance appraisals, and bonuses, are all based on how close we come to those goals. So at some point, we all need to concentrate on our own numbers."

The facilitator pressed further. "So, what will it take to change this?" he asked.

"Well, obviously," responded the employee, "if our bonuses depended on the sales of the whole team, then we'd be more interested. It's not that we're against working together—in fact, we're all pretty excited at what we might accomplish if we pooled our resources. But right now the bottom line depends on how much we sell—as individuals—not as a team."

The Transfer Environment

Case study #4 highlights an all-too-common scenario in organizations; that is, management purports to want employees to perform in teams, yet it does not support this behavior. In fact, it is a persistent theme in the transfer literature that a variety of crucial factors that occur after training (that is, back on the job) can have a profound impact on transfer of training in teams (Baldwin & Ford, 1988). These include a climate to support teamwork, performance measurement and reward systems, leader and team member support, relapse prevention, and team goals. The following sections describe each of these, with suggestions for managing them to optimize transfer.

Climate for Teamwork

Before learned teamwork behaviors will transfer to the job, a climate that supports teamwork must be in place. If team members do not believe that teamwork is valued in the organization, they are unlikely to display desired teamwork behaviors. For example, it has been found that when team members observe others being punished or rewarded for displaying teamwork, they adjust their behavior accordingly (Smith-Jentsch, Salas, & Brannick, 2001). Such a climate may manifest itself in several ways; clearly the factors discussed in the following sections are part of the message sent to team members about the value of teamwork.

> Recommendation 16: A positive climate
> for teamwork in the transfer environment
> will increase the likelihood that team
> training will transfer.

Performance Appraisals

Employees are most often are evaluated on individual rather than team performance, regardless of whether or not they work in a team. This may lead to goals that are more focused on individual behaviors than on team competencies. Team appraisals may be necessary to demonstrate that team members will be held accountable for their performance as a team. Further, team performance appraisals can provide team members with feedback regarding their teamwork processes as well as the outcome of their performance. As a result, they should enhance the degree of transfer of learned material. Hence, the following proposition is offered:

> Recommendation 17: Employ team-level
> performance appraisals that highlight
> the importance of teamwork and provide
> team-level feedback to enhance transfer
> of desired teamwork skills.

Reward and Performance Management Systems

Like performance appraisals, reward systems in most organizations are currently focused on individual compensation. Team member contribution is calculated and rewarded individually, and team members may never be rewarded for the team's output or for their use of team competencies. If not rewarded for team behaviors, team members may get the message that teamwork does not carry as much weight as their individual behaviors and outputs. Clearly, even well-learned teamwork skills will not transfer under such conditions. Our hypothesis in this regard is that transfer of team training will be enhanced if team-level performance is rewarded; therefore, the following proposition holds:

> Recommendation 18: Team-level reward systems designed to recognize and reward effective teamwork performance will increase the degree to which team competencies transfer back to the job; these should be designed as a companion to team training.

Team Goals

Related to team performance appraisals and reward systems, it is also well established that setting goals in the transfer environment can enhance the likelihood that trainees will apply learned material (Smith-Jentsch et al., 1998). Once again, much has been written about this phenomenon at the individual level, but very little at the team level. Some exceptions include the finding that team goals prevent social loafing (Hoffman, 1994) and may energize team members and reduce conflict among them (Sherif, 1958). Team goals may also direct attention, increase collaborative effort, and regulate team resource allocation. Taking these results and extrapolating individual findings, we expect that when trainees are encouraged to set goals for the entire team, they will be more likely to employ teamwork skills in the actual environment. The following proposition applies:

> Recommendation 19: Include team-level goals to focus the team's attention on team-level performance and encourage team members to transfer learned teamwork competencies.

Leader and Team Member Support

Supervisor support has been implicated as a factor affecting the transfer of learned material in individuals (Tannenbaum & Yukl, 1992). At the team level, it is reasonable to suggest that supervisors back on the job who are supportive of the team and of the use of teamwork skills will enhance team-level transfer (Smith-Jentsch et al., 2001). At the team level, it is also possible for team members to support one another. Smith-Jentsch et al. suggest that informal support from other team members may be a strong motivator. In this case, we would expect that transfer is increased since team members have the opportunity to model their teammates' behavior and are reinforced for displaying desired team competencies. In this area, we provide the following proposition:

> Recommendation 20: Support for displaying targeted team behaviors from team leaders and teammates can increase the degree of team training transfer obtained; interventions designed to foster this behavior should be implemented.

Relapse Prevention

Evidence from the individual level indicates that relapse prevention measures can be introduced for trainees who are at risk to fall back into pretraining behaviors (Tannenbaum & Yukl, 1992). No research that we know of has extended this work to the team level. However, it is reasonable to expect that team members who are at risk for not applying what they have learned can be targeted for relapse prevention measures. Further, at the team level, other members of the team can be involved in relapse prevention. In fact, we hypothesize that relapse prevention may be easier to implement and more successful when teammates are involved. The following proposition is offered:

> Recommendation 21: Relapse prevention programs, especially those designed to involve team members, will increase the likelihood of teamwork transfer.

Summary

In summary, we contend that many of the same practices employed at the individual level can be applied to maximize team training transfer. However, a few issues are unique to teams. For example, the decision to train intact or ad hoc teams is one unique to team training. In addition, concepts such as metacognition may be extended to the team level, but are likely to differ from the original (individual-level) construct. In other cases, team transfer may actually be easier than individual transfer because team members themselves can provide mutual support (for example, with relapse prevention).

As we have noted, we are not able to provide definitive, empirically verified recommendations for the transfer of team training. However, by applying what is already known and extrapolating from the individual level, we can derive some preliminary recommendations (see Exhibit 10.1). This does not mean that we are satisfied with the state of the art in this area—it is clear that team training transfer is a topic that has not received much attention in the literature.

**Exhibit 10.1. Recommendations
for Enhancing Team Training Transfer.**

Establishing Team Competencies

- Clearly specify the goals of team training.
- Conduct a team task analysis to determine the team competencies required for successful performance on the task or job.

Team Characteristics

- Assess team aptitude—for both team and task aspects of training—prior to training.
- Provide remedial teamwork skills training for trainees who lack these competencies.
- If the task requires knowledge of teammate characteristics, train in intact teams.
- Measure collective efficacy prior to training.
- Provide remedial interventions to raise collective efficacy if it is low.

Exhibit 10.1. Recommendations
for Enhancing Team Training Transfer, Cont'd.

Team Characteristics

- Design training to build collective efficacy early in training.
- Assess collective orientation prior to training.
- Develop interventions to raise low collective orientation in trainees.
- Remove trainees with low collective orientation from team training.
- Assess team members' attitudes toward teamwork prior to training.
- Develop interventions to raise low collective orientation in trainees.

Team Training Design

- Provide advance organizers that explain complex team and task relationships.
- Provide pre-practice briefs that explain team roles and clarify expectations.
- Train team-level metacognitive skills so that team members can track their own learning (of team-level competencies).
- When interdependence is high in the task, maximize task fidelity in training.
- When behavioral discretion is high, train in intact teams (that is, with real teammates) when possible.
- Train team members to provide intrateam feedback and self-correction behaviors.
- Develop a positive climate for teamwork in the transfer environment.

The Transfer Environment

- Develop and provide team-level performance appraisals.
- Implement team-level reward systems.
- Provide a supportive environment for teamwork by involving supervisors and other team members.
- Encourage team members to develop team-level goals.
- Develop relapse prevention programs for team members at risk to not transfer learned teamwork skills.
- Involve teammates in relapse prevention where possible.

In fact, virtually all of our assertions and recommendations lack rigorous empirical testing. Obviously, we believe that this situation should change. This is especially true given the growing reliance on teams in industry, and the importance of tasks typically performed by teams (for example, flying planes, performing surgery). We hope that the thinking that we have begun here prompts others to study this crucial area.

References

Baldwin, T., & Ford, J. (1988). Transfer-of-training: A review and directions for future research. *Personnel Psychology, 41,* 63–105.

Blickensderfer, E., Cannon-Bowers, J., & Salas, E. (1997). Theoretical bases for team self-correction: Fostering shared mental models. *Advances in Interdisciplinary Studies of Work Teams, 4,* 249–279.

Blickensderfer, E., Cannon-Bowers, J., & Salas, E. (1998). Cross-training and team performance. In J. A. Cannon-Bowers & E. Salas (Eds.), *Making decisions under stress: Implications for individual and team training* (pp. 299–311). Washington, DC: American Psychological Association.

Bowers, C., Baker, D., & Salas, E. (1994). Measuring the importance of teamwork: The reliability and validity of job/task analysis indices for team-training design. *Military Psychology, 6,* 205–214.

Campion, M., Medsker, F., & Higgs, A. (1993). Relations between work group characteristics and effectiveness: Implications for designing effective work groups. *Personnel Psychology, 46,* 823–850.

Cannon-Bowers, J., Rhodenizer, L., Salas, E., & Bowers, C. (1998). A framework for understanding pre-practice conditions and their impact on learning. *Personnel Psychology, 51,* 291–320.

Cannon-Bowers, J., & Salas, E. (Eds.). (1998). *Making decisions under stress: Implications for individual and team training.* Washington, DC: American Psychological Association.

Cannon-Bowers, J., Salas, E., & Blickensderfer, E. (1998, April). Making fine distinctions among team constructs: Worthy endeavor or "crewel" and unusual punishment? In R. Klimoski (Chair), *When is a work team a crew and does it matter?* Symposium presented at the 13th annual conference of the Society for Industrial and Organizational Psychology, Dallas, TX.

Cannon-Bowers, J., Tannenbaum, S., Salas, E., & Volpe, C. (1995). Defining competencies and establishing team training requirements. In R. Guzzo and E. Salas (Eds.), *Team effectiveness and decision making in organizations* (pp. 333–380). San Francisco: Jossey-Bass.

Driskell, J., & Salas, E. (1992). Collective behavior and team performance. *Human Factors, 34,* 277–288.

Fowlkes, J., Dwyer, D., Milham, L., Burns, J., & Pierce, L. (1999, November). Team skills assessment: A test and evaluation component for emerging weapon systems. [CD-ROM]. *Proceedings of the 21st Annual Interservice/Industry Training, Simulation and Education Conference,* Orlando, FL, 640–648.

Gist, M. (1997). Training design and pedagogy: Implications for skill acquisition, maintenance, and generalization. In M. A. Quinones & A. Ehrenstein (Eds.), *Training for a rapidly changing workplace: Applications of psychological research* (pp. 201–222). Washington, DC: American Psychological Association.

Guzzo, R., Yost, P., Campbell, R., & Shea, J. (1994). Potency in groups: Articulating the construct. *British Journal of Social Psychology, 32,* 87–106.

Helmreich, R., Foushee, C., Benson, R., & Russini, W. (1986). Cockpit resource management: Exploring the attitude-performance linkage. *Aviation, Space, & Environmental Medicine 57* (12, sect 1), 1198–1200.

Hill, G. W. (1982). Group versus individual performance: Are n+1 heads better than one? *Psychological Bulletin, 91,* 517–539.

Hoffman, R. (1994). Overcoming social loafing through goal setting and feedback. *Dissertation Abstracts International 53*(7-B), 3820.

Ilgen, D. (1999). Teams embedded in organizations: Some implications. *American Psychologist, 54*(2), 129–139.

Ilgen, D. R., Fisher, C. D., & Taylor, M. S. (1979). Consequences of individual feedback on behavior in organizations. *Journal of Applied Psychology, 64,* 349–371.

Kraiger, K., Ford, J. K., & Salas, E. (1993). Application of cognitive, skill-based, and affective theories of learning outcomes to new methods of training evaluation. *Journal of Applied Psychology, 78*(2), 311–328.

Kraiger, K., Salas, E., & Cannon-Bowers, J. (1995). Measuring knowledge organization as a method for assessing learning during training. *Human Factors, 37,* 804–816.

Mayer, R. (1989). Models for understanding. *Review of Educational Research, 59,* 43–64.

Modrick, J. A. (1986). Team performance and training. In J. Zeidner (Ed.), *Human productivity enhancement: Training and human factors in systems design* (Vol. 1, pp. 130–166). New York: Praeger.

Nadler, A. (1979). The effects of feedback on task group behavior: A review of the experimental research. *Organizational Behavior and Human Performance, 23,* 309–338.

Salas, E., & Cannon-Bowers, J. (1997). Methods, tools, and strategies for team training. In M. A. Quinones & A. Ehrenstein (Eds.), *Training for a rapidly changing workplace: Applications of psychological research* (pp. 249–279). Washington, DC: American Psychological Association.

Salas, E., Fowlkes, J., Stout, R., Milanovich, D., & Prince, D. (1999). Does CRM training improve teamwork skills in the cockpit? Two evaluation studies. *Human Factors, 41*(2), 326–343.

Salas, E., Rozell, D., Mullen, B., & Driskell, J. (1999). The effect of team building on performance: An integration. *Small Group Research, 30*(3), 309–329.

Sherif, C. (1958). Superordinate goals in the reduction of intergroup conflict. *American Journal of Sociology, 63,* 349–356.

Smith-Jentsch, K., Salas, E., & Brannick, M. (2001). To transfer or not to transfer? Investigating the combined effects of trainee characteristics and team transfer environments. *Journal of Applied Psychology, 86*(2), 279–292.

Smith-Jentsch, K., Zeisig, R., Acton, B., & McPherson, J. (1998). Team dimensional training. In J. A. Cannon-Bowers & E. Salas (Eds.), *Decision making under stress: Implications for individual and team training.* Washington, DC: American Psychological Association.

Steiner, I. D. (1972). *Group processes and productivity.* New York: Academic Press.

Swezey, R., & Llaneras, R. (1997). Models in training and instruction. In G. Salvendy (Ed.), *Handbook of human factors and ergonomics* (2nd ed., pp. 514–577). New York: Wiley.

Tannenbaum, S., Beard, R., & Salas, E. (1992). Team building and its influence on team effectiveness: An examination of conceptual and empirical developments. In K. Kelley (Ed.), *Issues, theory, and research in industrial/organizational psychology* (pp. 117–153). Amsterdam: Elsevier.

Tannenbaum, S., Cannon-Bowers, J., Salas, E., & Mathieu, J. (1993). *Factors that influence training effectiveness: A conceptual model and longitudinal analysis.* (Naval Training Systems Center, Human Systems Integration Division Tech Rept. No. 93–011). Orlando, FL: Naval Air Warfare Center.

Tannenbaum, S., Smith-Jentsch, K., & Behson, S. (1998). Training team leaders to facilitate team learning and performance. In J. A. Cannon-Bowers & E. Salas (Eds.), *Making decisions under stress: Implications for individual and team training* (pp. 247–270). Washington, DC: American Psychological Association.

Tannenbaum, S., & Yukl, G. (1992). Training and development in work organizations. *Annual Review of Psychology, 43,* 399–441.

Tulving, E., & Thompson, D. (1973). Encoding specificity and retrieval processes in episodic memory. *Psychological Review, 3,* 112–129.

Vroom, V. H. (1964). *Work and motivation.* New York: Wiley.

Weiner, E., Kanki, B., & Helmreich, R. (Eds.). (1993). *Cockpit resource management.* San Diego: Academic Press.

PART FOUR

From Performance Capability to Sustained Performance

CHAPTER 11

Transfer Is Personal

Equipping Trainees with Self-Management and Relapse Prevention Strategies

Robert D. Marx
Lisa A. Burke

For management consultants and practitioners, the transfer problem is more one of professional credibility and survival than one of intellectual curiosity. This chapter provides practitioners with a research-based set of practical transfer strategies customized to fit the specific concerns of each trainee. The relapse prevention strategies described in this chapter can be applied to a wide variety of training programs and the step-by-step instructions provided require little additional instruction for knowledgeable trainers. Perhaps of most importance is the consideration of an organization's transfer climate as a guide to maximizing the impact of the relapse prevention strategies. By fine-tuning these transfer strategies to fit the needs of individual trainees *and* the transfer-readiness of the organization, an optimal outcome for the participants, the practitioners, and the company can be attained.

Another executive development program entered its final hours and, for Meredith Parker, the hope for improving her delegation skills was marred by recollections of past disappointments once she returned to the workplace. Parker, one of the company's youngest vice presidents, managed a highly productive management team. Her record indicated that she was extremely intelligent, industrious, and inspiring to her team. There was, however, one pattern that showed up repeatedly in the "needs improvement" portion of her performance reviews. Parker tended to take over a project when a deadline approached, often overriding the progress of her management team.

She understood that today's employees thrive on autonomy and self-managed work teams, but she almost unknowingly reverted to a highly directive supervision mode whenever she perceived a deadline or crisis approaching. Consequently, her team had not learned to make crucial decisions under pressure. Although they had not complained openly, there had been talk of her need to control the decision-making process. Despite the team's appreciation of her talents, it was becoming apparent that her failure to delegate appropriately could limit her professional advancement and deny her subordinates the experiences they needed to grow professionally.

Meredith Parker's attention returned to the delegation skills program she was attending. She had participated enthusiastically in this well-designed three-day program, hoping to break out of her self-defeating pattern. But she also knew that understanding how and when to delegate did not automatically result in appropriate use of this skill. Under the pressure of deadlines, the workshop lessons seemed just as likely to be mysteriously unavailable to her as those she'd received in the past.

"Using the skills you have learned here when you return to work can be a lonely process," she heard the presenter say—and she knew that was true. Practicing delegation skills with a trainee group in the executive development program provided her with a supportive environment that didn't exist back at work.

"Nobody is impressed if you stop drinking at the Betty Ford Center or behave like a leader at the Center for Creative Leadership," the trainer continued. "What's impressive is maintaining those behaviors after the conclusion of training programs. Unfortunately, abstinence and skill retention following special programs often takes place under treacherous conditions. You don't have that constant support and feedback anymore, and your new behaviors must be exhibited in an environment for which you're unprepared.

"To succeed in transferring these new skills, a different form of training is required. We will learn a completely different set of skills that will serve as a parachute to help you land safely in dangerous terrain (your work environment) armed with strategies tailored to your specific circumstances. This training is designed to help you implement your new skills effectively by anticipating the problems you are likely to face."

Parker was fully attentive now. The trainer had touched on the key element of her past failures—loneliness once back from the training programs and lack of training to apply her new skills while coping with the realities of the workplace. As she heard him proclaim, "This afternoon I would like to introduce you to the Relapse Prevention Model," she felt a sense of hope that her delegation deficit might soon become a thing of the past.

Individuals' Role in the Transfer of Training Process

Review articles on the transfer of training problem (Baldwin & Ford, 1988; Tannenbaum & Yukl, 1992;) have explored a broad array of variables impacting transfer strategy effectiveness. These include trainer variables, organizational factors, content and delivery of training programs, and trainee characteristics. For example, Broad (Chapter Six of this volume) argues that organizations do not adequately support skill retention efforts once employees return to work; she suggests the creation of a role called "learning transfer manager" to facilitate the process. Schermerhorn (1979) found that skill retention efforts floundered in organizations because of lack of top-down support, measurement difficulty, and executive attention to bottom-line outcomes rather than analysis of the complex processes required to attain those outcomes.

Although these organizational factors are important in understanding the training transfer puzzle, it is ultimately each trainee's actions that will determine whether a newly trained skill will survive. To paraphrase an old sports axiom, coaching can only do so much: ultimately, the athlete must play the game.

Relapse prevention (RP) training is a set of cognitive and behavioral self-management strategies grounded in social learning theory (Bandura, 1977). Recent transfer literature reviews acknowledge the potential of relapse prevention training for being among the best practices for enhancing training transfer (see Burke & Baldwin, 1999; Burke, 2001). Originally conceived by Marlatt and Gordon (1980, 1985) for treating addictive disorders (drinking, smoking, gambling, and the like), the model recognizes that a single lapse (or slip) in one's intention to abstain from addictive behavior can lead to a permanent lapse or relapse, depending on how well prepared the addict is to cope with the lapse. Marlatt and

Gordon found that addicts could identify the circumstances of their initial lapses, and could thus be prepared with RP strategies to prevent relapses. They also found that, although addicts were able to maintain high abstinence rates during treatment, 90 percent reverted to addictive behavior within three months when supports of the treatment environment were removed and addicts were on their own.

Marx (1982, 1986) originally adapted the Relapse Prevention Model to the training transfer problem. Designed to increase trainee awareness of threats to skill retention, the model introduces a set of strategies that help the trainee identify high-risk situations for relapse and develop skills to cope with them. Thus each trainee is taught two distinct sets of skills—training content (for example, leadership, coaching, teamwork) and post-training RP strategies. The strategies shift the focus to identifying potential threats to post-training skill retention. The core of the RP model is identification of high-risk situations that might sabotage trainees' intention to implement a newly learned skill.

Consistent with the S-O-B-C (Stimulus-Organism-Behavior-Consequences) framework applied to organizational learning by Luthans and Davis (1979) and Kreitner and Luthans (1984), trainees are taught to anticipate high-risk threats to skill retention (stimulus), deal with overwhelming thoughts or feelings (organism) interfering with rational responses to initial lapses, learn additional coping skills (behavior) to overcome the high-risk situations, and develop strategies to create meaningful rewards (consequences) otherwise absent. The RP framework is unique because it is largely based on principles of behavioral self-management (Manz & Sims, 1980) and does not assume that any of the support, feedback, and direction present in the skill acquisition aspect of training (largely under the control of the trainer) will be available during the skill transfer and retention period following training (largely under the control of the trainee and the organization).

Empirical support for the effects of RP training in clinical settings is quite impressive. For example, RP Training has been particularly effective with weight loss clients (Perri, Shapiro, Ludwig, Twentyman, & McAdoo, 1984) and in smoking cessation programs (Stevens & Hollis, 1989). Unfortunately, despite frequent mention and widespread conceptual support for RP in the organizational training literature, empirical research on the effects of RP on working adults in naturally occurring organizational learning contexts has been slow to emerge.

An RP Intervention at the Front

One instructive example of the investigation of an RP intervention at the corporate front is the second author's investigation of a coaching skills program in a large pharmaceutical firm (Burke, 1996; Burke & Baldwin, 1999). Seventy-eight research scientists were involved in the research, all supervisors who had attended a training program—designed and delivered entirely independent of the researcher. The program addressed the role of coaching in supervising employees, examined opportunities for coaching, identified ways coaching could make a supervisor's job easier, and provided practice opportunities.

Acutely aware of the transfer problem, the organizational sponsors of the training were concerned that the R&D supervisors would return to their jobs and encounter numerous critical deadlines and work pressures that would dilute the potential application of skills from the program. Especially for research scientists, who often prefer autonomous work environments, the immediate gratification of completing their own tasks instead of taking time to coach their subordinates was likely to tempt them into coaching lapses. As such, high-risk situations would threaten the trained supervisors' use of their new coaching skills, blind them to opportunities to coach, and make them lose confidence in their ability to coach—and thus eventually relapse.

The sponsor's concern translated into its receptiveness for an RP intervention and thus a rich opportunity to test RP effects in an industrial organization context. Two different RP modules were ultimately administered and tested. Also included was a control group whose members received the coaching module but no RP. The first RP module examined was a full-blown version as originally proposed by Marx (1982)—it contained all the traditional RP elements, including goal-setting, decision matrix, coping skills, and self-monitoring. The second RP module was a scaled-down version that included select elements of RP to see if a more time-efficient method was effective in enhancing skill transfer.

The results of the RP intervention revealed several points that can inform training researchers and professionals. First, as expected, a supportive individual transfer climate significantly increased the scientists' use of transfer strategies back on the job, confirming that trainees' work context is largely responsible for their ultimate use of training on the job. Second, consistent with its clinical cousin, the full-blown RP training enhanced maintenance outcomes—self-report coaching session frequency, subordinate measure of supervisory coaching effectiveness, and a self-report measure of transfer strategy use—but only in *unfavorable* transfer climates. It seems that a full RP intervention produces the greatest effects in the most hostile climates—those least conducive to transfer.

On the other hand, the scaled-down version of RP training enhanced maintenance in *favorable* work climates. That is, the modified RP (and control) group tended to produce greater transfer rates in the more supportive climates. This is encouraging in that it points to the possibility that just a modest intervention can help skill maintenance. It also suggests that in cases where the climate is supportive the additional RP elements may be superfluous. Overall, this study points to the importance of climate and contextual factors in assessing the need for, and ultimate design of, post-training interventions such as relapse prevention.

Interesting qualitative data were also collected in this corporate setting. Trainees in the full-blown RP condition were asked how useful they considered each component in their post-training transfer intervention. Accordingly, 67 percent reported the goal-setting component to be useful; a small 33 percent agreed the decision matrix was useful; 67 percent thought it was helpful to predict their first slip; 50 percent claimed that it was beneficial to generate coping skills to enhance their transfer (step 6); and finally, 80 percent found the self-monitoring tool to be useful (step 7). Thus, employees viewed an on-the-job tracking mechanism as useful, as well as goal-setting exercises and predicting their first slip, while other RP elements were less well received by these employees.

We think it is also important to note that, while generally well received, the RP applications were not without their detractors. Several of the most critical comments (Burke, 1996, p. 40) are worth considering:

No matter what you do, there is still the problem of "not enough time." Work pressures and project timelines do not allow enough opportunity to apply all of the new skills that we learn. . . . The best I can do is to pick and choose from the highlights.

I found that the moment I walked out of the class I began to forget what I learned. A big part of it is the fact that my team does not know anything about coaching nor is it interested in it. Thus I find it difficult to apply certain things. Part of the problem too is my boss doesn't use these skills either.

In practice, total workload really did prevent the relapse training being useful.

The training was not useful. There is nothing new that I didn't know. This kind of training should be done one-on-one and for specific issues encountered.

Those comments indicate the imposing challenge of making training stick in organizational contexts where time is a precious resource and people are not inclined to learn for the sake of learning. The consummate challenge with any post-training transfer intervention may be to convince employees who face many urgent projects and tasks that they need to stay for *more* training to make the training they just sat through more effective.

Taken together, this study and others (for example, Marx & Karren, 1988, 1990) point to some predictors of successful (and unsuccessful) application of RP interventions. Perhaps most important, RP seems to work best when used with other transfer strategies. For instance, in a clinical weight loss study (Perri et al., 1984) RP training was optimally effective when combined with behavioral treatment and post-treatment contact with the therapist. In organizational settings, centrality of the skill to professional development appears to be a prerequisite to skill retention, and overall transfer climate is critical as well. Certainly, trainers cannot simply insert RP interventions at the end of every program in their organization and expect immediate on-the-job skill application. Rather, a holistic and systematic approach that considers the nature of the training, the immediate boss support, attitudes of peers, and transfer climate should help to determine the need for, as well as the design of, RP or other post-training modules. That said, the emerging body of empirical work does support that RP training can be an important tool for helping address the training transfer problem.

Applying the Relapse Prevention Model: The Meredith Parker Case

Although Meredith Parker has been spared the physiological component that poses such a major challenge for addicts, in other respects she faces a similar post-training environment with a broad array of challenges to her intention to retain her fledgling delegation skills. Two basic assumptions make RP training particularly appropriate for post-training skill retention. First, the trainees cannot count on support, feedback, or external rewards for maintaining their chosen skill. These processes must be self-managed. If the organization develops internal processes such as appointing a learning transfer manager, then less self-management may be required, but ultimately trainees will need to function independently.

Second, each individual trainee perceives and experiences the skill-training program from a unique perspective and has different sets of obstacles to overcome. What Burke and Baldwin (1999) call "different organizational climates," even for trainees working in the same company, holds true for the nature of the post-training work environment. Each trainee returns with a different profile of strengths and vulnerabilities.

The case of Meredith Parker illustrates one such example, but the RP model is designed to accommodate the individual differences one might expect in a diverse group. The worksheet illustrated in Exhibit 11.1 depicts the recommended steps that Parker will follow to prepare for her return to the work setting. The next section explains each worksheet step using the Meredith Parker case.

Completing the Relapse Prevention Worksheet

I. Choosing a Skill to Retain

Because RP is based on self-managed behavior, the behavior to be changed must be *voluntary*. Parker may want to learn to delegate under time pressure to improve her advancement opportunities and to help her employees develop their decision-making skills. In either case, her motivation to change is a necessary prerequisite to effective skill retention.

Target behaviors most appropriate to RP are those *susceptible to relapse*. Some technical behaviors, automatic once learned (for example, logging on to a computer), are typically unlikely to relapse. Delegation may be susceptible to relapse for Parker when certain environmental conditions are present (such as time pressure or confrontational subordinates).

The skill to be maintained must be operationally defined and therefore *countable*. That is, it is important to go from the vague "I need to delegate more" to the more precise "I will delegate to my management team an average of two important decisions per week. To assure that the

Exhibit 11.1. Relapse Prevention Worksheet.

I. Choose a Skill: Voluntary _____ Susceptible to Relapse _____ Countable _____

II. Set the Goal: Specific _____ Realistic _____

    A. Skill Retention _____

    B. Slip (temporary lapse) _____

    C. Relapse (permanent lapse) _____

III. Commitment to Retain the Skill

	Advantages	Disadvantages
Retaining		
Not Retaining		

IV. Apply the Strategies

    Strategies to Increase Awareness

    1. Observe differences between training and work _____

    2. Create an effective SUPPORT network _____

    3. Identify high-risk situations _____

    4. Recognize Seemingly Unimportant Behaviors That Lead to Errors (S.U.B.T.L.E.) _____

    Strategies to Increase Rational Thinking

    5. Reduce dysfunctional emotions (The Commitment Violation Effect) _____

    Strategies to Diagnose and Practice Related Support Skills

    6. Diagnose support skills necessary to retain your new behavior _____

    Strategies to Provide Appropriate Consequences for Behavior

    7. Identify organization support for skill retention and create meaningful rewards and punishments when they don't exist _____

V. Predict the Circumstances of the First Lapse

VI. Practice Critical Skills

VII. Monitor Behavior

	M	T	W	T	F
Behavior retained = X					
Behavior not retained = O					
Slip = S					
Relapse = R					

delegation of decision making is clear, my signature and that of a team member will appear on a page describing the task to be delegated."

Key point: Selection of an appropriate skill to be retained requires trainee-trainer collaboration. Research indicates that RP strategies work best with skills central to the trainees' performance (that is, number of decisions delegated under time pressure rather than the number of daily to-do lists to improve time management skills).

II. Setting the Goal

Setting a specific and challenging goal is an important prerequisite to *skill retention*. The parameters of a slip (temporary lapse in skill use) and a relapse (more permanent lapse) must be quantified. For Meredith Parker, two delegated decisions per week would be considered skill retention. Psychologically, she might feel that any week without any decisions being delegated to her management team would be a warning or *slip* and four weeks without a delegated decision would be designated a *relapse* or permanent lapse.

Key point: Designation of retention, slip, and relapse is likely to vary among individuals and departments, but can be designated for a large group of trainees. For example: Three consecutive days without completing a to-do list is a slip.

III. Making a Commitment to Retain the Skill

Advantages and disadvantages of retaining and not retaining the target behavior are elaborated on the worksheet in the commitment grid:

	Advantages	*Disadvantages*
Retaining	When Parker delegates under pressure, employees trust her, feel empowered. She builds their skills and looks more promotable.	Parker will have to undergo a significant change in a long-standing habit. She will have to worry that a poor result from her team will reflect badly on her competency.
Not Retaining	When she doesn't delegate under pressure, the work gets done more quickly and under her control.	Her experience in training will be another failure. Her adaptability will be questioned and her relationship with her employees may deteriorate as they sense her rigidity.

Key point: Weight loss research indicates that the long-term benefits of reduced caloric intake were no match for the instant gratification of ice cream when trainees were depressed. By creating this matrix of the consequences of not retaining the skill, trainees are reminded of their original *commitment* to behavioral change.

IV. Applying the Strategies

The following seven strategies make up the core of relapse prevention training. The first four are designed to increase awareness, while the remaining three increase rational thinking, help diagnose and practice related support skills, and provide appropriate consequences, respectively.

1. *Observe differences between training and work.*

   Skills learned in a supportive training environment may be difficult to transfer to chaotic work settings. Planning implementation of the new skill given the realities of work will help skill retention.

2. *Create effective support network.*

   It would have been useful for Parker to attend training with a colleague so they could monitor each other's behavior. Although this would be easier to arrange in advance, it may be possible to arrange support partnerships during the training.

3. *Identify high-risk situations.*

   This is the critical RP strategy. By reviewing past difficulties in retaining new learning and anticipating skill implementation problems, trainees can engage in cognitive fire drills to identify cues that threaten skill retention. These include

   - *Intrapersonal:*   Parker worries excessively about the group's failing to make an effective decision, thus reflecting poorly on her judgment.
   - *Interpersonal:*   Parker does not like some team members very much even though their work is exemplary.
   - *Environmental:*   Tasks delegated late in the month are more susceptible to slips because Parker has less time to work with team members before monthly reports are due.

4. *Recognize seemingly unimportant behaviors that lead to errors.*

   The acronym SUBTLE can be a useful mnemonic for this point. When Parker schedules task assignments toward the end of her meeting agenda, they don't get delegated because there "isn't time" to sort out who should take on the task, or because some people have to be elsewhere and the appropriate representation is unavailable. SUBTLEs are small behaviors in a chain of events that can eventually result in the trainee's fledging skills being overwhelmed.

Key point: Virtually all awareness-increasing strategies are based on information that the trainee already knows, but that most training programs avoid. RP training, in contrast, treasures these data as a normal part of the trial-and-error learning process.

5. *Reduce dysfunctional emotions.*

This is often referred to as the commitment violation effect. Parker can reframe a lapse in her delegation behavior as trial-and-error learning and discover what lack of awareness on her part contributed to the slip rather than feeling guilty and losing concentration for the next delegation opportunity.

Key point: When addicts violate a commitment to abstain, binge drinking, compulsive eating, or other addictive behavior can occur in order to deal with their guilt. In contrast to such dysfunctional emotional reactions, Parker is simply recognizing she has not yet sufficiently developed her skill to delegate in that difficult situation.

6. *Identify what related skills are necessary to support the new behavior.*

Parker finds it difficult to delegate because she has not been taught leadership models that help managers determine when directing employees is necessary and when it is redundant and demotivating. Time management deficiencies also thwart her ability to apportion tasks appropriately over the monthly cycle.

Key point: Careful review of high-risk situations can serve as a personal needs assessment for future skill training. Most skill retention requires additional support skill enhancement.

7. *Identify organizational support for skill retention and create meaningful rewards and punishments when nonexistent.*

There are no formal rewards for delegation in Parker's company. Her support partner has agreed to buy her lunch each time she delegates appropriately (short-term consequence). Parker will treat herself to a new laptop (long-term consequence) when her performance review mentions her progress in this area.

Key point: While the organization may offer a reward (promotion, raise) for a successful outcome such as group productivity, the small steps that form the process leading to such outcomes must be self-managed.

V. Predicting Circumstances of the First Lapse

Most trainees, after being exposed to the RP strategies, find it easy to imagine the combination of circumstances likely to occur that could sabotage their new learning. When Parker returns to work following training, she knows she will be several days behind because of her absence and likely to take control of a project that her team is capable of handling.

Key point: Predicting the initial lapse ironically creates some control over a previously unanticipated high-risk situation. This helps ready the trainee for the initial errors in the trial-and-error process.

VI. Practicing Critical Skills

The journey through the RP strategies culminating in the prediction of the initial lapse has identified several skills requiring improvement. Parker can practice leadership models and time management skills during the RP program by using other trainees to role-play her management team.

Key point: If the same skills are mentioned by several trainees as crucial to learning delegation, these data can serve as a form of needs assessment that can shape future training offerings. RP training should take up half a day in a three-day program, but it should not be the final half day, which should refocus on the new skill to be learned.

VII. Monitoring the Behavior

How does Parker know if she is retaining her skill? If the earlier steps of skill choice and goal setting have been carefully done, then behavior monitoring is straightforward. For research or internal data collection, a paper record of the behavior is helpful.

Key point: Initial estimates of frequency necessary for skill retention may change after trainees complete the remainder of the RP training. Refining the definition of the skill to be retained throughout the program results in more effective monitoring procedures.

What Can You Do About Transfer?

This SIOP volume addresses several approaches to the training transfer problem, including use of specialists such as the learning or transfer manager, diagnostic tools such as the Learning Transfer System Inventory, and trainee motivation strategies. When added to these state-of-the-art interventions, relapse prevention training offers a number of distinct attributes:

- It is solidly based on well-established behavioral self-management principles.
- It takes into account individual differences, especially differing high-risk situations and available support skills across individuals.
- It can attach to virtually any existing training program.
- It does not require extensive additional training for a knowledgeable trainer.
- It does not require extensive organizational follow-through, being designed to help the trainee function in an environment where organizational follow-through is minimal.

As the research accumulates specifying what self-management skill retention strategies are most effective under which organizational conditions, RP training can be enacted on an experimental basis. RP demonstrates how previewing the post-training environment during the formal training period can maintain trainee focus on the additional set of skills received, which will allow the trainee to anticipate high-risk situations most likely to sabotage new learning.

> Meredith Parker hardly participated in the usual "after-training" socializing. Her mind had fast-forwarded to the day the following week that she had predicted her first lapse would occur. She thought about the coping skills she had practiced and how she would respond if it didn't all turn out perfectly the first time. Of all the new lessons Parker had absorbed in this intense afternoon, the most memorable was "transfer is personal."

Let the delegation begin!

References

Baldwin, T. T., & Ford, J. K. (1988). Transfer of training: A review and directions for future research. *Personnel Psychology, 41,* 63–106.

Bandura, A. (1977). *Social learning theory.* New Saddle River, NJ: Prentice Hall.

Burke, L. A. (1996). Improving transfer of training: A field investigation of the effect of relapse prevention training and transfer climate on maintenance outcomes. *Dissertation Abstracts International, 57–04A,* 1725. Accession no: AAG9627025.

Burke, L. A. (Ed). (2001). *High-impact training solutions.* Westport, CT: Quorum Books.

Burke, L. A., & Baldwin, T. T. (1999). Workforce training transfer: A study of the effect of relapse prevention training and transfer climate. *Human Resource Management, 38*(3), 227–242.

Kreitner, R., & Luthans, F. (1984). A social learning approach to behavioral management: Radical behaviorists "mellowing out." *Organizational Dynamics, 13,* 47–65.

Luthans, R., & Davis, T. (1979). Behavioral self-management: The missing link in managerial effectiveness. *Organizational Dynamics, 8*(1), 42–60.

Manz, C. C., & Sims, J. P., Jr. (1980). Self-management as a substitute for leadership: A social learning perspective. *Academy of Management Review, 5,* 361–367.

Marlatt, G. A., & Gordon, J. R. (1980). Determinants of relapse: Implications for the maintenance of behavior change. In P. O. Davidson & S. M. Davidson (Eds.), *Behavioral medicine: Changing health life styles* (pp. 410–452). New York: Brunner/Mazel.

Marlatt, G. A., & Gordon, J. R. (Eds.). (1985). *Relapse prevention: Maintaining strategies in the treatment of addictive behaviors.* New York: Guilford Press.

Marx, R. D. (1982). Relapse prevention for managerial training: A model for maintenance of behavioral change. *Academy of Management Review, 7,* 433–441.

Marx, R. D. (1986). Improving management development through relapse prevention strategies. *Journal of Management Development, 5*(2), 27–40.

Marx, R. D., & Karren, R. J. (1988, August). *The effects of relapse prevention training and interactive follow-up on positive transfer of training.* Paper presented at annual Academy of Management meeting, Anaheim, CA.

Marx, R. D., & Karren, R. J. (1990, August). *The effects of relapse prevention and post-training follow-up on time management behavior.* Paper presented at the annual Academy of Management meeting, San Francisco, CA.

Perri, M. G., Shapiro, R. M., Ludwig, W. W., Twentyman, C. T., & McAdoo, W. G. (1984). Maintenance strategies for the treatment of obesity: An evaluation of relapse prevention training and post treatment contact by mail and telephone. *Journal of Consulting and Clinical Psychology, 52,* 404–413.

Schermerhorn, J. R. (1979). The health care manager's role in promoting change. *Health Care Management Review, 4*(1), 71–79.

Stevens, V. J., & Hollis, J. F. (1989). Preventing smoking relapse: Using an individually tailored skills-training technique. *Journal of Consulting and Clinical Psychology, 57*(3), 420–424.

Tannenbaum, S. I., & Yukl, G. (1992). Training and development in work organizations. *Annual Review of Psychology, 43,* 399–441.

CHAPTER 12

Managers as Transfer Agents

Reid A. Bates

Managers and supervisors play a critical role as transfer agents when they use their managerial skills and abilities to support and influence employee learning transfer, help training generate the outcomes for which it was intended, and enhance the return their organization realizes from training investments. This chapter chronicles the case of Betterway Technology to illustrate how this role can be played. First, some guidelines are presented to describe how managers and supervisors can build a foundation for success as a transfer agent by understanding the fundamental factors that contribute to training effectiveness so that sound training decisions can be made; establishing and communicating to trainees and other stakeholders the presence of learning-transfer-performance improvement linkage; and identifying critical leverage points for change and support activities that can improve learning transfer. Discussions and case study vignettes demonstrate how managers and supervisors can apply fundamental managerial competencies (for example, using rewards, providing coaching and feedback, building self-management skills in subordinates, supplying the necessary resources to support desired performance, and using assessment to measure results) to improve learning transfer in their organization. Finally, the chapter provides a short list of first-step actions for managers who believe learning transfer is important for their organization and who want to start being more effective as transfer agents.

Betterway Technology, a manufacturer and retailer of computers and teller-machines, is feeling the strain of a tight economy, increasing customer demands, and intense competition in a highly aggressive industry. Dr. Emma Lewis, CEO of Betterway, knows that making Betterway more successful in this environment will require efforts on multiple fronts. But one of the key competitive advantages that Betterway has traditionally enjoyed has been its attention to customer service and its ability to deliver effective service to customers when and where they need it most. Unfortunately, over the past two years the profitability of the customer service department has tailed off dramatically. Increasingly complex technology coupled with a wide variety of made-to-order designs to meet specific customer needs has meant field engineers are taking nearly twice as long to complete service calls compared to a year or even six months ago. The Customer Service Task Force, a committee of senior managers and subject matter experts from the Research and Development, Manufacturing, and Service and Maintenance Divisions, has spent the last two months studying ways in which customer service calls can be made more efficient. They have come up with a number of new techniques and technologies, approaches they believe can significantly reduce service time and increase the profitability and customer satisfaction of service calls.

However, these solutions won't work until the field engineers who make the service calls learn and implement the new approaches. Making this happen has become the responsibility of Bob Falk, the manager of the Service and Maintenance Division at Betterway, and his regional service and maintenance supervisors.

The challenge facing Bob and Betterway—and all managers and organizations that attempt to use training as a performance improvement strategy—is one of learning transfer. They may not know it now, but there are two fundamental truths about learning transfer with which they will need to contend. First, training is unlikely to improve job performance without a work environment supportive of learning transfer. Second, although a number of work environment variables can influence learning transfer, research and best training practices increasingly highlight the central role that managers and supervisors play in transfer success. So beyond Betterway's training program or what the field engineers learn in training, the capacity of Bob and his regional supervisors to support learning transfer will be critical in making sure that the training generates the performance improvement outcomes it is supposed to generate.

Unfortunately, the literature offers little guidance about what exactly managers and supervisors must know or do to facilitate employee learning transfer. This chapter attempts to address this issue by presenting a view of managers and supervisors as transfer agents. *Transfer agents* are those individuals most capable of acting both as a means through which learning transfer occurs and a force capable of improving organizational transfer systems. Managers and supervisors function as transfer agents when their actions are instrumental in helping employees successfully apply learning and helping their organization generate performance improvement outcomes from training. The concept of managers and supervisors as transfer agents is crucial because it underscores the unique, profound, and broad capacity they have to improve learning transfer and the subsequent return organizations are able to realize from their investments in training.

Managers and supervisors who are effective transfer agents have taken fundamental managerial competencies and applied these to improving learning transfer in their organization. For example, the capacity to be an effective transfer agent encompasses the following competencies common to most high-performance managerial and supervisory competency models:

- Take self-initiated action to solve problems and improve results.
- Analyze problems, identify cause-effect relationships, and create and prioritize solutions.
- Optimize systems and processes to improve performance.
- Build productive relationships.
- Measure and assess results.
- Develop and actualize human potential.
- Use data to influence others to improve business results.
- Manage resources to achieve business goals.
- Facilitate meaningful change.

Laying the Foundation for Effective Learning Transfer

Developing the ability to be an effective transfer agent requires managers and supervisors to focus the listed capabilities specifically on improving learning transfer and increasing the payoff from training investments. This chapter describes and illustrates ways to do this, with the help of case study vignettes. The goal is to provide some concrete guidance about how managers and supervisors can become more effective transfer agents.

Rational Decisions About Training

To be effective as transfer agents, one of the primary competencies managers and supervisors must develop is the ability to make sound, rational decisions about training. This includes the capacity to ensure that training meets acceptable design and evaluation standards, fits the requirements of the job being targeted, and is aligned with organizational goals and values. The instructional systems design (ISD) model best encapsulates the fundamental elements of this approach (Goldstein, 1991). The ISD model provides managers and supervisors with a foundation for understanding what is needed to make sure that training generates the performance improvement outcomes it is supposed to generate. Effective transfer agents therefore must have a fundamental understanding of this model and its implications for systematic, effective training.

Bob feels a little bit overwhelmed with the responsibility he has been given for this change. He knows that fixing the customer service problem is important for the organization. Fortunately, Betterway has already devoted a lot of resources to figuring out some solutions that can speed customer service calls. He thinks, "I want to do everything I can to make this work. I know it will involve training the field engineers on the new technical approaches, but I have never devoted much attention to training. To be honest I always thought that training was kind of a no-brainer, just common sense."

But he realizes that to make sure this training works, he had better understand at least the fundamentals of what makes for effective training. Since this was never covered in any of his MBA courses, he goes to Sylvia Jones, the training manager at Betterway, for some guidance.

"Sylvia, you know the Customer Service Task Force has been working on figuring out how to streamline the field engineers' maintenance and customer service calls. I'm responsible for rolling out these changes, making sure the engineers get the proper training and apply the new stuff on the job. And I don't know beans about training; how am I supposed to decide what to do? What's the best practice these days? What can I do to make this effort pay off?"

Sylvia replies, "I'm glad you came to see me, Bob. Managers like you can be a big asset when it comes to making training work. And that's more complex than you might think. The basic principles," says Sylvia, "are pretty well encompassed in what is called the Instructional Systems Design Model. The ISD model emphasizes some basic points:

"You have to base the design of training programs on systematic needs assessment to assure the content of training meets job-related performance needs.

"Then you have to select material, media, and instructional procedures not because they are popular or faddish but because they have a basis in scientific research and are appropriate for the capabilities of your target audience.

"The idea is to develop instructional events that make sure what is learned can be applied and maintained on the job.

"And then you have to evaluate the training against the criteria of effectiveness that were identified in the needs assessment."

The ISD model presents a logical and systematic approach to formulating training that can pay off in individual and organizational performance improvement. Unfortunately, the truth is that most managers and supervisors don't understand the ISD model or make rational training decisions based on that model (Dipboye, 1997). A common tendency is to rely on the appeal of a current training fad or the hope of a quick and painless fix rather than a thorough understanding of how that training will address real organizational needs (Gordon, 1994; Lewinson, 1992). These kinds of decisions all but extinguish the ability of training investments to improve performance or produce an economic return for the organization. They are also poison to the development of a performance improvement culture because they send an unmistakable message to employees that training is not something that is highly valued as a performance improvement tool.

On the other hand, managers and supervisors who have a sound, fundamental understanding of the ISD model are better equipped to make effective decisions about training. They are better positioned to make sure that training is job-relevant because they can demand that it be based on a systematic assessment of performance needs. They can also monitor the training to see that it is designed and delivered in a way that facilitates learning and transfer, and they can make sure that programs are evaluated based on relevant criteria and that the resulting information is used to improve future training.

When Bob considers the field engineer training in the context of the ISD model he recognizes that Betterway has started down the right road. First, he knows that high-quality customer service is a key goal of Betterway and improving its ability to deliver that service has become a critical need. Second, the analysis and assessment activities of the Customer Service Task Force identified a number of improvements in maintenance and service that have the potential to solve some of the company's most pressing customer service problems. The next step is to design and develop the training that will enable the field engineers to learn and use these improvements on the job.

Of course, training design isn't Bob's responsibility, and he knows that Sylvia and her people in the Training Department have a good reputation in Betterway for being effective at what they do. But because of the importance of this training effort, Bob wants to do all that he can to make sure it works. He decides to do two things that he hasn't done with past training initiatives. First, he reviews the field engineer training program developed by the Training Department to confirm the program is consistent with the learning requirements identified through the Customer Service Task Force's report.

Second, he decides to make a commitment to do all he can to support Sylvia and the Training Department in this effort. At the end of a meeting with Sylvia to discuss the design of the upcoming field engineer training, Bob gets a chance to put this commitment to work.

Sylvia says, "You know, I really like meeting with you like this, but I'm not the one you need to impress most. You can jump-start the whole training process if you make sure the field engineers are absolutely clear about how the training is supposed to help them do their jobs better. And if you really want to hit a home run, make sure they know just how important the training is to the people at the top of this organization."

"You want me to send out a memo? OK, what should I say?"

"A memo isn't enough. Talk to the engineers about what an opportunity this is. Come visit the class and say it again. The more of yourself and your own time you put into this, the surer they'll be that this time it really means something, and the company isn't just going through the motions."

Link Learning, Transfer, and Performance Improvement

To be effective transfer agents, managers must be crystal clear, before training begins, about how learning, application of that learning on the job, and individual and organizational performance improvements are linked. Then they must communicate this linkage to the employees who will be attending the training and make sure they understand why the training is being conducted, what will be learned, and how it will improve performance.

Although communicating this information may seem rather mundane, managers routinely overlook it. Employees are frequently uncertain about the purpose of training, how it will improve job performance, or what it will contribute to organizational goals. As a consequence, they have very little reason to value training—and often do not. When managers and supervisors fail to tell employees what training is about and why it is important, they miss an important opportunity to increase the motivation and learning readiness of employees.

> One of Bob's key objectives as an effective transfer agent is to make sure the field engineers understand how important this training is to the organization and how learning and transfer are linked to performance improvement.
>
> Bob knows that the Betterway CEO, Dr. Lewis, views this training as critically important to the organization. He concludes it might be a good opportunity to ask her to get involved in communicating this to all the training stakeholders including the field engineers, their immediate supervisors, and the training staff—after all, if his time will help persuade the engineers to pay attention, hers will do even more. He considers setting up a pretraining orientation session that includes Dr. Lewis, Sylvia and her trainers, and the field engineers and their supervisors. He knows that Dr. Lewis is highly regarded by employees, and if she could talk about the purpose of the upcoming training, its intended link to job performance, and its importance to the organization, this would send a powerful message to those involved in making this training work.

Effective transfer agents must make sure that all the key stakeholders in the training effort including top management, trainers, trainees, and the trainees' immediate supervisors understand the following points (Brinkerhoff & Gill, 1994):

Why the training is being delivered.

What will be learned.

How the learning will improve job performance.

How the learning will benefit the organization.

Effective transfer agents communicate this information *before training begins* to set the stage for generating the maximum benefits from training. It clarifies and publicizes training and performance improvement expectations and is a powerful tool for creating a shared vision among the stakeholders about the importance of training and what it will accomplish for employees and the organization. For the trainees themselves, it is a critical first step in shaping positive attitudes about the usefulness of training. It creates a need for training in employees' minds and signals to them that training has performance improvement value. It helps build commitment to the training and motivates employees to learn and to use that learning on the job.

Diagnose Transfer Problems Before Training

Effective transfer agents diagnose transfer problems before training to identify catalysts, barriers, and solutions.

Kozlowski and Salas argue that the training of individuals is "embedded in team- or unit-level technology, coordination processes, social system contexts, [and] broader contextual constraints originating at higher system levels" (1997, p. 249). In other words, in addition to individual employee factors such as motivation, technical or cognitive ability, and so on, a wide variety of factors can influence learning transfer. Holton (Chapter Four in this volume) conceptualizes these factors as a transfer system, defined as all individual, training-related, team or group, and organizational factors that influence learning transfer.

This systems view of transfer suggests that if managers and supervisors are going to be effective transfer agents they must identify key transfer system elements that can be used to improve learning transfer. In this sense, effective transfer agents are comparable to coaches preparing a baseball or football field before a game. They examine a range of team-related factors to make sure all the key elements needed for the winning game are working and in place before the game is played. If they find a problem, they have to take steps to fix it before the team takes the field. It's the same with learning transfer. **The payoff from training will be maximized when managers and supervisors use their leadership skills, managerial ability, and decision-making power to diagnose and foster change in the transfer system before trainees take their learning into the workplace.**

Bob proposes to Sylvia that they do some up-front analysis to make sure the field engineers don't run into any obstacles when it comes to applying their training back on the job. "Let's take a look at what kinds of support the field engineers will need when it comes to using this learning on the job. My understanding is that there are lots of things beyond the trainer or the content of the training that can help or hurt employees trying to use new learning on the job."

Sylvia says, "Yes, there has been some very practical research in this area. In fact, I know of a survey instrument, the Learning Transfer Systems Inventory (LTSI), that may help us. From what I know the survey is sound from a measurement perspective, easy to use, and has helped some trainers I know get more job improvement from training. We could use the LTSI as a 'pulse-taking' diagnostic tool to get more information about what kinds of support the field engineers will need to use the training back on the job."

Bob and Sylvia distribute the LTSI to all the field engineers at the conclusion of the orientation meeting with Dr. Lewis, three weeks prior to the beginning of the training program. To analyze the responses, they calculate some simple averages to get an indication of what might be potential strengths and weaknesses of the transfer system facing the field engineers. To make sure they have a clear picture of how these factors might be affecting learning transfer they conduct several focus groups with the field engineers. What they find is both good and bad. The good news is that the motivation of the field engineers is a big plus.

Field engineers have a high level of confidence in their own ability to use new learning on the job, they are motivated to use new learning on the job, and their expectations that training will help them do their job better are high.

In addition, the fact that field engineers work in two-person teams appears to be another supportive factor for learning transfer. They found that work partners actively help each other identify and take advantage of opportunities to apply training. They also see training as a way to acquire new skills that can improve their job performance.

The bad news is that a couple of key elements of the transfer system could be more supportive. They found that field engineers did not believe that using training to improve job performance was very rewarding. They did not feel they got much in the way of formal or informal recognition for using training on the job. Moreover, there were times when those who were successful at using learning to improve performance suffered as a result. They were frequently given additional work or more difficult work than others who were not as effective in applying their training. In short, the data suggested the need for more positive, effective feedback (rewards) for using training on the job.

Second, the work environment of the field engineers must provide greater support for the application of learning on the job. The field engineers reported difficulty getting opportunities to apply new skills because the material and supplies they used when learning new techniques in training were often not available at the end of training. For example, a recent training program focused on the use of new diagnostic software. But the field engineers did not get the new software to use in their service calls until several weeks after the training. By this time much of their learning had been lost. In addition, the field engineers' workload created tremendous pressure to complete repair and maintenance jobs as quickly as possible. This limited their personal capacity (time and energy) to try new things.

Finally, the data also indicated that past training frequently was not presented in a manner that made the learning easy to use on the job. The field engineers noted they often got too much material dumped on them too fast and that the training would be better if there were less lecture and discussion and more chance to try out the techniques and get some hands-on experience at making them work. Sylvia adjusted the planned training to make greater use of clear examples, experiential exercises, application activities, and other active learning techniques that could help the field engineers learn how to use the learning in real work situations.

Managers and supervisors wishing to enhance the performance return on learning investments must understand the factors that can affect learning transfer. Advance diagnosis of the learning transfer system is a crucial form of feedforward control that enables effective transfer agents to build support for transfer and anticipate and fix problems. As we can see from Bob and Sylvia's efforts, advance diagnosis of the learning transfer system is a vital prerequisite for

- Recognizing critical leverage points (catalysts and barriers) for changing the learning transfer system.

- Generating specific information to clarify how and why those catalysts and barriers are influencing learning transfer.
- Providing guidance in identifying the kinds of support activities or transfer interventions that have the greatest potential for improving learning transfer.

Supporting and Influencing Learning Transfer

But figuring out what is good and bad about a transfer system is only half the battle. This information is only valuable to the extent that it leads to corrective action. Managers who are effective transfer agents must have the capacity to change learning transfer systems by putting into place appropriate configurations of systems, policies, and other work-related factors to increase learning transfer. Not only is transfer more likely to succeed in such environments, managers risk creating a debilitating cycle in which current transfer failure undermines future efforts when transfer barriers exist and no action is taken to overcome them (Mathieu, Tannenbaum, & Salas, 1992). Our systems perspective suggests that in most cases change, support, and influence will be required on multiple fronts. The remainder of this chapter examines some specific actions and strategies characteristic of high-performing transfer agents.

Build Partnerships with Key Stakeholders

One of the keys to effectively supporting and influencing learning transfer is to decide where and how energy and resources can most effectively be directed to maximize the performance improvement potential of training. To do so, effective transfer agents must not only rely on their advance diagnostic information but must also recognize that effective transfer is dependent on the active participation of a variety of individuals including trainees, trainers, coworkers, supervisors, and upper management. In fact, a crucial source of strength in building effective transfer systems is the working partnerships that effective transfer agents build with other key transfer players. These partnerships, oriented toward sharing transfer system information, clarifying and defining transfer responsibilities, and managing transfer system elements to foster learning transfer, are key to generating and maintaining the application of learning on the job.

We have already seen that one of the first things that Bob did was to begin building effective working partnerships with other stakeholders in the training process. He partnered with Sylvia to learn more about training and the ISD model. With Sylvia's cooperation, he initiated a training partnership with top management at Betterway. The advance orientation meeting in which Bob enlisted the help of CEO Lewis and others was highly effective in communicating realistic information about the purpose and importance of training—so much so that enthusiasm for the upcoming training had never been higher among the field engineers and their supervisors, as well as among the training staff.

Bob also put some time and effort into facilitating a three-way partnership between the training staff, field engineers, and their supervisors. Since the diagnostic data indicated that past training often included too much lecture and discussion and not enough structured job-related skill practice, the initial focus of this partnership was on getting input from the field engineers and supervisors about how training might be made more active and hands-on. It made sense to call on this expertise and explore ways to facilitate the involvement of the recipients in training design. He found that this kind of involvement also generated feelings of ownership of the training and increased training-related motivation and commitment to transfer. As it turned out, not only did these employees appreciate the opportunity to have direct input into training, their understanding of the job and its requirements was so helpful to the training staff that Bob and Sylvia decided to provide an avenue for their input in all key training efforts.

Use Goal Cues to Improve Learning Transfer

Goal setting as a performance improvement strategy is not new to effective managers. Goals can improve subordinates' performance because they provide a visible target for performance and provide a basis for tracking progress. A good deal of research has established that the most effective goals are specific (focused on distinct task-related outcomes rather than fuzzy "do your best" goals), challenging rather than easy to attain, and measurable in ways that allow progress to be monitored by both managers and employees. It is probably fair to say that most managers have never applied their goal-setting skills to learning transfer.

However, used effectively a set of transfer goals can provide the framework for a learning application plan for each employee. Effective transfer agents in most cases must address multiple layers of goals. For example, first they must distinguish between learning goals and transfer goals (Elliott & Dweck, 1988) and use goal-setting processes to maximize the effectiveness of each set of goals. For example, research suggests that setting difficult transfer goals prior to or during training may actually interfere with the learning and skill acquisition process (Kanfer & Ackerman, 1989). Effective transfer agents therefore treat learning and transfer as separate goal-setting incidents: they facilitate the identification of learning goals early in the training and delay identification of transfer goals until training is completed or nearing completion.

Second, effective transfer agents also understand that goal setting can be an effective tool not only with trainees but also with their direct supervisors. Trainees' direct supervisors are ideally located to provide critical support to learning transfer efforts. Managers who are effective transfer agents can facilitate a goal-setting process in which these individuals identify and set objectives for supporting their subordinates' transfer efforts.

Bob decides to take a two-pronged approach to transfer-related goal setting. First, he asks Sylvia for her help in conducting an advance orientation session with the regional supervisors. The goal of this session will be to discuss learning transfer and the importance of active supervisory support in making transfer happen, and to help the supervisors set some concrete, realistic goals for themselves in terms of what they plan to do to support the field engineers' transfer efforts. He recognizes that the supervisors' goal plans will be most effective in motivating, guiding, and evaluating transfer support efforts if they are formalized in a written "statement of goals" that can be shared and discussed. He works with each of his regional supervisors to develop such a plan.

Second, he knows the field engineers themselves will have to develop some transfer-related goals. If their supervisors are involved in this planning, if the goals are shared or set with the supervisors' participation, they will probably be more forceful in motivating and guiding the field engineers' learning and transfer efforts. Bob takes a "tell and sell" approach with the supervisors to encourage them to work with the field engineers to develop two sets of goals. First, he wants to see learning goals developed prior to or very early in the training program. These will serve to guide and motivate what the field engineers learn. Toward the end of the program, after the learning content has largely been mastered, he wants the supervisors to work with the field engineers to develop specific transfer goals. Both sets of goals should be formalized into written statements.

Effective transfer agents use goal setting to establish learning and transfer as important work-related outcomes. Participative goal setting, in which managers and supervisors work with each other and with employees to plan goals, communicates expectations and identifies standards of excellence for learning, transfer, and support. But goal setting without follow-up is an empty promise. It is critical that once goals are set, managers and supervisors demonstrate their commitment to those goals by providing consequences for goal attainment and supporting subordinates' goal-directed efforts. They understand that if employees interpret the goals as "merely wishes, with no accountability and no consequences for not attaining [them]" the goals will have little motivational value (Baldwin & Magjuka, 1997, p. 102). In other words, effective transfer agents manage the meaning that employees attach to their learning and transfer goals. The use of reward power is one way managers and supervisors can do so.

Use Reward Power to Support Learning Transfer

The presence of a supportive reward system for learning transfer can be a potent factor to improve performance. High-performing transfer systems will invariably include processes for providing organizational members with rewards that support the acquisition and use of learning. Rewards represent a clear policy statement about the value placed on learning transfer (Kozlowski & Hults, 1987), and have the potential to motivate transfer behavior and lead to improved transfer results. Effective transfer agents understand that effective transfer reward systems are key components in the ongoing maintenance of learning transfer.

> Bob and his regional supervisors decided their goal-setting efforts would have more teeth if they could tie accomplishment of those goals to some kind of rewards that the field engineers value. They decided to use a simple but multifaceted approach that included the following measures:
> *Use of informal rewards.* Field engineers and their supervisors were encouraged to record incidents in which knowledge or skills learned in training made dramatic improvements in the quality and timeliness of a service or maintenance call. Every two weeks these brief success stories were posted on the company Web site along with the names and pictures of the employees who made the success. Bob sent personal notes of appreciation to those involved.

Follow-up status meetings. Six weeks after the training ended, Bob held a follow-up meeting with the field engineers and their supervisors. Betterway provided lunch. During this meeting Bob outlined the positive outcomes of the training program so far and recognized individual field engineers and supervisors for goal-related accomplishments. Plaques were awarded for outstanding transfer and transfer-support successes. Results were publicized in the Betterway monthly newsletter.

More publicity for transfer successes. Three months after the training, Bob wrote an article for the Betterway monthly newsletter that recognized by name the individual efforts of specific field engineers and their supervisors in applying the new service and maintenance skills and techniques learned in training. He also made a point of recognizing the training staff for their efforts in making the training work.

For the newsletter article, Bob provided a summary of the data he had collected about how service call time had been reduced since training ended. He used this data to provide an estimate of the savings to the organization as a result of the use of the new service and maintenance techniques.

Although skill-based pay, incentive compensation, and other performance-based reward systems hold great promise for improving learning transfer, they are rarely applied in organizational training settings (Baldwin & Magjuka, 1997). Because of the cost, complexity, and potential risks of developing such systems, these are probably long-term goals in the development of high-performing transfer systems.

On the other hand, there is evidence that far less complicated and costly reward efforts such as those used by Bob and his colleagues can be effective in supporting learning transfer. In fact, experience suggests that informal public reward processes such as impromptu verbal praise, casual notes recognizing successes or failures, or other types of inexpensive public recognition can significantly influence the transfer behavior of employees. Transfer agents must recognize that informal rewards are most effective under the following conditions:

- Employees value them and perceive them as positively reinforcing.
- They are closely tied to increases in transfer performance and are seen as distinguishing between better transfer performers and poorer ones.

- They are delivered in ways that support feelings of accomplishment, personal worth, responsibility, increased competence, and self-determination.

Effective transfer agents understand that using new learning in work situations can be difficult, and that when productive transfer efforts are ignored or not rewarded it can easily give way to relapse or doing things "the way they have always been done." In essence, effective transfer agents must be good at catching employees "doing something right" and rewarding that behavior.

Provide Ongoing Coaching in Ways That Continuously Improve Transfer

Ongoing coaching represents the concrete involvement of managers and supervisors in work-related transfer efforts. It is a key competency for effective transfer agents. Coaching's unique value lies in its ability to fundamentally transform the transfer situation from one that is solely dependent on the employee for success to a team-based structure (Olivero, Bane, & Kopelman, 1997) in which employee and manager or supervisor work together to build transfer results. Coaching involves the provision of periodic feedback and advice concerning transfer efforts and results.

> As experienced managers, Bob and his supervisors had done lots of coaching as a part of their daily activities. This experience enabled them to work together to develop effective ways to apply the same coaching skills and techniques to learning transfer they had used for other performance issues. For example:
>
> The regional supervisors worked with each field engineer team to develop specific transfer action plans. These action plans were tied to the goal statements the field engineers had produced but were more specific in describing what was going to be done to meet those goals. They included a section that identified the activities, roles, and responsibilities that both the supervisors and the field engineers would undertake to make transfer happen. Like the goal statements, the action plans were formalized in writing and represented a "transfer contract." In developing the action plans, Bob and his supervisors did their best to encourage realistic expectations about transfer success and help the field engineers develop an understanding that transfer is challenging but possible, and that it is ultimately a shared responsibility.

A key element in the productiveness of transfer coaching is the feedback that transfer agents provide. Because of their power and proximity, managers and supervisors are the best equipped to provide transfer-related feedback. Such feedback serves several critical functions. It can increase employee motivation and feelings of competence by providing information that employees can use to evaluate the extent to which they meet transfer goals (Bandura, 1991). It can facilitate the adjustment of transfer behaviors to maximize transfer results (Cormier, 1987), and it can allow employees to correct errors in transfer behaviors before they become bad habits (Dansereau, 1985). Action plans not only lay out a guide for transfer efforts but also serve as an important mechanism for transfer-related feedback: they provide the medium through which information about transfer efforts and results can be shared and discussed.

Build Transfer Self-Management Skills

To be effective, transfer agents, managers, and supervisors must recognize that they will not always be present to provide supportive coaching or reinforcement. Ultimately it is the employee who must make the transition from learning to application (Marx, 2000), and employees encounter different transfer obstacles and opportunities in the post-training work environment than they do during training.

Transfer agents respond to these challenges by helping their employees develop transfer-related self-management skills. In fact, self-management skills have been shown to be effective tools for enhancing employee learning and transfer in a number of work contexts (Burke, 1997; Burke & Baldwin, 1999; Noe, Sears, & Fullencamp, 1990; Tziner, Haccoun, & Kadish, 1991).

When employees develop self-management skills, it means they are capable of managing their own transfer efforts. Fostering transfer-related self-management skills involves managers and supervisors in the use of strategies and techniques that help employees build the skills needed to alter their work environment and self-motivate themselves to achieve successful learning transfer. There are a number of ways this can be done. For example, including a relapse prevention module in the training program can help employees identify threats to transfer and develop strategies to cope with those threats before they happen. Marx discusses in detail how relapse prevention can be used to support learning transfer in Chapter Eleven of this volume.

> At Betterway, Bob worked with Sylvia and his supervisors to develop a number of straightforward and inexpensive strategies to help the field engineers develop transfer self-management skills. For example, they took the following steps:
>
> 1. *They used the personal transfer action plans to build self-management skills.* These plans supported transfer self-management by providing the field engineers with countable milestones or objectives against which they could continuously track their progress. Bob and his supervisors built on this by facilitating regular periodic reviews in which they worked with the field engineers to reflect on and change the action plans based on what had been learned from their transfer successes and failures.
>
> 2. *They helped the field engineers develop personalized transfer performance charts.* These charts, based on the employee goal statements and action plans, were essentially checklists designed to enable the field engineers to track their personal history of transfer behavior (when and how often they used the knowledge, skills, and abilities learned in training). The tracking sheets also had space for the field engineers to record comments about their use of new learning and the successes that accrued as a result.
>
> 3. *The supervisors allowed the field engineers to select specific job assignments or tasks that offered high potential for successful use of new learning.* Providing employees with some discretion in defining when, where, and how new learning can be used fosters transfer self-management by building intrinsic motivation into the transfer process (Manz, 1986).

Obtain and Commit Resources That Support Learning Transfer

Research has demonstrated that the lack of proper technology, job-related information, required services, material and supplies, money, time, human resources, and attributes of the physical environment can present substantial obstacles to learning transfer (Latham & Crandall, 1991). These factors can directly influence transfer when, for example, the technology an employee is trained on does not match the technology back in the workplace. They can also indirectly influence transfer by decreasing motivation and self-efficacy beliefs, and by increasing job-related frustration (Baldwin & Magjuka, 1997; Peters, O'Connor, & Eulberg, 1985). Managers must therefore be capable of identifying and providing the technical, logistic, or human resources needed to make transfer happen.

> Bob and his supervisors made sure that all the field engineer units had the tools or other technology on their trucks when they returned from training to make sure they could use their learning on the job. These elements were all ordered and received before training began to make sure they would be available the day the field engineers returned to work.

Managers and supervisors who are effective transfer agents also recognize that they are key gatekeepers in providing employees with opportunities for on-the-job skill practice (Quinones, Ford, Sego, & Smith, 1996). Providing opportunities to use new skills back on the job is a key element in transfer because the direct task experience gained through such practice enhances skill retention and generalization (Ackerman & Humphreys, 1990). A number of strategies and techniques are available for providing on-the-job practice opportunities.

> For instance, Bob and his supervisors took the following steps:
>
> 1. *They eased the service and maintenance workload for several weeks immediately after training to create some "open space" in the field engineers' work schedule.* In the short run this made the service call times a bit longer. But its long-term effect was to cement the use of the new skills on the job. It not only allowed the field engineers time to use their new learning, it lowered stress levels so they felt comfortable enough to do what needed to be done to experiment with the new skills, tools, and techniques they had learned in training.
>
> 2. *They adjusted the job priority list.* That is, when it was appropriate they moved up those repair and maintenance jobs that provided the best and most immediate opportunity to use new learning.
>
> 3. *They allowed some field engineer teams to double up on service and maintenance calls that provided challenging opportunities to use new learning.* Allowing multiple teams of field engineers to work on a single service call meant quicker turnaround times, which pleased customers. More important for transfer, it gave more field engineers an opportunity to have meaningful transfer experiences, and it helped build a supportive transfer culture among the field engineers themselves.

Effective transfer agents should consider several factors when committing resources to increase job-related practice opportunities. First, as a general rule, it is safe to assume that the greater the number of new skills learned in training, the more opportunities for practice will be required for skill maintenance. Second, it may be important to consider how frequently trained tasks will be performed on the job. Important tasks that are rarely used on the job will require the provision of regular, periodic practice opportunities to support skill retention. Frequently performed tasks, on the other hand, will probably get the early and repeated practice needed without scheduling any ongoing practice opportunities. Third, the number and frequency of practice opportunities will probably need to increase as the difficulty of the transfer task increases: more difficult tasks will likely require more on-the-job practice (Ford, Quinones, Sego, & Sorra, 1992).

Develop a System for Assessing the Results of Transfer Efforts

Although billions of dollars are spent annually on formal training in the United States, the vast bulk of this training is not assessed to determine if learning has in any way changed job performance (Bassi & Cheney, 1996). And when some assessment is done it is rarely rigorous, relying mostly on employee reaction surveys ("smile sheets") that fail to address the learning–behavior change–job performance linkage (Saari, Johnson, McLaughlin, & Zimmerle, 1988; Sackett & Mullen, 1993). A major reason for this "evaluation evasion" is managers' acute antipathy toward assessing the outcomes of training. Whether this stems from fear of scrutiny or the erroneous assumption that learning during training automatically ensures transfer to the job, often the last thing a manager wants to do is undertake a formal, systematic, and revealing assessment of training (Kerr, 1975).

This is not to say that every training program should be evaluated. Evaluation takes time, money, and other resources. If program outcomes are not intended to improve performance, not meaningful to high-placed decision makers, and if the results of the assessment are not important or will not be used, then assessment resources may be better used elsewhere (Swanson & Holton, 1999). But if these things matter, then evaluation is essential.

Bob had wrestled with the idea of assessment since this training program began. Frankly, it made him nervous. But he knew the training was important for the organization and it was clear they would need to have some kind of data about whether the training was effective in reducing service call time. Bob also didn't want this assessment to get too time-consuming. He wanted to use what existing resources he could to make the best and most efficient assessment possible. Not surprisingly, Bob found that Betterway had a number of things already in place that helped him produce a very credible assessment. First, Sylvia and the training department routinely assessed both trainee learning and satisfaction with training programs. Using these established processes they were able to include the following end-of-training learning and reaction data in the assessment:

- *Written responses to multiple-choice and short-answer test questions.* This data represented a fairly thorough assessment of the field engineers' knowledge and understanding of the new service and maintenance tools and techniques.
- *Work sample tests.* These tools provided an assessment of the field engineers' ability to use some of the learned skills, tools, and techniques in a simulated setting. Since the training department had included a variety of hands-on techniques in the training, it was relatively simple to modify these for use as work sample tests.
- The standard trainee satisfaction-with-training survey used in nearly all Betterway training was modified slightly to improve its measurement of trainee perceptions of job-related utility of training and their satisfaction with how training was designed and delivered.

The biggest challenge for Bob and his colleagues was determining if the training and its application on-the-job really reduced the time required to complete service and maintenance calls. After all, this was what the training was all about. But to his knowledge, training at Betterway had never been assessed in this way. Although this meant that his superiors' expectations for this kind of an assessment might not be high, it also meant they were operating in new territory. They decided to simplify, using what was available and what was familiar.

To find out if the field engineers were using the training on the job, they developed a simple five-question survey that asked them to rate their own transfer behavior. For example, they asked field engineers to rate how successful they felt they had been at using what they learned in training, and to estimate (0 to 100 percent) how much of their learning they had been able to apply on the job. The field engineers had used self-rating instruments in the past for employee development purposes so this type of survey was familiar and nonthreatening. Bob and Sylvia expected to get relatively honest responses.

To get some indication about whether the transfer of training made a difference in service call time, Bob went to the Betterway database. Betterway routinely collected information about what tasks are performed on service calls and how much time those tasks require. Using existing data, Bob was able to compare completion times for specific service and maintenance tasks for the sixty days before training with those for the sixty days following training. He was also able to translate these findings into increased profitability figures for the Service and Maintenance Department.

The assessment of transfer results is critical to systematic transfer improvement. But assessment cannot just stop with trainee reaction or learning measures. These say nothing about changes in job performance or the value that these changes have created for the organization. Effective transfer agents strive to collect information about the effectiveness of training (for example, learning) and about the extent to which that learning contributes to performance improvement. This kind of assessment links training programs with the outcomes they are supposed to generate; it makes trainees, trainers, transfer agents, and others accountable for transfer success; and it helps create a culture that values learning and its application on the job. Without assessment, employees are far less likely to feel committed or responsible for learning and transfer, and will be less motivated to engage in or support either.

Where (or How) Can I Start?

Time-pressed managers—who are already struggling to deal with a generous helping of planning, organizing, motivating, and controlling responsibilities—may well be reacting to this chapter by thinking, "Sounds good, but I can't possibly do all of this." Don't despair just yet; there is still hope. The last section of this chapter is intended to help those of you interested in improving the learning transfer of your employees and the performance improvement you get from training by pointing to a few first-step areas in which your efforts as a transfer agent may pay substantial dividends. In other words, if you can't do it all, here are some focused steps you can take to begin to make a difference.

Start Small

First, as you have probably begun to realize, moving into the role of transfer agent can be a relatively ambitious undertaking. Most managers have probably not devoted a great deal of attention or energy to the management of employee learning transfer. And you can expect that initial attempts at improving transfer and transfer systems will most likely be challenging.

Therefore it is important that you pick your early battles carefully. Experience suggests that, early on, it is important to start small and choose projects that have a high chance of success. Big, high-profile training events attract a lot of attention, can be threatening to participants, and put a lot of pressure on transfer agents to be successful—something you don't need when experimenting with a new role. Choose a manageable project that has value to your organization and in which you have a good chance of demonstrating success. If you are successful—even in a small way—you will have built the confidence and competence of all involved and laid a good foundation for future efforts.

Make It a Team Effort

Building and using partnerships to support learning transfer is perhaps the most important element in changing and improving transfer systems. The active involvement of the training staff, employees, supervisors, top management, and other stakeholders not only makes the job easier but also increases the probability of success. A key component in making transfer a team effort is making sure that you and all the key stakeholders in the training effort (organizational leaders, trainers, trainees, and trainees' immediate supervisors or others) understand why the training is being delivered, what will be learned as a result of the training, how the learning will improve job performance, and how those improvements in performance will benefit the organization. Clearly, accomplishing this will first require some understanding on your part of the performance problem that training is intended to address. And it may require that you ask some difficult questions about the goals, outcomes, or relevance of training. But, as noted earlier, confirming this linkage and making it crystal clear is a critical first step in building employee motivation to learn and transfer and in establishing a broad coalition of support and commitment to successful transfer efforts.

Establish a Positive Transfer Expectations–Performance Cycle

One of the most important characteristics of effective transfer agents (indeed, of superior managers in general) is the ability to set high expectations for employees, communicate confidence in their ability to meet those expectations, and reward them when they do so. Common sense (and a good deal of research) tells that when a positive link is established between high expectations, performance, and rewards this linkage has the potential to build upon itself such that early successes lead to increasingly higher expectations and performance. In short, it provides an immediate mechanism for making "transfer winners" of your employees and it establishes the foundation upon which further transfer efforts can be built.

Building this linkage involves three straightforward but valuable steps. First, as a manager you must establish high transfer expectations: make it clear to employees what constitutes good transfer performance. Obviously, there are a number of ways this can be done. Collaborative goal setting is one option that was described earlier in this chapter. You may have other preferred methods. The important point is that your expectations about transfer are explicit and clear to each employee.

Once expectations or goals are established, employee progress toward those objectives should be regularly monitored. I recommend informal assessments: they are easy and efficient and less threatening to employees. For example, simply walking around and asking employees how well they are managing to transfer their new learning verifies to them that you are serious about transfer. It also helps establish employee accountability for transfer and provides a source of feedback information that may be helpful to you in providing further transfer support.

Finally, reinforce transfer efforts and successes whenever you find them. In other words, catch employees meeting your transfer expectations and reward them for it. As noted earlier, effective rewards need not be costly or complex. But they do need to communicate to employees that your transfer expectations have been met or exceeded.

Conclusion

Although managers and supervisors can play a crucial role in making training pay off in performance improvement, their commitment and ability to do so is often flawed. Many decisions about what training to provide or how it should be provided fail to conform to norms of rationality. Efforts to facilitate transfer fall short because the value of training is not recognized or communicated to employees, the resources needed to support learning transfer are not provided, and transfer efforts are not evaluated. Despite a new emphasis on training as a strategic organizational investment (one that makes the transfer agent role even more important), managers and supervisors have not gotten a great deal of help from academic or practitioner literature about how to fulfill this role.

This chapter has attempted to put some meat on these bones by describing managers and supervisors as transfer agents and emphasizing the importance of this role for helping employees use new learning on the job. Guidelines and an extensive case example have been used to describe, first, how managers and supervisors can build a foundation of successful learning transfer by

- Understanding the fundamental factors that contribute to training effectiveness so that sound training decisions can be made.
- Validating and communicating to trainees and other stakeholders the presence of learning-transfer-performance improvement linkage, and value of this linkage to the organization.
- Diagnosing learning transfer systems to identify critical leverage points for change and support activities that can improve learning transfer.

Second, this chapter illustrated how skills and competencies that effective managers already have (such as using rewards, providing coaching and feedback, building self-management skills in subordinates, supplying the necessary resources to support desired performance, and using assessment to measure results) can be applied to learning transfer. Effective transfer agents were described as those managers and supervisors who use these skills to support and influence learning transfer, help learning generate the outcomes for which it was intended, and enhance the return organizations are able to realize from their investments in learning.

Third, the chapter provided a short list of first-step actions for managers who believe learning transfer is important and who want to engage the transfer agent role. It was suggested that if you can start small, make transfer a team effort, and establish a positive transfer expectation–performance cycle with your employees you will have gone a long way toward being a successful transfer agent.

Finally, please recognize that much of what was discussed in this chapter represents an ideal that managers can aspire to as learning and learning transfer becomes more important in their organizations. Certainly Bob's experience at Betterway could easily be criticized as painting too rosy a picture of what might happen (or how easy it might be) when attempting to change and improve learning transfer. We all know that life in organizations may never be this easy. However, it is also true that if you are willing to undertake the responsibility for changing the transfer system in your organization you will set in motion a process that can dramatically increase performance improvement from training and integrate and unite those you choose to involve in the process.

References

Ackerman, P. L., & Humphreys, L. G. (1990). Individual differences theory in industrial and organizational psychology. In M. Dunnette & L. M. Hough (Eds.), *Handbook of industrial and organizational psychology* (2nd ed., vol. 1, pp. 223–282). Palo Alto, CA: Consulting Psychologists Press.

Baldwin, T. T., & Magjuka, R. J. (1997). Training as an organizational episode: Pretraining influences on trainee motivation. In J. K. Ford, S.W.J. Kozlowski, K. Kraiger, E. Salas, & M. S. Teachout (Eds.), *Improving training effectiveness in work organizations* (pp. 99–127). Mahwah, NJ: Erlbaum.

Bandura, A. (1991). Social cognitive theory of self-regulation. *Organizational Behavior and Human Decision Processes, 50,* 248–287.

Bassi, L. J., & Cheney, S. (1996). *Results from the 1996 benchmarking forum.* Alexandria, VA: American Society for Training and Development.

Brinkerhoff, R. O., & Gill, S. J. (1994). *The learning alliance: Systems thinking in human resource development.* San Francisco: Jossey-Bass.

Burke, L. A. (1997). Improving positive transfer: A test of relapse prevention training on transfer outcomes. *Human Resource Development Quarterly, 8,* 115–128.

Burke, L. A., & Baldwin, T. T. (1999). Workforce training transfer: A study of the effect of relapse prevention training and transfer climate. *Human Resource Management, 38*(3), 227–242.

Cormier, S. M. (1987). The structural processes underlying transfer of training. In S. M. Cormier and J. D. Hagman (Eds.), *Transfer of learning: Contemporary research and application* (pp. 151–181). New York: Academic Press.

Dansereau, D. F. (1985). Learning strategy research. In J. W. Segal, S. F. Chipman, & R. Glaser (Eds.), *Thinking and learning skills* (Vol. 1, pp. 209–239). Hillsdale, NJ: Erlbaum.

Dipboye, R. L. (1997). Organizational barriers to implementing a rational model of training. In M. A. Quinones & A. Ehrenstein (Eds.), *Training for a rapidly changing workplace: Applications of psychological research* (pp. 31–60). Washington, DC: American Psychological Association.

Elliott, E. S., & Dweck, C. S. (1988). Goals: An approach to motivation and achievement. *Journal of Personality and Social Psychology, 54,* 5–12.

Ford, J. K., Quinones, M., Sego, D., & Sorra, J. (1992). Factors affecting the opportunity to use trained skills on the job. *Personnel Psychology, 45,* 511–527.

Goldstein, I. L. (1991). Training in work organizations. In M. D. Dunnette & L. M. Hough (Eds.), *Handbook of industrial and organizational psychology* (2nd ed., vol. 2, pp. 507–619). Palo Alto, CA: Consulting Psychologists Press.

Gordon, J. (1994). Madame Z. *Training, 31,* 8.

Kanfer, R., & Ackerman, P. (1989). Motivation and cognitive abilities: An integrative/aptitude-treatment interaction approach to skill acquisition. *Journal of Applied Psychology, 74,* 657–690.

Kerr, S. (1975). On the folly of rewarding A, while hoping for B. *Academy of Management Journal, 18,* 769–783.

Kozlowski, S. W., & Hults, B. M. (1987). An exploration of climates for technical updating and performance. *Personnel Psychology, 40,* 539–563.

Kozlowski, S. W., & Salas, E. (1997). A multilevel organizational systems approach for the implementation and transfer of training. In K. Ford & S.W.J. Kozlowski (Eds.), *Improving training effectiveness in work organizations* (pp. 247–287). Mahwah, NJ: Erlbaum.

Latham, G. P., & Crandall, S. (1991). Organizational and social factors. In J. Morrison (Ed.), *Training for performance: Principles of applied human learning* (pp. 259–285). Chichester, England: Wiley.

Lewinson, H. (1992). Fad, fantasies, and psychological management. *Consulting Psychology Journal: Practice and Research, 44,* 1–12.

Manz, C. C. (1986). Self-leadership: Toward an expanded theory of self-influence processes in organizations. *Academy of Management Review, 11*(3), 585–600.

Marx, R. (2000). Transfer is personal: Equipping trainees with self-management and relapse-prevention strategies. *Advances in Developing Human Resources, 8,* 36–48.

Mathieu, J. E., Tannenbaum, S. I., & Salas, E. (1992). Individual and situational influences on measures of training effectiveness. *Academy of Management Journal, 35*(4), 828–847.

Noe, R. A., Sears, J., & Fullencamp, A. M. (1990). Relapse training: Does it influence trainees' post training behavior and cognitive strategies? *Journal of Business and Psychology, 4*(3), 319–328.

Olivero, G., Bane, K. D., & Kopelman, R. E. (1997). Executive coaching as a transfer of training tool: Effects on productivity in a public agency. *Public Personnel Management, 26*(4), 461–470.

Peters, L. H., O'Connor, E. J., & Eulberg, J. R. (1985). Situational constraints and work outcomes: The influences of a frequently overlooked construct. *Academy of Management Review, 5*(3), 391–397.

Quinones, M. A., Ford, J. K., Sego, D. J., & Smith, E. M. (1996). The effects of individual and transfer environment characteristics on the opportunity to perform trained tasks. *Training Research Journal, 1,* 29–48.

Saari, L. M., Johnson, T. R., McLaughlin, S. D., & Zimmerle, D. M. (1988). A survey of management training and education practices in U.S. companies. *Personnel Psychology, 41,* 731–743.

Sackett, P. R., & Mullen, E. J. (1993). Beyond formal experimental design: Towards an expanded view of the training evaluation process. *Personnel Psychology, 46,* 613–627.

Swanson, R. A., & Holton, E. F., III. (1999). *Results: How to assess performance, learning, and perceptions in organizations.* San Francisco: Berrett-Koehler.

Tziner, A., Haccoun, R. R., & Kadish, A. (1991). Personal and situational characteristics influencing the effectiveness of transfer of training improvement strategies. *Journal of Occupational Psychology, 64,* 167–177.

CHAPTER 13

Creating a Climate for Learning Transfer

Jerry W. Gilley
Erik Hoekstra

It has been well documented that the work environment (climate) greatly affects learning transfer. Work environments that encourage learning transfer help employees feel good about their self-development plans. Further, organizations that develop such climates will be empathetic entities focusing their energies on building relationships and fulfilling the developmental needs of every employee. Three types of strategies are examined in this chapter. First are macro organizational and environmental strategies, which include creating a developmental culture, developing self-esteeming organizations, overcoming fear in the workplace, and linking compensation and reward programs to employee growth and development. Second are organizational leadership actions—adopting a development philosophy, adopting the characteristics and actions of the learning organization, and establishing rapport with employees. Third are developmental strategies that provide organizations with unique and creative ways of improving performance capacity and capability: transforming performance appraisals into developmental evaluations, instituting employee growth and development plans, and identifying employee strengths. Collectively these strategies guide managers' and HRD professionals' action and keep them focused on real, practical solutions to complex learning transfer barriers.

Corporate and government spending on training activities aimed at improving employees' job performance represents an enormous budget commitment in the United States. In 1999, organizations earmarked over $62 billion in direct training dollars (Buckingham & Coffman, 1999). With the addition of the indirect costs and other informal on-the-job training efforts, estimates range from three to six times that amount (Carnevale & Gainer, 1989). It is widely thought that less than 10 percent of these total training dollars actually result in improved performance in job settings (Baldwin & Ford, 1988; Georgenson, 1982; Hoffman, 1983).

While the exact amount of learning transferred to the job setting is speculative, the problem is believed to be so pervasive that leading writers suggest they have not yet found a learning-performance situation in which no transfer problem occurs (Broad & Newstrom, 1992). Given that grim reality, it is incumbent on the people development profession to continue searching for means to improve that statistic in their quest to improve individual and organizational performance.

Effects of Workplace Environment on Learning Transfer

One of the hopeful streams of research into the motivational side of training transfer is the study of workplace climate. According to several researchers, the work environment (climate) greatly affects learning transfer (Baumgartel, Reynolds, & Pathan, 1984; Ford, Quinones, Sego, & Sorra, 1992; Holton, 1996; Huczynksi and Lewis, 1980; Tracey, Tannenbaum, & Kavanaugh, 1995). *Transfer climate* can be regarded as perceptions describing characteristics of the work environment that may facilitate or inhibit the use of trained skills. These characteristics can include immediate supervisor's influence, the nature of employee attitudes toward training, and the extent of formal training policies and practices that exist to support training initiatives. Transfer climates may, therefore, be described as either supportive (favorable, positive) or unsupportive (unfavorable, negative) in relation to these characteristics.

Several factors have been identified that affect the relationship between work environment and learning transfer. Tziner, Haccoun, and Kadish (1991) identified three factors that affect individual employees' relationships with their managers. These include feedback or performance coaching activities used to encourage the use of learning on the job, amount of support employees receive for using new learning, and the extent to which managers actively promote or oppose using new knowledge and expertise. Xiao (1996) identified two factors that affect the work group: support peers provide for using new learning, and the extent to which the group norm is open to change. Finally, two factors address the reward systems: the extent to which the outcomes for the person are positive or negative (Holton, 2000).

Work climate is a critical condition in determining whether employees (trainees) apply skills on the job after training (Tracey et al., 1995). The employees' perceptions of supervisory support in terms of discussing learning goals, listening to and championing new ideas, and allowing for experimentation are all factors that increase learning transfer (Huczynksi & Lewis, 1980). Noe (1986) reported that environmental favorability and increased learning transfer are positively correlated. Furthermore, Ford et al. (1992) discovered that when employees described their immediate work groups as supportive, they performed more complex and difficult tasks more easily.

Roullier and Goldstein (1993) reported that in locations with more positive transfer climates, as rated by managerial coworkers at each location, employees demonstrated significantly more trained behaviors and functioned more effectively on the job. From this study, they developed a conceptual framework for transfer climate consisting of two general types of workplace cues: situational and consequence. From these, eight distinct and observable variations were identified. Situational cues are those that remind employees (trainees) of what they have learned or provide the opportunity for them to use what they have learned. There are four variations of situational cues: goal, social, task, and self-control. On the other hand, consequence cues are those on-the-job outcomes that affect the extent to which training is transferred. There are four variations of consequence cues as well: positive feedback, negative feedback, punishment, and no feedback.

Tracey et al. (1995) replicated this study and expanded on it using thirty-three items from Roullier and Goldstein's (1993) instrument and twenty-four others designed to measure continuous-learning culture. Drawing on data gathered from more than five hundred supermarket managers from more than fifty stores, the researchers found similar results to Roullier and Goldstein—transfer climate and a continuous learning culture were directly related to post-training transfer effectiveness by way of demonstrating learned behaviors.

Burke and Baldwin (1999) reported that a supporting (positive) transfer climate is a key variable in training effectiveness. They found immediate workgroup climate to be such a strong indicator of transfer effectiveness that the impact of their core hypotheses related to relapse prevention would have been missed had they not included transfer climate in the study. In fact, Burke and Baldwin call for training researchers to consider the effect of climate in ongoing research, stating, "much of prior training research could be subject to re-interpretation if contextual factors and trainee perceptions had been measured and reported. This does not mean abandoning the core of training research, but it does mean more careful attention to the variables that have been ignored or controlled for" (p. 237). This warning had earlier been sounded by Holton, Bates, Seyler, and Carvalho (1997, p. 97) when they asserted that "without controlling for the influence of the transfer climate, evaluation results are likely to vary considerably and lead to erroneous conclusions about intervention outcomes." These researchers reinforce the need for HRD professionals to reexamine the impact of transfer climate and to make certain that such climatic factors are more strongly represented in research regarding learning transfer.

Principles for Creating Learning Transfer Climates

When creating learning transfer climates, several principles can guide managers' action and keep them focused on real, practical solutions to complex learning transfer barriers:

• *Employees tend to be problem-centered in their outlook.* Employees are pragmatic, desiring learning transfer climates that help them cope with real-life situations or ones that help them achieve tasks or solve problems (Zemke & Zemke, 1995). As a result, employees will transfer learning when it helps them perform tasks or deal with problems they confront.

Employees will embrace learning transfer when it addresses their immediate personal and professional problems (Knowles,

Holton, & Swanson, 1998). Thus, managers should identify the problems that employees are presently facing and together determine the best course of action in resolving them. For example, employees may fail to support learning transfer unless they believe that they are being fairly treated.

- *Personal growth, development, and advancement is a powerful motivational force.* Employees are motivated by a desire to improve their lives or future job prospects (Bradshaw, 1981). Therefore, employees are interested in learning transfer opportunities that benefit them personally and professionally. Since such appeals to self-interest will often work, employees should be questioned about their interests and desires for personal gain.
- *Motivation for learning transfer can be increased.* A majority of employees are very responsive to external motivation such as promotions, advancements, increased compensation, recognition, and other rewards (Flannery, Hofrichter, & Platten, 1996). However, the most influential motivators are intrinsic—those motivational strategies that enable employees to increase their job satisfaction, self-esteem, and quality of life while acting on and demonstrating their values and beliefs (Facteau, Dobbins, Russell, Ladd, & Kudisch, 1995). When establishing appropriate recognition and rewards, managers need to identify those that encourage employees to embrace learning transfer. Further, employees respond favorably to positive reinforcement, embracing honest and constructive feedback designed to improve their skills, abilities, and competencies (Gilley, Boughton, & Maycunich, 1999).

Managers can enhance employees' motivation to transfer learning by helping them understand how a learning opportunity will benefit them. Important questions to consider include

What are the employees' present levels of motivation for transferring learning?

How obvious are the benefits to employees?

What can be done to increase employee motivation?

- *Feedback and recognition should be planned.* Employees should be provided with ample opportunity to receive feedback on their efforts to implement transfer learning to the job (Peterson &

Hicks, 1996). As a result, managers will need to know employees well. In particular, managers and HRD professionals should provide the type and frequency of feedback and recognition most likely to be successful with each employee (Bradshaw, 1981).

• *Employees incorporate and implement learning transfer in different ways.* Thus managers and HRD professionals should identify employees' learning styles, account for differences, and incorporate them into the learning transfer process (James & Galbraith, 1984). Interpersonal and learning style assessment may include surveys, questionnaires, or one-on-one discussions.

• *Learning transfer initiatives should accommodate employees' continued growth and changing values.* Employees' interests and needs change throughout life. Effective learning transfer initiatives adapt to these changes by discovering employees' values and determining what people need and want. This allows managers and HRD professionals to isolate issues associated with those values that will correspond with employees' needs (Bradshaw, 1981).

Learning transfer initiatives should take into account employees' experience, self-esteem, and uniqueness. When facilitating learning transfer, it is therefore important to remember that employees have a great deal of firsthand experience that can positively or negatively influence learning transfer opportunities, as well as strong habits and attitudes that are difficult to alter but possess the ability to impact learning transfer (Knowles et al., 1998; Zemke & Zemke, 1995).

Employees also have very tangible things (reputations, job security, status and influence, relationships) to lose during learning transfer. Thus they demonstrate a considerable amount of pride that should be accounted for accordingly. Each of these factors should be incorporated into the learning transfer process to enhance the likelihood of change. Finally, an employee's personal and professional experiences, relationships, assumptions, beliefs, and values can either accelerate or impede the learning transfer process (Knowles et al., 1998). When past experiences create a negative predisposition to learning transfer, managers and HRD professionals will need to isolate the problem and provide corrective action designed to alter the erroneous assumptions and maximize learning transfer opportunities (Gilley & Maycunich, 2000).

Creating Learning Transfer Climates

To enhance learning transfer, managers and HRD professionals need to create a climate that fosters it. Gilley, Quatro, Hoekstra, Wittle, and Maycunich (2001) contend that by creating such environments they help employees feel good about their contributions, involvement, and accomplishments. When such climates are developed, organizations will be empathetic entities focusing their energies on building relationships and fulfilling the developmental needs of every employee (Morris, 1995). To develop such climates, organizational and environmental strategies, organizational leadership action strategies, and developmental strategies can all prove useful.

Organizational and Environmental Strategies

The organizational and environmental strategies focus on macro issues critical to creating learning transfer climates. This approach also focuses attention on the work climate within organizations. Strategies include creating a developmental culture, developing self-esteeming organizations, overcoming fear in the workplace, and linking compensation and reward programs to employee growth and development.

Creating a Developmental Culture

Most organizations publicly attribute their ultimate success to their employees and claim that employees are their number-one priority. To provide substance to such claims, organizations provide resources needed to enhance employee satisfaction and development. In some situations, such statements are absolutely true. On closer examination, however, organizational reality is considerably different. In many organizations, employees are treated as consumable resources to be used and disposed of as the organization sees fit, like pawns in a great competitive contest among the mighty lords of industry (Gilley & Maycunich, 2000). Because of this approach, many of an organization's best employees leave, seeking opportunities for growth, development, and appreciation in other organizations. To overcome this problem, organizations need to create a developmental culture.

The primary purpose for creating a developmental culture is to provide a work environment that encourages change within an individual. One way to foster this type of environment is by engaging in critical reflective activities (Mezirow, 1997). The outcome of such change is known as *new meaning,* which we define as reconfiguration and understanding of oneself. Morris (1995) contends that such revelations alter individuals to the point that they can never return to their original state. Consequently, individuals desire to change the way they interact on a daily basis.

Another purpose of a developmental culture is to create conditions where *continuous growth and development* is encouraged. Gilley and Maycunich (2000) suggest that continuous growth and development is a process of never-ending expansion, taking into account new and different things, the outcome of which is improved *renewal and performance capacity.* As a result, employees improve their reservoir of performance capabilities, which can be drawn upon when needed. Accordingly, their organizations improve their competitive readiness, avoiding the plateau periods of maturity as well as the slippery slopes of decline.

Too many organizations establish training or career development programs to help employees overcome their weaknesses. They mistakenly believe the prevailing myth that fixing employee weaknesses will improve their performance and enhance the organization's competitive readiness. Strategies such as these actually sabotage efforts to improve employee performance while communicating that something must be wrong with the firm or its employees. Further, fixing employee weaknesses only makes their performance normal or average, not outstanding (Buckingham & Coffman, 1999; Clifton & Nelson, 1992). Excellence is the result of building on employee strengths while managing their weaknesses, not by ignoring their strengths and attempting to eliminate their weaknesses (Gilley & Boughton, 1996).

Another myth involves managers' and employees' belief that anything is possible regardless of its difficulty or the obstacles that prevent effective performance. In reality, certain things just aren't feasible no matter how much effort is expended. Oversimplifications such as "if at first you don't succeed, try, try again," "practice makes perfect," or "if I can do it you can do it" overshadow potentially complex organizational issues—frustrating or demotivating those attempting to master an unattainable goal. This belief erroneously assumes that all people are the same, possessing identical talents, abilities, and competencies. As we all know, individuals have a finite and eclectic set of strengths, weaknesses, skills, knowledge, and competencies—they're not clones (Gilley & Boughton, 1996).

In summary, creating a developmental culture requires organizations to foster an environment where employee growth and development is paramount. It also encourages organizations to create conditions where employees are encouraged, rewarded, and appreciated for their individual growth and development. Furthermore, developmental cultures need leaders who prescribe to a philosophy that demonstrates their appreciation for and value of employee contributions—one that reveals a lifelong commitment to employees and a dedication to their well-being.

Developmental Culture at Mercer Human Resource Consulting

Mercer Human Resource Consulting (formerly William M. Mercer, Inc.) is the world's largest compensation, benefits, and human resource consulting firm; it employs more than 9,000 people in 120 offices worldwide. The firm's revenues exceed $1.2 billion annually. As with all professional service firms, Mercer's primary competitive advantage is its people. These include managing consultants (senior consultants), practice consultants specializing in communications, pensions, health care, compensation, defined contribution, and human resources, technical professionals (technical analysts), and administrative professionals that provide direct or indirect consulting services. To maintain its market advantage, Mercer's senior management team has implemented programs that encourage the continuous development of its employees. One such program focuses on mentoring and professional development where practice consultants and technical professionals are assigned a senior practice consultant or managing consultant as a mentor to look after their long-term professional development activities. This mentoring program, in turn, helps create an organizational culture supportive of development. We'll return to Mercer in subsequent sections to describe how it applies the other concepts developed in this chapter.

Recommendations for creating a developmental culture: Morris (1995) and Simonsen (1997) both contend that creating a developmental culture within an organization is essential to fostering positive learning transfer climates. In addition, they contend that trust is the essential ingredient required in the creation of such cultures. Simonsen points out that the building blocks of trust within organizations include straight talk, listening for understanding, making commitments, reliability, respect, and honesty. These are absolutes in creating a developmental culture where managers and employees work side by side to improve employees' competencies and career potential, and ultimately improve their effectiveness through learning transfer activities. Although they are difficult to change, organizational cultures can be made more performance enhancing, providing managers and HRD professionals the opportunity to create climates conducive to learning transfer.

As Gilley et al. contend, a developmental culture allows an organization to focus all of its energy and resources on enhancing the collective talents of its employees for the purpose of better serving customers in an efficient, effective manner. They add, "Such a culture is a strongly focused philosophical shift that must be made if organizations plan to continue the long, challenging journey toward organizational success. Within a developmental culture, leaders philosophically recognize that members of the entire organization must be involved in the realization of its mission, vision, and goals for all to enjoy prosperity" (1999, pp. 190–191).

Pragmatically, developmental cultures will not be successful unless leaders, managers, supervisors, and employees collectively blend their talents toward achieving an organization's strategic business goals and objectives. Improper treatment and utilization of human resources inhibits performance outputs. Organizational efficiency and effectiveness cannot be achieved without enhancing the skills, expertise, talents, and intellectual capital of all organizational members, which can only be accomplished if the proper learning transfer climate is established.

Creating Self-Esteeming Organizations

Another way of building a positive learning transfer climate is to enhance working relationships with employees—sometimes referred to as self-esteeming. *Self-esteeming* can be defined as mutual and reciprocal respect and confidence when two parties work collaboratively to achieve desired results (Gilley & Boughton, 1996). Because self-esteeming is based on collegial partnerships between managers and their employees, it relies on two-way communication, trust, honesty, and interaction, and should be nonjudgmental and free of fear, both personal and professional (Bolton, 1986).

Bradshaw (1981) believes that the self-esteem process is reciprocal. As such, both managers and their employees benefit by working and interacting together. How can both individuals increase their self-esteem at the same time? It's easy. As a result of developing an understanding of employees, accepting them as unique individuals, and becoming personally involved with them as professionals, a manager develops a higher level of trust and honesty, which in turn increases employee confidence. As their confidence increases, employees are more willing to attempt transfer of learning activities. Thus employees are able to demonstrate success on the job as well as learn new and exciting ways of performing their jobs. Such success, if positively reinforced, will in turn increase their own self-esteem. Further, Bradshaw notes, improving employees' self-esteem encourages them to take on increasingly difficult assignments that initiate learning transfer within an organization. On the other hand, managers have the opportunity to develop an understanding of their employees on a personal level. Thus they are able to identify what is important to them and can select motivational strategies that challenge and stimulate them. This helps improve managers' performance coaching and change management skills, thus increasing their confidence and self-esteem. Moreover, managers and HRD professionals benefit by increasing their professional involvement with their employees. This can energize them, motivating and challenging them to become the best managers possible, which enhances their self-esteem.

Mercer Human Resource Consulting: An Example of a Self-Esteeming Organization

Let us illustrate how self-esteeming works on a practical level. A managing consultant at Mercer Human Resource Consulting assigns one of her employees a project to create a consulting strategy designed to compete in the international marketplace. The managing consultant and employee have a strong, trusting, honest relationship, and have worked together for five years. The managing consultant clearly explains the parameters of the project, its outcomes, time line, quality specifications, and the employee's level of decision-making authority. The employee is now free to assemble a project team to work with and begin the task of designing and developing a new consulting strategy. As the employee begins to work on the project several roadblocks emerge, and the employee asks the managing consultant for her assistance in removing them. The managing consultant makes some suggestions for dealing with each of the barriers and reaffirms her confidence in the employee's abilities and skills. Several weeks into the project the managing consultant asks for an update and provides positive feedback regarding the completion of important tasks. In addition, the managing consultant and employee discuss other upcoming challenges that will affect the project's completion. This activity is repeated several times during the life of the project. At the completion of the project, the managing consultant rewards and recognizes the employee and her team for a job well done. The employees feel great and are appreciative of the assistance, feedback, and recognition received. In return, the employee shares with the managing consultant her appreciation for being allowed to lead such a challenging project and for the support and guidance received. As a result, the working relationship between the managing consultant and employee is dramatically improved. Thus self-esteeming has been successfully achieved.

Recommendations for creating self-esteeming organizations: As managers interact with employees every day, both sides have opportunities to enhance or diminish their self-esteem. To increase employees' self-concepts, managers can use one of four sources of growth and development:

- Achievement, accomplishment, and mastery
- Power, control, and influence
- Being cared about and valued
- Acting on values and beliefs (Bradshaw, 1981, p. 23)

Each of these sources provides an opportunity for employees to enhance their self-esteem. The more positive these experiences are, the higher self-esteem will rise. Self-esteeming is a process that organizations must strive for and build upon. It is one of the basic tenets of organizational effectiveness, and must be encouraged, embraced, and achieved to successfully meet business results.

Self-esteeming organizations can also be created by allowing employees to view each other as learning resources and as instruments of encouragement and reinforcement (Holton et al., 1997). This requires an environment where managers become involved with their employees. Unfortunately, it is one of the most difficult things for managers to master because it requires them to have the courage to relinquish control and dominance over their employees. A participatory approach requires a gentle shift away from authoritarian control and toward allowing employees to participate in the implementation of learning (Gilley, 2001). It also allows employees to become involved, which helps them support their own decisions, eliminate isolationism, enhance dialogue and group decision making, improve collaboration and teamwork, and establish high expectations for learning transfer (Ash & Persall, 2000). In this way learning transfer becomes less threatening to employees.

Overcoming Fear in the Workplace

Work environments that are full of fear are very unpleasant, full of tension and anxiety (Ryan & Oestreith, 1998). Under such conditions, it is difficult for employees to implement learning on the job. Nonetheless, some managers do not think they have done a good job unless all their employees fear them, which is simply wrong—a classic example of managerial malpractice (Gilley & Boughton, 1996).

Fear is one of the primary reasons that employees do not successfully implement learning on the job (Jensen, 1998). Moreover, fear destroys employee morale and confidence, damages lives, destroys relationships, stifles growth, and limits entrepreneurial spirit. To eliminate fear, managers need to stop treating employees with a lack of respect and with a cavalier, dismissive attitude (Ryan & Oestreith, 1998).

Creating Fear-Free Environments
Mercer Human Resource Consulting

Within the competitive world of consulting, it is common for consultants and technical analysts to be working on several important projects simultaneously. Such competing activities increase workplace stress and tension. As a way of addressing this issue, Mercer's senior management team implemented an organization-wide team-building initiative. The program's principal objective was to create self-directed work teams responsible for delivering quality results in a timely manner while maintaining a sense of belonging and commitment for each project team member. Additionally, every project was evaluated to determine the degree to which it met this objective, and managing consultants and project team leaders were held accountable for achieving this objective.

The team-building initiative was founded on two fundamental beliefs:

- Employees possess a greater knowledge of job-related problems than their leaders do, because they perform job tasks on a regular basis and thus are familiar with the components of each job.
- Leaders have the authority to solve job-related problems and are in a position to exercise control and influence related to each job.

As a result, Mercer's goal was to make certain that leaders' knowledge of job-related problems increased while employees' authority to solve job-related problems advanced. In this way, team leaders and employees worked together to increase a team's autonomy and freedom to decide which problems to address, encourage collaborative problem solving, increase trust among all team members, and encourage the identification of solutions that employees would support.

Recommendations for creating fear-free environments: To create work environments free of fear, organizations need to encourage managers to champion employee performance growth and development. Over time, organizations will benefit by unleashing the collective minds of their employees. Quite simply, encouraging learning acquisition and transfer allows employees the opportunities to grow and develop, which could result in a windfall of productivity, profitability, and revenue enhancement. Organizations may also be surprised at the effects such encouragement will have on employee morale, attitudes, and commitment.

Of course, fear can be healthy. Healthy fear is the type that stimulates employee development. It drives and challenges employees to take responsibility for what they do. For example, sales staff may have a fear of making cold calls on potential clients while realizing that success is impossible without making such calls. This realization helps salespeople overcome their fear of meeting with clients. The critical difference with this type of fear is that employees do not feel that they are going to be belittled, embarrassed, or humiliated when they attempt to use new skills and knowledge for the first time. Instead, they feel a sense of accomplishment, hope, and positive reinforcement for a job well done.

Further, managers need to take time to create environments that are devoid of retribution. Such environments can be developed if managers support their employees' learning transfer efforts and allow them to take risks without fear of reprisal. Unfortunately, too many managers punish employees for "thinking outside the box" or for behaving differently from the norm. In fact, organizations with homogeneous populations that operate like robots are less effective in addressing performance problems than are ones whose employees are encouraged to foster and demonstrate creativity, independence, and diversity (Gilley & Maycunich, 1998).

Adopting Reward Systems That Reinforce Learning Transfer

The purpose of any organization is to secure results: increase market share, improve profitability, boost quality. Therefore, managers' sole challenge is to "get results through people" (LeBoeuf, 1985, p. 63). We believe that it makes tremendous sense to reward people for their growth, development, and commitment, which is a philosophy that works wonders in improving employee performance and achieving the results needed by the organization.

Typically, compensation and reward programs are linked to performance. However, employee performance increases dramatically when organizations link their compensation and reward programs to employee performance growth and development activities (Williams & Sunderland, 1998). As a result, compensation and rewards become a vehicle for ever-increasing employee development, which is long-term focused as opposed to the short-term focus of performance-based programs. The intent is not to reduce the importance of performance, but to clarify that performance without growth and development will stagnate or even decline (Gilley & Maycunich, 2000). Moreover, shifting compensation and reward programs to encourage employee growth and development guarantees that employees' skills and competencies continue to evolve.

The way people are rewarded says volumes about an organization, its culture, and its expectations of itself and employees. Compensation and rewards remain among the most effective tools available for motivating people to transfer learning (Flannery et al., 1996). Therefore, an innovative compensation and reward strategy is crucial to creating positive learning transfer climates.

Jensen (1998) contends that short-term, immediate rewards are not an effective strategy for creating a climate for learning transfer. By contrast, he believes, eliminating threats in the workplace, setting performance goals, providing positive reinforcement and continuous feedback, and celebrating learning successes are excellent techniques for enhancing learning transfer over a period of time.

Rewarding Growth and Development at Mercer Human Resource Consulting

One longstanding policy at Mercer Human Resource Consulting is its financial support for employee growth and development. For example, pension and defined contribution consultants are encouraged to participate in a certification program offered by the Society of Actuaries. Consultants are reimbursed for successfully completed classes. The certification program consists of ten courses that address every aspect of pension and retirement consulting including fiduciary accountability and federal laws governing retirement planning. The program has two separate designations: associate and fellow. The associate designation is awarded after a participant successfully completes five courses; the fellow designation is awarded for the successful completion of ten courses and an examination. Mercer consultants receive a minor salary increase for achieving the associate level and a significant salary increase for achieving the fellow designation. Once consultants receive the fellow designation, they are eligible to be promoted to either associate or principal partner status, which qualifies them to participate in the organization's annual bonus program. Such an opportunity can increase a consultant's annual income by several thousand dollars. The organization benefits by having consultants that have achieved the industry's highest professional status, which enables them to vouch for the accuracy of pension programs at organizations where Mercer has a fiduciary responsibility. In summary, this is an excellent example of linking compensation and rewards to learning transfer for the betterment of employees and the organization.

Strategies for linking learning transfer to compensation and reward programs: One of the best ways of improving organizational performance capacity is by linking compensation and rewards to the growth and development of employees (Gilley & Maycunich, 2000). When growth and development is rewarded and reinforced, it will be repeated. In this way, organizations encourage employees to develop their performance competencies such that they will be better able to produce desired organizational results. Another benefit is that it enhances employees' commitment and loyalty. This straightforward, commonsense approach enhances employee performance, involvement, and development. By becoming developmentally oriented, organizations adopt an approach that will help them systematically respond to the challenges facing them.

Williams and Sunderland (1998) believe that in order for growth and development to be linked to compensation and reward programs, they must be tied to business strategy. Accordingly, the program's objectives must be clearly articulated so that employees know how growth and development is being rewarded and why. Such programs must support the organization's culture and be linked to actual business performance. As with all compensation and reward programs, the design must be adaptable to changing business conditions. Additionally, employees' participation in program design would be advantageous, as they must perceive that the program has value. Finally, all elements of the program should be regularly reviewed to determine how effective the program is in meeting its overall objectives. Each of these attributes is critical in linking rewards to learning transfer. When implemented, these attributes help create a positive learning climate within an organization.

Organizational Leadership Strategies

Organizational leadership strategies include those things that leaders can do to help foster a learning transfer climate. These include adopting a developmental philosophy, adopting the characteristics and actions of the learning organization and the principles and practices of servant leadership, and developing communication and feedback skills to establish rapport with employees.

Adopting a Developmental Philosophy

A developmental philosophy recognizes that members of the entire organization must be involved in the realization of its mission, vision, and goals for all to enjoy prosperity. Pragmatically, such a philosophy will not be successful unless leaders, managers, supervisors, and employees collectively blend their talents toward achievement of strategic business goals and objectives. Quite simply, organizational efficiency and effectiveness cannot be achieved without enhancing the skills, expertise, talents, and intellectual capital of all organizational members.

All too often, organizations believe that employees are easily replaced. Consequently, they adopt a human resource philosophy that reinforces the belief that an abundant supply of qualified replacements exists in the marketplace. Gilley et al. (1999, p. 1) refer to this approach as a "revolving door philosophy" toward human resources. When this philosophy is executed, employees are often treated with a lack of dignity and respect due to management's belief that people are disposable. Moreover, this philosophy produces an attitude of corporate indifference, where organizational leaders and managers refuse to mentor and develop their employees, tending to wash their hands of any responsibility for their employees' performance. Further, employees are quickly dismissed when they fail to meet performance expectations. These actions degrade employee morale and productivity, severely limiting loyalty and commitment.

Recommendations for adopting a developmental philosophy: Gilley (2000) believes that at the center of this controversy is the overriding need of organizations to maintain an optimal number of qualified, talented employees to produce the products and services demanded by clients. He suggests that this need can be fulfilled in two ways. First, organizations can acquire needed resources from the open market, given an adequate supply of talented individuals. Second, they can grow and develop employees within the organization. When organizations choose the latter approach, they understand that the specialized knowledge, skills, and competencies they need to remain competitive are not easily found on the open market and can deteriorate quickly. They also understand that employee morale can be affected by a lack of opportunity or challenges available within the organization, and that new employees may need additional development to maximize their performance and productivity. Either strategy requires organizations to adopt a developmental philosophy to achieve competitiveness, productivity, and profitability requirements. Regardless of which approach is used, organizations more easily retain talented employees when they provide career development opportunities (Buckingham & Coffman, 1999).

Adopting the Characteristics and Actions of a Learning Organization

Marquardt (1996) suggests that the learning organization is an institution that learns powerfully and collectively, continually transforming itself to better manage and use knowledge for corporate success, empowering people within and outside the organization to learn as they work and to employ technology to maximize learning and production. He also contends that a number of important characteristics of the learning organization are critical in creating a climate for learning transfer. First, learning organizations require a work climate that encourages, rewards, and accelerates individual and group learning. Such a climate focuses on creativity and generative learning and encourages change. It is a climate where surprises and even failure are viewed as opportunities to learn. The climate encourages agility and flexibility, and all employees are driven by a desire for quality and continuous improvement. Such a climate promotes the adoption of learning activities that are characterized by aspirations, reflections, and conceptualization, and it continuously adapts, renews, and revitalizes itself in response to the changing environment. Finally, learning organizations maintain a climate where learning is continuous.

Furthermore, as Senge (1990) points out, "Learning has very little to do with taking in information. Learning, instead, is a process that is about enhancing capacity. Learning is about building the capabilities to create that which you previously could not create" (p. 191). Quite simply, learning ultimately relates to action; information does not. The principal assumption of learning organizations, therefore, is this: If the learning reservoir of individuals is improved, organizational performance capacity will also improve.

Recommendations for adopting the characteristics and actions of a learning organization: To make the transition from the traditional to the learning organization, organizational leaders must take the following steps (Marquardt, 1996, pp. 180–191):

1. Alter the environment to support and encourage learning.
2. Link learning to business operations.
3. Communicate the importance of the learning organization.
4. Demonstrate their commitment to learning.
5. Transform the organizational culture to one of continuous learning and improvement, establish organization-wide strategies for learning, and eliminate organizational bureaucracy.

6. Encourage employee involvement.
7. Embrace continuous, adaptive, improvement-oriented learning approaches throughout the organization.

When these steps have been accomplished, organizational leaders will have demonstrated the importance of improving learning capacity as well as encouraging self-directed learning behavior on the part of all employees. Learning organizations are as concerned about market share, productivity, and profitability as traditional organizations are, but they understand that learning is the key to acquiring greater business results. Nevertheless, the orientation of the learning organization is simply *learning,* which requires a climate for learning transfer (Morris, 1995).

Establishing Rapport with Employees

One of the best ways of creating positive learning transfer climates is for leaders to develop unconditional positive regard for their employees. This is sometimes described as *rapport.* It is not simply a superficial relationship but a deep concern for the well-being of employees. It is demonstrated when leaders are as interested in their employees as they are in the results they produce. In short, rapport is established through the sincere interest in, and acceptance of, employees.

When rapport has been established, employees feel free to express their opinions, ideas, beliefs, and attitudes. At that point, employees are encouraged to engage in learning transfer activities, without which many employees may never attempt to apply new knowledge or skills on the job.

Establishing Rapport with Employees at Mercer Human Resource Consulting

Most professional service firms—including Mercer Human Resource Consulting—generate business results through formal client projects. Such projects require the cooperation and contribution of many team members from varying practice areas. Mercer's senior management team strongly believes that project success begins with a well-defined and clearly articulated set of goals and objectives. Further, they believe that all project team members should be informed of the project's deliverables and their individual responsibilities in achieving them. They also believe that every project team member affects the overall outcome of a project and that its deliverables will be weakened if its weakest team member isn't up to the job. Additionally, Mercer's senior management team believes that every project team leader is responsible for creating a work climate free of fear and based on honesty, respect, encouragement, and support. Consequently, it is extremely important for project leaders (managing consultants) and project team members to develop positive working relationships (rapport). When developed, rapport helps improve communications and decision making and encourages seamless interaction among team members.

At the conclusion of a project, project leaders are responsible for determining the outcomes of the project, examining its strengths and weaknesses, identifying each member's contribution, examining the quality of the working climate, and identifying strategies for improvement. Additionally, leaders need to celebrate the success of the project with team members. The aggregate outcome of this type of evaluation is to improve the quality of future projects in terms of their deliverables as well as the working environment (rapport) produced during project execution.

Recommendations for establishing rapport with employees:

- *Increase interaction with employees.* To successfully create a learning transfer climate, organizational leaders and employees need to interact on a regular basis. Interaction is more than communication because it implies a personal engagement with employees. Accordingly, leaders should take the time to discuss growth and development issues and learning transfer problems with employees. They must also take time to get to know their employees on a personal level, which requires face-to-face interaction. Unfortunately, many leaders spend very little time interacting with employees, even though research has clearly demonstrated that employee satisfaction can be greatly enhanced through collaborative interaction with their leaders (Bolton & Grover Bolton, 1996).

- *Adopt an acceptance attitude.* Acceptance requires respect for employees as persons of worth. As organizational leaders begin interacting more and more with their employees, they discover the differing characteristics of each employee. They realize that each is an individual with a unique personality, life experience, and professional path. Leaders need to understand that strength lies in these individual differences, and that it is their responsibility to challenge employees to capitalize on their unique gifts. Once this attitude is clearly evidenced, employees' self-esteem will be enhanced, which will improve their willingness to apply new knowledge and skills on the job.

• *Increase personal involvement.* Acceptance is a prerequisite to personal involvement, which requires organizational leaders to spend significant time with each of their employees. Without this involvement, leaders will never be able to develop the type of transfer climate required to improve organizational performance and quality. Personal involvement requires leaders to engage in conversations that help create a personal bond with employees. One useful technique for improving personal involvement is known as self-disclosure. Self-disclosure requires leaders to open up, sharing information both personal and professional and revealing to employees that they are real human beings with feelings and emotions—in short, demonstrating that they are real people.

• *Demonstrate respect.* All employees, whether inside an organization or in their personal lives, must be *respected as persons of worth* (Goleman, 1998; Rogers, 1961). Quite simply, creating a climate for learning transfer begins with treating employees with dignity and respect so that they reciprocate in kind. In the workplace, this need is met through positive interactions with coworkers and leaders (Bradshaw, 1981). Unfortunately, this basic need is rarely met because many leaders treat employees with little respect while demanding that they perform at high levels (Jensen, 1998).

• *Encourage trust and honesty.* One reason learning fails to be transferred to the job is the lack of trust between organizational leaders and their employees (Peterson & Hicks, 1996). Therefore, leaders should spend a great deal of time cultivating trust with their employees. When trust is established, employees will feel comfortable applying new learning to the job. The cycle of mistrust begins with negative assumptions that produce self-protective behaviors in a self-reinforcing pattern that repeatedly traps both leaders and their employees (Ryan & Oestreith, 1998, p. 20). As a consequence, leaders and employees adopt negative beliefs about each other's intentions, style, or behavior. When creating a climate for learning transfer, Peterson and Hicks discovered, trust leads to honesty. Consequently, employees begin sharing more and more information with their leaders as the level of professional intimacy increases.

- *Demonstrate empathy.* When organizational leaders demonstrate the ability to understand their employees' vantage points, they are practicing empathy. Empathic leaders understand and appreciate other people's worldviews. Becoming empathic is key to overcoming personal criticism of employees. Empathetic understanding is the ability to recognize, sense, and understand the feelings that people communicate through their behavioral and verbal expressions, and to accurately communicate this understanding to them (Gilley, 2000).

- *Demonstrate understanding.* Understanding can take two forms—external and internal. External understanding is organizational leaders' awareness of their employees' actions and behaviors. Internal understanding is the ability of leaders to step into the perceptual world of their employees, including their fears, successes, and failures. Both types of understanding help create positive learning transfer climates.

- *Demonstrate genuineness.* Genuineness is the ability to recognize one's own feelings, accept them, live them, and express them (Quatro, Hoekstra, & Gilley, 2002). This enables organizational leaders to be who they are, not what people want them to be. In other words, genuineness requires authenticity and transparency. Genuineness also refers to leaders' ability to be themselves in all work situations rather than playing a part or role. Furthermore, genuineness implies being honest and candid with employees during learning transfer initiatives.

Developmental Strategies

To create positive learning transfer climates, organizations can employ several developmental strategies. When they do so, they establish unique and creative ways of improving performance capacity and capability. These strategies include transforming performance appraisals into developmental evaluations, instituting employee growth and development plans, and identifying employee strengths and identifying and managing employee weaknesses.

Transforming Performance Appraisals into Developmental Evaluations
The oldest technique used to improve individual production and performance is the performance appraisal. The principal purpose

of a performance appraisal is to assess past performance, which serves as a foundation for future decisions. The focus of a performance appraisal is on the review of the past, using judging methods, ratings, and descriptions established by the organization. Organizational leaders are the primary evaluators, and past accomplishments are viewed as the basis of the review, which is known as the *evaluation approach.*

Unfortunately, the term *performance appraisal* restricts one's ability to work collaboratively with employees in their development. To overcome this problem, Gilley et al. (1999) suggest referring to performance appraisals as *developmental evaluations.* This approach motivates and directs individual performance and career development efforts. The focus is on future planning; counseling and interaction between the leader and the employee is the primary methodology. Emphasis is placed on goal setting as well as review. Leaders and employees share equal responsibility in this type of appraisal process. The basis of the review is future goals and plans for future development.

Recommendations for creating developmental evaluations: Organizational leaders should use development evaluations to ascertain satisfaction of internal and external stakeholders with performance outputs produced by employees. Moreover, at the heart of every developmental evaluation lies the concept of feedback. In this way, developmental evaluations and coaching are very similar activities. The fundamental difference between the two is that coaching is an ongoing minute-by-minute, day-by-day feedback opportunity, while developmental evaluations are designed to be formal, summative evaluations. In some respects, both coaching and developmental evaluations are designed to achieve the same end—to provide feedback so that employees can continue to grow and develop. Accordingly, coaching and developmental evaluations must be specific and timely if employees are to make the types of corrections and improvements required to bring about desired business results.

Another activity of a developmental evaluation is to assess employee strengths and weaknesses. In this way, developmental evaluations provide organizational leaders with opportunities to analyze employees' knowledge, skills, and attitudes, and determine those areas of excellence or needing improvement. Such evaluations also present opportunities for leaders and employees to discuss current and future developmental goals and objectives, and how employees plan to achieve them. Most critically, developmental evaluations are a vehicle for discussion of future growth and development activities that will enhance employees' abilities and competencies as well as advance their careers.

As a result, developmental evaluations are an excellent tool for analyzing employee performance and making recommendations for improvement. Since many employees fail to perform adequately because of barriers that prevent exemplary performance, the developmental evaluation approach can help isolate these obstacles and formulate strategies for overcoming them. As a result of these discussions, employees participate in interactions that improve the work environment and general conditions under which they are asked to perform. Moreover, employees can participate in analysis of job design and assist in identification of improvements and efficiencies in the execution of job tasks.

As discussed, developmental evaluations provide employees with feedback on their performance, help recognize their strengths and achievements over a specific period of time, identify areas where they can continue to grow and develop, define performance goals for the next six months to a year, and review the fit between the organization's expectations and their own. Developmental evaluations help organizations make decisions regarding employee performance and aid in construction of developmental and career planning activities that enhance their work.

Instituting Employee Growth and Development Plans

The primary purpose of developmental evaluations is for organizational leaders and employees to discuss ways of enhancing performance results and future career development opportunities. These conversations include an examination of employees' strengths, weaknesses, and areas for improvement. Additionally, they become the focus of employee growth and development plans and should be perceived as a long-term learning transfer strategy instead of a quick fix.

Instituting Growth and Development Plans at Mercer Human Resource Consulting

At the beginning of every fiscal year, all Mercer employees are responsible for identifying their professional growth and development needs and constructing a plan for addressing them. This plan consists of the following components:

- Job responsibility
- Knowledge or skills to be developed
- Performance objectives
- Learning and resource strategies
- Target date for completion of the development plan
- Learning transfer strategy
- Indicators of accomplishment
- Criteria and means of validating indicators
- Ways of reporting results
- Possible rewards and recognition for accomplishment

At the conclusion of the year, the employees each meet with their immediate supervisor to review and discuss the results of their development engagement. These conversations are documented and become a part of the employee's permanent record. Growth and development plans can help determine future work assignments, promotion opportunities, and additional responsibilities within the organization.

Recommendations for developing growth and development plans: Organizational leaders and employees must mutually design growth and development plans. These plans should be realistic, specific, attainable, and tied to a timetable. Additionally, they should be initiated as a result of a developmental evaluation and implemented immediately—delaying the applications of a growth and development plan may diminish its effectiveness, importance, and value. Delays also give leaders who are not truly interested in their employees' growth and development the opportunity to procrastinate.

Employees engage in the design and construction of performance growth and development plans by

- Identifying developmental and performance objectives
- Specifying learning sources and strategies they will use to acquire new skills and knowledge

- Identifying transfer of learning strategies that promote application of new learning to the job
- Identifying project completion target dates
- Assisting in the measurement of learning acquisition and transfer on the job

Organizational leader participation includes providing employees with performance feedback and reinforcement, conducting performance measurement activities, and examining learning acquisition during future developmental evaluation reviews.

Identifying Employee Strengths

Clifton and Nelson (1992) introduced one of the most important strategies for creating climates that encourage learning transfer: build strength, manage weakness. This concept was further popularized by Buckingham and Coffman (1999) and refined by Buckingham and Clifton (2001). It is based on the notion that employees' performance improves dramatically when they are allowed to build on their strengths rather than being required to conform to all aspects of an inherited job design. The latter requires employees to do things that they cannot do well, do not enjoy doing, or simply cannot perform adequately, all of which are sometimes referred to as *weaknesses* (Clifton & Nelson, 1992).

In certain professions, individual expertise is easily demonstrated, measurable, or noticeable by others—athletes, musicians, surgeons, and the like come to mind. These individuals have certain strengths upon which they capitalize, and are usually strategically placed to take advantage of these skills to the fullest. Capitalizing on strengths makes sense; asking employees to perform outside their arenas of expertise wastes valuable talent. Why, then, do organizations spend millions of dollars every year on developmental fix-it strategies unrelated to employee strengths? Often, the answer lies in organizational ignorance of the value of focusing on strengths, inability to identify strengths in employees, or a combination of both.

Recommendations for identifying employee strengths: Identifying strengths challenges organizational leaders and employees to analyze their behaviors and successes. Clifton and Nelson (1992) identified four characteristics indicative of individual strengths:

- *Internal burning* refers to an individual's internal self-talk that fuels the initiative to try new things, creating an attraction to or curiosity about a subject or activity. Curiosity leads to heightened interest, which, if allowed to flourish over time, forms genuine expertise. People who participate sufficiently and possess basic, innate abilities often build proficiencies that eventually become strengths.
- *High satisfaction level* refers to completing tasks or activities that bring about enjoyment and pleasure each time an employee performs them.
- *Rapid learning* refers to an employee's ability to grasp and perform new tasks and activities quickly.
- *Performance in the zone* involves executing a task or series of tasks without any conscious awareness of the steps involved. When this occurs, employees feel invincible and powerful, wanting to repeat the performance over and over again.

Each of these provides evidence of employee strength. When employees are allowed to engage in such activities their self-esteem and job satisfaction increase dramatically (Buckingham & Coffman, 1999). Moreover, repetition brings improvement, which leads to expertise and mastery—a cycle organizations should employ to enhance learning transfer.

Building on Strengths at Mercer Human Resource Consulting

In 1994, Mercer's senior management team realized it had a problem. The organization had a long-standing policy that every managing consultant was responsible for business development as a part of the job. In other words, every managing consultant was responsible for generating new or renewable revenue with existing or new clients. Some managing consultants excelled in this area of responsibility but others did not. Although this requirement appeared to be reasonable, Mercer's senior management team realized that not every managing consultant had the ability to generate new business. Quite simply, some managing consultants did not possess business development skills as a fundamental strength, even though they performed other duties, such as project management, at very high levels. Instead of requiring those that did not have the ability to generate new business to participate in additional training or punish them in some other fashion, Mercer elected to employ a *building on strengths* strategy. The firm went through an exhaustive analysis of all managing consultants and separated them into two categories: client relationship consultants and project management consultants. Those selected to be client relationship consultants were assigned business development activities as their primary responsibility while project management consultants were given the responsibility of managing complex and technical projects. Both of these responsibilities were viewed by Mercer's senior management team to be equal in importance and the new assignments were recognized as equivalent career paths. Over time, this strategy has paid dividends for Mercer because revenue growth has grown to over 1.2 billion.

Recommendations for building on strengths: As a way of maximizing strengths, Clifton and Nelson (1992) suggested that employees develop personal master lists of strengths. They believe that the four characteristics previously discussed can be used as a guide. After employees compile the personal master list, organizational leaders should ask them to isolate a single strength to be developed for a month. Employees should

1. Select a strength they will have an opportunity to employ on a regular basis.
2. Use this strength as often as possible during the month.
3. Record *how* it is used and the *outcomes* that result.

Simultaneously, organizational leaders should

1. Informally discuss the employee's efforts throughout the month, providing encouragement and praise when appropriate.
2. Discuss how many times the strength was used and its results at month's end.
3. Ask employees how they felt about using the strengths and whether performance improved.

This activity creates conditions that encourage learning transfer and development. As a result, it helps improves performance, job satisfaction, work relationships, and employee confidence. Further, this experience emphasizes employees' special skills and abilities, providing a foundation they can build on in the future. Finally, organizational leaders should realize that employees enjoy improving their performance when allowed to build on strengths rather than fix weaknesses. This process should be repeated until all strengths have been fully developed.

Conclusion

While acknowledging the fact that the amount of training transferred to the workplace has been disappointingly low, leaders should take heart and pay specific attention to workplace climate issues that may increase the transfer challenge. Recent research and practice cited here should provide the impetus to move the field of training to increased attention to the issue of workplace climate and building positive relationships with employees to enhance training and organizational effectiveness. The benefits of positive workplace climate are many—greater trust, honesty, commitment, and productivity, which ultimately will yield emotional and financial rewards for training participants and the organization at large.

References

Ash, R., & Persall, J. (2000). The principal as chief learning officer: Developing teacher leaders. *NASSP Bulletin 84,* 5, 15–22.

Baldwin, T. T., & Ford, J. K. (1988). Transfer of training: A review and directions for future research. *Personnel Psychology, 41,* 63–105.

Baumgartel, H., Reynolds, M., & Pathan, R. (1984). How personality and organizational climate variables moderate the effectiveness of management development programmes: A review and some recent research findings. *Management and Labor Studies, 9,* 1–16.

Bolton, R. (1986). *People skills: How to assert yourself, listen to others, and resolve conflicts.* New York: Simon & Schuster.

Bolton, R., & Grover Bolton, D. (1996). *People styles at work: Making bad relationships good and good relationships better.* New York: AMACOM.

Boyett, J. H., & Boyett, J. T. (1995). *Beyond workforce 2000: Essential strategies for the new American corporation.* New York: Dutton.

Bradshaw, P. (1981). *The management of self-esteem: How people can feel good about themselves and their organizations.* Upper Saddle River, NJ: Prentice Hall.

Broad, M. L., & Newstrom, J. W. (1992). *Transfer of training: Action-packed strategies to ensure high payoff from training investments.* Cambridge, MA: Perseus.

Buckingham, M., & Clifton, D. O. (2001). *Now, discover your strengths.* New York: Free Press.

Buckingham, M., & Coffman, C. (1999). *First, break all the rules: What the world's greatest managers do differently.* New York: Simon & Schuster.

Burke, L., & Baldwin, T. T. (1999). Effects of relapse prevention training and transfer climate on the use of trained skills. *Human Resource Management, 38,* 227–242.

Carnevale, A. P., & Gainer, L. J. (1989). *The learning enterprise.* Alexandria, VA: American Society for Training and Development and the Employment and Training Administration, U.S. Department of Labor.

Clifton, D. O., & Nelson, P. (1992). *Soar with your strengths.* New York: Delacorte.

Collins, J. (2001). *Good to great: Why some companies make the leap and others don't.* New York: HarperCollins.

Facteau, J. D., Dobbins, G. H., Russell, J.E.A., Ladd, R. T., & Kudisch, J. D. (1995). The influence of general perceptions of the training environment on pretraining motivation and perceived training transfer. *Journal of Management, 21,* 1–15.

Flannery, T. P., Hofrichter, D. A., & Platten, P. E. (1996). *People, performance and pay: Dynamic compensation for changing organizations.* New York: Free Press.

Ford, J. K., Quinones, M. A., Sego, D. J., & Sorra, J. (1992). Factors affecting the opportunity to perform trained tasks on the job. *Personnel Psychology, 45,* 511–527.

Georgenson, D. L. (1982). The problem of transfer calls for partnership. *Training and Development Journal, 36*(10), 75–78.

Gilley, J. W. (2000). Understanding and building capacity for change: A key to school transformation. *International Journal of Educational Reform, 9*(2), 109–119.

Gilley, J. W. (2001). Taming the organization. *Human Resource Development International, 4*(2), 217–233.

Gilley, J. W., & Boughton, N. W. (1996). *Stop managing, start coaching.* New York: McGraw-Hill.

Gilley, J. W., Boughton, N. W., & Maycunich, A. (1999). *The performance challenge: Developing management systems to make employees your greatest asset.* Cambridge, MA: Perseus.

Gilley, J. W., & Maycunich, A. (1998). *Strategically integrated HRD: Partnering to maximize organizational performance.* Cambridge, MA: Perseus.

Gilley, J. W., & Maycunich, A. (2000). *Beyond the learning organization: Creating a culture of continuous growth and development through state-of-the-art human resource practices.* Cambridge, MA: Perseus.

Gilley, J. W., Quatro, S., Hoekstra, E., Wittle, D. D., & Maycunich, A. (2001). *The manager as change agent: A practical guide for high performance individuals and organizations.* Cambridge, MA: Perseus.

Goleman, D. (1998). *Emotional intelligence: Why it can matter more than IQ.* New York: Bantam Books.

Greenleaf, R. K. (1996). *On becoming a servant leader.* San Francisco: Jossey-Bass.

Hoffman, F. O. (1983). Is management doing the job? *Training and Development Journal, 37*(1), 34–39.

Holton, E. F., III. (1996). The flawed four level evaluation model. *Human Resource Development Quarterly, 7,* 5–21.

Holton, E. F., III. (2000). What's really wrong: Diagnosis for learning transfer system change. In E. F. Holton III, T. T. Baldwin, & S. S. Naquin (Eds.), *Managing and changing learning transfer systems.* San Francisco: Berrett-Koehler.

Holton, E. F., III, Bates, R., Seyler, D., & Carvalho, M. (1997). Toward construct validation of a transfer climate instrument. *Human Resource Development Quarterly, 8,* 95–113.

Huczynski, A. A., & Lewis, J. W. (1980). An empirical study into the learning transfer process in management training. *Journal of Management Studies, 17,* 227–240.

James, W., & Galbraith, M. W. (1984). Perceptual learning styles: Implications and techniques for practitioners. *Lifelong Learning, 7,* 10, 20–23.

Jensen, E. (1998). *Teaching with the brain in mind.* Alexandria, VA: Association for Supervision and Curriculum Development.

Knowles, M. S., Holton, E. F., III, & Swanson, R. A. (1998). *The adult learner* (5th ed.). Houston: Gulf.

LeBoeuf, M. (1985). *Getting results: The secret to motivating yourself and others.* New York: Berkeley Books.

Marquardt, M. J. (1996). *Building the learning organization.* New York: McGraw-Hill.

Maxwell, J. C. (1998). *The 21 irrefutable laws of leadership: Follow them and people will follow you.* Nashville: Thomas Nelson.

Mezirow, J. (1997). Transformative learning: Theory to practice. In P. Cranton (Ed.), *Transformative learning in action: Insights from practice.* New Directions in Adult and Continuing Education, no. 79, pp. 5–12. San Francisco: Jossey-Bass.

Morris, L. (1995). Development strategies in the knowledge era. In S. Chawler & J. Renesch (Eds.), *Learning organizations: Developing cultures for tomorrow's workplace* (pp. 323–376). Portland, OR: Productivity Press.

Noe, R. A. (1986). Trainees' attributes and attitudes: Neglected influences on training effectiveness. *Academy of Management Review, 11,* 736–749.

Peterson, D. B., & Hicks, M. D. (1996). *Leader as coach: Strategies for coaching and developing others.* Minneapolis, MN: Personnel Decisions International.

Quatro, S. A., Hoekstra, E., & Gilley, J. W. (2002). Holistic model for change agent excellence: Core roles and competencies for successful change agency. In R. Sims (Ed.), *Changing the way we manage change: The consultants speak.* Westport, CT: Quorum Books.

Rogers, C. R. (1961). *Freedom to learn.* Columbus, OH: Merrill.

Rouillier, J. Z., & Goldstein, I. L. (1993). The relationship between organizational transfer climate and positive transfer of training. *Human Resource Development Quarterly, 4,* 377–390.

Ryan, K., & Oestreith, D. K. (1998). *Driving fear out of the workplace: Creating the high-trust, high-performance organization.* San Francisco: Jossey-Bass.

Senge, P. M. (1990). *The fifth discipline: The art and practice of the learning organization.* New York: Doubleday.

Simonsen, P. (1997). *Promoting a developmental culture in your organization: Using career development as a change agent.* Palo Alto, CA: Davies-Black.

Tracey, J. B., Tannenbaum, S. I., & Kavanaugh, M. J. (1995). Applying trained skills on the job: The importance of the work environment. *Journal of Applied Psychology, 80,* 239–252.

Tziner, A., Haccoun, R. R., & Kadish, A. (1991). Personal and situational characteristics of transfer of training improvement strategies. *Journal of Occupational Psychology, 64,* 167–177.

Williams, V. L., & Sunderland, J. E. (1998). Maximize the power of your reward and recognition strategies. *Journal of Compensation and Benefits, 2*(14), 11–17.

Xiao, J. (1996). The relationship between organizational factors and the transfer of training in the electronics industry in Shenzhen, China. *Human Resource Development Quarterly, 7,* 55–86.

Zemke, R., & Zemke, S. (1995). Adult learning: What do we know for sure? *Training, 32*(6), 31–40.

PART FIVE

Conclusion

CHAPTER 14

The Bottom Line

Talking Points for Transfer Improvement in Organizations

Timothy T. Baldwin
Elwood F. Holton III

In this final chapter, we take a step back and answer the question, What have we learned about how to improve learning transfer? Rather than write a lengthy narrative, we offer eleven short, succinct core messages that emerge from the book. They provide a set of talking points for change messages in your organization, as well as a concise guideline for action.

The impetus for this volume was our desire to explore a very practical question: What can be done to actively intervene and improve the persistently low transfer from organizational learning experiences? Consistent with the theme of the SIOP Professional Practice Series we thought it would be appropriate to use this postscript chapter to focus explicitly on what we have learned from the authors in this book regarding that practical question. And we wanted to do so in a way that might truly be useful to learning professionals. Our goal was to provide a short and succinct synthesis of the core messages in a form that could be easily consumed and perhaps used as "talking points."

We think the roadblocks to transfer are both informational and motivational. That is, while the need for more research-based evidence in support of various transfer interventions remains pressing, there is also a need to energize those with accountability for learning to use what we do know to be more proactive in making transfer happen.

Prior to listing our lessons for intervention, two of the core assumptions with which we began were reaffirmed throughout the various chapters and are the underlying logic for an active pursuit of better transfer interventions. First, the traditional tenets of learning success in organizations—great coursework, stimulating learning environments, and senior management support—are no longer sufficient. Learning must be viewed as helping the firm compete and win in the marketplace. So we contend that the focus of learning professionals has to be on transfer. Failure to transfer is both a waste of organizational resources and an opportunity cost where learners could be better deployed. Conversely, because the focus is on learner performance, effective transfer interventions can make money for the organization. The business case for transfer intervention is directly tied to performance improvement.

Second, transfer interventions can work. While rigorous empirical evidence is still the exception rather than the rule, the evidence we do have suggests that transfer is feasible. Moreover, though it is clear that the greatest influence on transfer will come from systemic assessment and intervention, it is not the case that improved transfer necessitates extensive new systems, labor, or infrastructure. Indeed, the emerging evidence suggests that transfer will be best achieved via integration with the organizational processes and systems that already exist and matter most in the firms.

The following is our attempt to provide a shorthand version of the core messages that we hope will help stimulate more effective interventions to improve transfer.

- *Focus your attention on transfer factors outside the learning environment.* Sustained transfer—when skills and knowledge are retained and maintained—is that most closely aligned with performance improvement in organizations and is the type of transfer most affected by factors in the transfer climate (both pre and post learning).

- *Involve and train your managers as transfer agents.* Direct supervisors often have more influence on employee behavior than any other source. They cannot rightly be left out of the transfer equation, but they generally need training to play their part well.
- *Use the transfer assessment tools and methods that exist.* Intervention without assessment is akin to treatment without diagnosis. Systematic assessment, even in abbreviated form, is essential to more effective transfer intervention.
- *Ensure that the primacy and challenge of transfer is communicated in every learning context in the organization.* Alert people to the prevalence of hostile transfer climates and the importance of self-management in navigating such climates.
- *Move away from unmanaged (first come–first served) entry into learning experiences.* Communicate to learners (and sponsors) the importance of transfer readiness, and seek to find ways to assess and select learners on that profile. At the same time, recognize that some part of your learning populations will not be highly predisposed to transfer. That reality should reinforce the importance of active management of transfer that is unlikely to occur on learner initiative alone.
- *Make new learning designs part of your transfer tool kit.* For example, work-based learning initiatives considerably shorten the distance between learning and performance and hold great potential for facilitating transfer.
- *At the same time, do not assume that just because you have moved away from classroom training (to measures such as e-learning, just-in-time training, or work-based initiatives) it means you have solved the transfer problem.* Particularly with respect to distant transfer—again that most aligned with the sustained performance we seek—the transfer problem in new learning environments is not solved, just changed.
- *Start where you can.* Significant impact on transfer is most likely to come from a systematic analysis and multidimensional approach. However, there is encouraging evidence that just modest attention to active management of transfer influences can improve outcomes.
- *Recognize that you cannot control many of the pre- and post-training factors shown to influence transfer—but go on bravely*

trying to influence them. All managers in today's complex organizations must influence factors outside their direct control that determine whether results are achieved. If the training doesn't result in job performance, it is the learning professionals who will be blamed. So get out of the comfort zone of learning and work to influence climate variables that will help turn learning into performance.

- *Transfer will be maximized when it is the explicit purpose of learning on the front end and not just a focus afterward.* Put another way, when learning is based on analyzed performance gaps the likelihood of transfer is correspondingly greater.
- *Get more systematic in managing the transfer process.* Many efforts to date have been haphazard and fragmented. Broad's process model in Chapter Six presents a particularly cogent strategy for formulating a transfer intervention in a systematic way.

Now onward to transfer greatness!

Name Index

Subject Index